"Let's go get 'em and then pound some Budweiser!"

With that cry, Joe Schultz, Jim Bouton's favorite manager, led his charged-up ball club straight into the jaws of defeat. But Joe is just one of baseball's masterminds you'll find on these pages. Here are the legends of the dugout like John McGraw and George Stallings, who raised profanity to a high art form. Here are the recent demi-gods like Casey Stengel and Leo Durocher, who turn out to have feet of clay and an abunda̶̶̶̶̶̶̶̶̶̶̶̶ ̶̶̶̶̶̶̶̶̶̶̶̶ ̶̶̶̶̶̶ ̶̶̶̶̶̶̶̶ubstance. And here are ̶̶ uk, who ran his ̶̶̶̶̶̶̶̶̶̶̶̶̶̶̶̶̶̶̶̶̶̶̶̶̶̶̶̶̶̶̶̶̶̶̶̶̶̶ Dick Williams, wh̶̶ and grew his hai̶̶̶̶̶̶̶̶̶̶̶̶̶̶̶̶̶̶̶̶̶̶̶̶̶̶̶̶̶̶̶̶̶̶̶̶̶ lges, who gave signals from the coach's box while standing on his head.

Jim Bouton has come up with his funniest book yet —freaking out baseball's stuffed shirts while turning the rest of us on.

"I MANAGED GOOD, BUT BOY DID THEY PLAY BAD"

Jim Bouton
with Neil Offen

A Dell Book

for Len

Published by
DELL PUBLISHING CO., INC.
1 Dag Hammarskjold Plaza
New York, New York 10017

Dell ® TM 681510, Dell Publishing Co., Inc.
Reprinted by arrangement with Playboy Press

Printed in the United States of America

First Dell printing—May 1974

Acknowledgments

"I Managed Good, But Boy Did They Play Bad" by Gilbert Rogin. Reprinted by permission. Copyright © by Gilbert Rogin. Originally appeared in *Sports Illustrated*.

"The Glory of His Time." Reprinted with permission of Macmillan Publishing Co., Inc. from *The Glory of Their Times* by Lawrence S. Ritter. Copyright © 1966 by Lawrence S. Ritter.

"From the Bench" is reprinted from *Pitching in a Pinch* by Christy Mathewson, published in 1912. Used by courtesy of G. P. Putnam's Sons.

"Musings of a Dugout Socrates" by Gilbert Millstein. Copyright © 1972 by The New York Times Company. Reprinted by permission.

"The Last Angry Old Man" by Edward Linn. Reprinted with permission from *The Saturday Evening Post*. Copyright © 1966, The Curtis Publishing Company.

"Which of Us Took the Greater Fall?" Reprinted by permission of G. P. Putnam's Sons from *The Hustler's Handbook* by Bill Veeck and Edward Linn. Copyright © 1965 by Bill Veeck and Edward Linn.

"Cornelius McGillicuddy—Mr. Mack" originally appeared under the title "Mr. Mack" by Bob Considine in *Life* magazine. Reprinted by permission of Bob Considine. Copyright © 1948 by Bob Considine.

"Manager with a Hair Shirt" by Melvin Durslag originally appeared under the title "Walt Alston, Manager with a Hair Shirt" in *Look* magazine. Reprinted by permission. Copyright © Cowles Communications, Inc., 1963.

"They Ain't Getting No Maiden" by Roger Kahn. Reprinted with permission from *The Saturday Evening Post*. Copyright © 1966, The Curtis Publishing Company.

"How Durocher Blew the Pennant" by William Barry Fur-

I'd like to thank Nancy Smith, an editor at *Scholastic*
magazine, and a close friend, who assembled the tables on managers. Thank you Nance.

—J.B.

I'd like to thank Carol Offen, a very close friend, for
proofreading and typing and lots of other things she
did. Thanks.

—N.O.

Contents

JOE MC CARTHY

DICK WILLIAMS

GEORGE STALLINGS

JOE SCHULTZ

Preface

People like to know how great works of art are created. So let me explain about this book.

My literary agent (what arrogance), Theron Raines, called me in July and said the Playboy book people wanted to put out an anthology on major-league managers. "Someone else will do the research and you'll do the introduction so they can put your name on the cover. It's an easy $2500 for you, $5000 for the researcher as an advance, and you'll split 50-50 if sales go beyond the advance."

"Okay," I said, "but I want to pick the researcher. The articles have to be a particular kind."

Book companies very often need a certain kind of book (sports) in a certain price range, and the quality doesn't really matter. Like most sports books of this kind, it won't sell great, but it'll sell a certain amount.

This may not have been Playboy's intention, but most book companies have a few books like this to sell. A nothing sports book with a recognizable name on the cover is guaranteed to sell 5000 copies. Harmless. And everybody makes a little money. Some stock to push while trying to move the top of the line.

I didn't want it to be that kind of a book. I wanted it to be a really good book, and when I saw Neil Offen buying Levi's in Bloomingdale's basement I knew it would be. Neil Offen wrote sports for the *New York Post* for three years. He was from the chipmunk school of sportswriting, meaning he thought there was more to sports than the scores, which was important. He was also out of work,

which was even more important. Nothing like a hungry
chipmunk for doing good work.

When I offered Neil the job of researcher he wanted to
know two things: First he asked me, "Do I get my name
on the cover?" And second he asked the salesman,
"Which floor for the Pierre Cardin Levi's?"

Offen spent four months living at the New York Public
Library. Since the book was going to have his name on
the cover, he felt the same way about it that I did. Most
important of all, we both wanted a book that would be
enjoyable to read. We weren't trying to make this book
definitive or encyclopedic. The pieces didn't have to cover
a manager's entire career up to the day of publication; if
they contained interesting information about the period
they did cover, it didn't matter if they were dated. We
decided that the pieces either had to be perceptive, in-
cisive, informative, or funny or unusual in some way.

Or, as Offen said, "easy to find."

With those as the criteria, some important managers
didn't make it. You'd think that a normal anthology
about managers would have to include Miller Huggins.
But we couldn't find an interesting enough piece on
him, so he doesn't get in. Sorry about that, Miller.

There were also some personal choices because I had
played for certain managers. In a book about 15 managers, you wouldn't expect to find a Ralph Houk or a Joe
Schultz. It's just their good fortune to have managed *me*.

After reading the pieces over and discussing the order in which they would appear, it occurred to us that
the stuff was too good to just put a cover on it and call
it an anthology. So we thought of *not* using a cover, or
calling it Seymour.

Then I decided I wanted to write some of my own com-
ments. And we figured if we were going to start off the
book with Rocky Bridges, who wasn't a major-league
manager, we had to end it with Joe Schultz, who really
wasn't one either. So we asked the greatest living authority (also the only) on Joe Schultz to write that chapter,
and I agreed.

If the Playboy people thought they were going to turn out a simple anthology, I think they got a lot more than they bargained for. I hope you feel the same way.

Jim Bouton
Englewood, N. J.

Introduction

With 24 Different Major-League Baseball Teams, How Come Jim Bouton Hasn't Been Named to Manage Any of Them?

I could never be a big-league manager. One reason is that no one would let me have it. Another reason is that I wouldn't want the job.

It seems to me that managers are lonely, and their lives aren't exciting enough. Also I'm not exactly enchanted with the idea of seeing places like Cincinnati and Cleveland for the 25th time. As a player I could get drunk in the back of the bus with the rest of the guys and forget where I was. As a manager I'd have to sit up in the front of the bus with the coaches. This is very similar to sitting alone.

Which is where organized baseball thinks I should be. The reason you'll never hear my name bandied about—I mean in a nice way—at the winter baseball meetings as a managerial prospect isn't because I'm not brilliant or handsome. It's because I was never an organization man. I'm not predictable. And it's also because baseball hates my guts, thanks to *Ball Four*.

The modern big-league manager, unlike me, is universally popular, a company man, up through the ranks, keeps his nose clean, doesn't rock any boats, knows the system. Guys like Ralph Houk, Eddie Kasko, Ken Aspromonte, Sparky Anderson and Whitey Lockman—all managers right now, in case you didn't know—would never stand out in a crowd. That's important, because a locker room full of today's modern, young, independent ballplayers can get awfully crowded.

As the players have changed through the years, so have managerial styles. Years ago, baseball players were glad just to have jobs playing baseball in the first place and were willing—because they had no choice—to take abuse from the manager. Over the past 20 years or so—possibly with the growth of the Players Association, partly because more athletes have been better educated, probably because society in general has become more rebellious and less blindly accepting—things have changed. Ballplayers have grown more secure, less dependent on baseball for their living and less willing to be pushed around by strong-willed, self-centered, dictatorial managers. What worked for Leo Durocher in 1951 wouldn't work—and didn't—in 1971. The modern manager understands that he must defer to his players, holds private discussions rather than shouts, blames himself instead of his players and uses the press to protect his team rather than prod it.

While managers were frequently dictators during the early years of baseball, they were also colorful. Over the last 20 years managers have stopped being dictators, but have remained colorful. Now they can't even be that anymore. Guys like Durocher, Casey Stengel, Charlie Dressen, John McGraw, George Stallings, Wilbert Robinson and others like them would never get their first chance to manage today. The fact that some, like Durocher and Harry Walker, are getting second and third chances only shows that baseball people are still willing to try something old before they try something new. They'd rather make the same old mistake than a new one.

The only new characters in the old mold hired to manage recently have been Baltimore's Earl Weaver, Philadelphia's Frank Lucchesi and Detroit's Billy Martin. But Weaver got his job because he'd been overwhelmingly successful in the Baltimore organization, almost forcing the Orioles to hire him. Lucchesi has been fired. And Billy Martin, remember, who had done a good job at Minnesota, was fired because he wasn't a company man, which meant he wouldn't go drink with owner Calvin Griffith and listen to lineup suggestions. (Maybe Martin will listen to Rangers' boss, Bob Short, more than he did to Griffin or Detroit's Jim Caldwell. But don't bet on it.)

And don't think drinking with the boss isn't important. I think that's the real reason there has never been a black manager in the big leagues. Most managerial jobs are given to old drinking buddies, cronies, friends of friends. Baseball owners and general managers don't have old black friends. *Or* young black friends. Not personal friends, anyway. And they're not about to *start* going out drinking with a black, or sit in planes with one, or trade girl friends with one, or lounge around a hotel suite discussing trades with one.

Another reason there aren't any black managers is that any blacks who would be strong enough personalities to be good managers wouldn't be company men, predictable, easily controlled. And any blacks who *would* fit the modern managerial mold—and be easily led by the front office—wouldn't command the respect of the black players.

That's why Frank Robinson, who's already earned that respect and who wants very much to manage, is playing it cool, being good. He's keeping quiet, or, when he does speak, talking like an elder statesman—respectable and traditional. He's managing in the winter league, always helping young players, never complains when he's traded—he's always being good. But as a young black remarked when asked to comment on Frank Robinson's new "establishment" ways, "Being good's a hustle, too, ain't it?" Yes, it is, and that's why Frank Robinson still makes baseball nervous. They think if he ever gets to be a manager he might quit "the hustle" and become the old outspoken Robinson, the boat rocker.

While we all wait for Frank Robinson or Maury Wills to become "good," baseball tries to ignore or belittle the problem of no black managers. Publicly, baseball says it's just a coincidence there are no black managers. Privately, baseball says things like "the fans aren't ready for it," "attendance would go down, and the kind of attendance would change," "the players aren't ready for it," "it would be impossible to fire one," etc. And very privately, maybe they say that they just don't *like* them.

Some baseball people try to deny that the problem even exists—like, for instance, Ralph Houk, the Yankee manager who likes to tell only good news. When asked about the lack of black managers, Houk conceded, "It's true there haven't been many lately."

Well, not since the beginning of time anyway.

Let's forget about whether a manager is black or white. Let's talk about the really important thing about a manager: How much does he contribute to the success or failure of a baseball team? This is one of the great questions of our time, on a par with what is the meaning of life and why do birds fly? The only difference is that the last two are easier to answer.

I'm convinced all managers play the game by the same book, the one that has all the same percentages, and so their on-the-field strategies tend to even themselves out in the long run. Charlie Dressen used to tell his players, "Stay close; I'll think of something." But at the same time, the opposing manager was likely to be thinking of the same thing.

That's why with some teams it didn't seem to matter who managed. The Yankees, for instance, were consistent winners under Huggins the dictator, McCarthy the aristocrat, Stengel the humorist, Houk the cheerleader and Berra the Yogi. Meanwhile, the Chicago Cubs couldn't win with or without nine rotating coaches.

But certain managers *are* better for certain teams—at certain times—than others. For instance, Harry Walker, the teacher, would be better with a young expansion team than with an established team of old pros. Young players would listen to the constantly talking Harry and learn a lot, while old pros resent the idea that they've still got things to learn. Leo Durocher, the prodder, is better in small doses; he should only be hired for the second half of a season and only for a contending team with talent, so he wouldn't lose interest. Houk should be hired by teams who've just fired guys like Walker and Durocher, teams where the players would be ready to appreciate Houk's best quality, which is that when he's not building you up, he's leaving you alone. But Houk should change teams every three years or so, because after a while even players who want to be deceived into thinking they're great can see through his smoke. When a popular manager like Houk leaves, he should be replaced by somebody within the organization, like Yogi Berra. In Pittsburgh they replaced Danny Murtaugh with Bill Virdon. This is so the players can't blame losing on some outsider who they think doesn't know their system or doesn't understand them, like the Yankee players blamed Johnny Keane.

And having someone to blame is important. Most people want to blame someone else for their failures and ballplayers are no different. Since only one team can win, most must lose. Which means lots of blaming. And who better to blame than the manager? Once you have a scapegoat, it becomes easier to lose. Give ballplayers a reason to lose and they will. "How can we be expected to bear down for this guy?" That's why a bad manager can hurt a ball club more than a good manager can help.

That's why the best manager I ever played for was Ralph Houk (not to be confused with Ralph Houk the worst general manager I ever played for). Houk holds the respect and affection of the Yankees not because he makes great on-the-field moves, or because he's a good instructor, or because he knows more baseball than other managers. They enjoy playing for Houk because he tells them where they stand, he alibis for their mistakes, he's continually building confidence by blowing that smoke—and he doesn't have a curfew. Don't underestimate that last part. Many ball clubs have had mutinies over the right to not sleep at the team hotel. Anyway, the players love Houk so much that they have only themselves to blame for losing and therefore they almost never throw in the towel. That explains why the Yankees surprise by bouncing back after losing streaks and why recently they've ended up higher in the standings than they had any right to be. (You know, I'll bet no one tells Ralph about this part of the book.)

Now, the best *field* manager I ever played for—the best strategist, the most knowledgeable, the most observant, the most thorough, the most daring manager I ever played for—was Harry Walker. But, as I said, Harry was not a good manager for teams like the Pittsburgh Pirates and the Houston Astros, teams that should have been contenders. Walker simply could not get players to play well for him the way Houk could. Even though Harry knew more about baseball, Houk knew more about baseball players. The ballplayers, particularly the older players, didn't like Harry because he was constantly pointing out what they were doing wrong or reminding them of what they should be doing. We'd be lounging in the Astro bullpen and Harry would call down to tell us to be alert so we could holler to our right fielder which base to throw to in the event he had to turn his back to get a ball off the wall. An important detail that could mean the ball game and only Harry Walker would think of it. Then we'd spend the rest of the game griping about what a pain Harry Walker was to interfere with our leisure time. When I was with the Astros, in 1969, we even had a players-only meeting where we decided we'd have to try to win the pennant in spite of Harry. We didn't. Because at the meeting we found our scapegoat, our excuse for losing, and we proceeded to take advantage of it.

While we're talking about things like players-only meetings, what can a manager do about dissension? Not very much, unless he's the cause of it, in which case he can retire. If it's not his fault, what he can do about it is what Dick Williams did with the dissension-ridden 1972 Oakland Athletics. That's the dissension-ridden 1972 World Champions, by the way. Instead of screaming at his players that they couldn't win if there was dissension, Williams told them it was normal and even healthy and maybe they'd win *because* of it. With exceptions like Oakland and the pennant-winning Yankee teams I played for (where there was more dissension than on my last-place Seattle Pilots), winning teams tend to have less dissension because players having good years are generally happier. Dissension is the result, rather than the cause, of losing.

Even if a manager is the cause of the dissension, he is probably not going to resign. Managers don't resign. Managers are not the type to say, "I'm not so good at managing, therefore, I quit." What happens is managers get fired. And managers live in constant fear of getting fired. That's because when a team loses there must be a cause and a remedy. One remedy would be to replace the players who did the losing, but that takes time and would be an admission that someone—like the general manager or the owner—made 25 or 30 different mistakes. It's easier for the general manager and/or owner to admit there was only one mistake and fire him. Managers cannot fire general managers for providing poor players.

In a 12-team league this puts tremendous pressure on 11 managers. It's not possible for them all to win, no matter how well they manage or how well their players play. It's like putting 12 brilliant scientists in a high-school science class and grading them on a curve. No matter how smart they all are, some are going to fail. This always makes me think of Vince Lombardi, who said he won at football because of his philosophy that winning is everything. I always wondered how he'd do in a league full of Vince Lombardis. I also wonder what it would be like playing for some of those teams. I also wonder what it would be like in the Black Hole of Calcutta.

Harry Walker, when he managed the Astros, came as close as I've ever seen a manager come to taking the blame for losing. On the first day of spring training, Harry would have a meeting to say he handled it all wrong last year, that he was too lenient and this year he was going to be tough. Or that last year he was too tough and this year he was going to be lenient. Either way, the season ended up the same—with Harry being tough. That's because for some reason losing makes managers angry, and when they get angry they crack down. A month or two would go by under Harry's lenient policy —no curfew, snacks allowed, no workouts—and still we'd be losing. Then Harry would have a meeting to say that he gave us a chance but it didn't work and now he had to get tough. Twelve o'clock curfew. No snacks. No golf. No swimming. No cards. No laughing. Workout to-morrow.

What if they did that to the 11 brilliant scientists who didn't finish number one in their class? What about those scientists who finished near the bottom? What if they got screamed at by the manager of the Atomic Energy Commission? What if they got laughed at in the newspapers? Or booed by the people? What if they had to explain about it on television? What if they got sent to Jablib, Wisconsin, to think about it? Under that kind of pressure we might have a cure for cancer by now. That's the answer. Put Harry Walker in charge of our scientists. He'd tell them they're not discovering things the way they used to in the old days.

The day that scientists and managers switch will be the day baseball players will be emotionally mature enough so that it won't matter what personality type is managing. When that day comes, the best managers will be the ones who work the hardest and know the most about baseball. Harry Walker can hardly wait.

And maybe some manager in the future will even lis-ten to Walter Lappe. Right now Walter Lappe can't get an audience with a groundskeeper. Walter Lappe is a man who has devoted the last 20 years of his life to charting baseball games (really) to see if teams really are making the best use of percentages. They aren't, according to Walter. What Walter has concluded is that baseball man-agers don't understand their own game. I've seen his find-ings and I think he's right. I also thought he was right be-fore I even met him.

Statistics are about as interesting as first-base coaches, so I'm only going to tell you about two percent of what

Walter's discovered. One of his findings is that some pitchers tend to yield grounders, while others tend to yield flies. Okay, big deal. But wait, there's more. Walter has also discovered that when a hitter pulls the ball it tends to be a grounder, and when he hits to the opposite field, more often than not it's a fly ball. Fantastic, sure, but what good is it? Here's the good of it. If a grounder-causing right-hander is pitching, it's foolish to pinch-hit a pull-hitting lefty because the probability that he will hit a grounder is doubled. And yet in that situation all managers blindly use the lefty-righty percentage without regard to whether the hitter pulls the ball or not. And even if the lefty pinch-hitter normally goes well to the opposite field, he probably won't even get instructions to do exactly that. According to Walter Lappe, the best choice for a manager in that situation is to pinch-hit a righty with instructions to hit to the opposite field. That's because the tendency of the pitcher to cause a grounder combines with the tendency of the opposite field hitter to cause a fly, producing a line drive which is the best chance for a hit. Or, as Walter says, "the vector of a fly and a grounder is a line drive." Since a right-hander's pitch usually breaks away from a righty hitter, it's easier for the righty hitter to hit to the opposite field than it is for the lefty hitter to hit a ball that's breaking in on him to *his* opposite field. If you understand all that, you know it means that in that particular situation baseball managers have been pinch-hitting the wrong man only forever.

Maybe it will be a long time before baseball people listen to Walter Lappe. Maybe this book will make him famous. Maybe Walter Lappe will make me famous. Maybe no one will ever hear of either one of us again. Someday, I guess, there will be a manager with the foresight to use Walter Lappe's information, but it's not likely to be soon. There aren't any managers I know of who would be able to stand up in front of their tobacco-chewing club in the spring and say, "Fellows, I want you all to listen to Walter Lappe here. He's going to tell us how we can win the pennant." It won't happen soon because too many managers still have some Joe Schultz in them: "Aww, I don't want to see your statistics. I can see what's going on with my own eyes." Can't you just see Joe Schultz on that word "vector"?

But maybe—*maybe*—the manager of the future won't have Joe Schultz's love for details. Maybe he'll have other things going for him like the luck of Yogi Berra, the bank account of Herman Franks, the batting average of Ted Williams, the chutzpah of Charlie Dressen, the wardrobe of Leo Durocher. Maybe he won't have the pigment of Whitey Herzog, but maybe he will have the friends of Casey Stengel, the larynx of Harry Walker, the ballplayers of Ralph Houk's imagination, the vocabulary of Joe Schultz and the seriousness of Rocky Bridges.

And maybe I'll be named commissioner of baseball.

Rocky Bridges

COMMENTS

My all-time-favorite manager is Rocky Bridges. He never managed in the major leagues, and I never played for the minor-league teams that he managed. In fact, I've never even met him.

However, I've spent a good piece of my life sitting in bullpens around the country listening to different ball-players talk about how much fun it was when they played for Rocky Bridges. Ethan Allen Blackaby (that's his real name) tells a typical story.

On one of those hot nights in July when even the thought of putting on spikes can make you tired, Rocky Bridges decided the way to wake everybody up was to give the signs from the third-base coaching box while standing on his head.

Of course, Blackaby, the hitter, had to stand on his head in the batter's box to receive the sign properly.

Being in the minors does loosen up some managers. People like Frank Lucchesi and Earl Weaver, almost normal when they are managing in the big leagues, did weird things when they managed in the minors. Things like climbing up a flagpole, or stealing second base—and then keeping it.

But being in the minors doesn't loosen up all managers. Most of them take things very seriously because they want very badly to manage in the big leagues and you don't get there by building a reputation as a flake.

One nice thing, though: It's more intimate in the minors, and players get to know their managers better because they deal directly with them, while big-league man-

agers have coaches to act as buffers. You don't get to
know a big-league manager as well. The relationships are
more personal in the minors.

The minor-league manager dresses with the players,
sometimes drives the bus, hangs out in the same bars and
actually gives advice. The best advice I ever got in baseball came when I was 19 years old and playing my first
professional season in the rookie league.

The first day I joined the team I wanted to meet the
manager, so I went up to his hotel room and knocked on
the door. Jimmy Gleeson, 60 years old with white hair,
shook my hand, said hi, and then he said, "Son, I'm going to tell you something I don't want you to ever forget.
As long as you're in professional baseball, don't *ever*
come up to the manager's hotel room without first calling from the lobby telephone. You can never tell who he
might have up in his room, you know what I mean? It's
okay now with me, but remember that for the future."

I always remembered. It may have kept me in the big
leagues.

And strangely enough the best pep talk I've ever heard
of came from a minor-league manager. When Don Hoak
was manager of the Triple A Columbus Jets in the International League, he called the players together before an important game and said, "Men, I'm just going to
say one thing." He held up his thumb and forefinger
about an inch apart. "I just want to remind every one of
you that you're only this far away from big-league pussy."

The difference between Rocky Bridges and Gleeson
and Hoak is that Gleeson and Hoak were serious. Bridges
rarely was. Take, for example, his line on what it was
like to play against a Japanese baseball team. "An hour
after the game," he said, "you want to go out and
play them again."

The reason Bridges was a great manager was that he
understood that baseball is supposed to be mainly fun.
That's probably why my favorite manager has never
managed in the big leagues.

"I Managed Good, But Boy Did They Play Bad"

by GILBERT ROGIN

"To begin with," says Rocky Bridges, the manager of the San Jose Bees, "I'm a handsome, debonair, easygoing six-footer. Anyway, that's what I told them at the Braille Institute. As *you* can see, I'm really a five-foot-eight-and-a-halfer and I weigh 190, but what you may not know is that my weight is very mobile—it's all moved around in front of me."

This is Rocky's first year as a manager, but he has come prepared, for he is one of the best stand-up comics in the history of baseball. "I'm back in the California League, where I started my slump," he says. "I'm the only man in the history of the game who began his career in a slump and stayed in it. I could play here as well as manage, but I have no guts. In 1947 I hit .183 for Santa Barbara and I'll be damned if I'll try again. I always wanted to be a baseball player. Now that I've quit playing, I still entertain that idea."

No man ever had a greater love for the game of baseball than Rocky Bridges. He considered it a privilege just to sit on the bench in the big leagues, which is a good thing because that was his usual position. "It was like being a little boy forever," he says. "I got a big charge just out of *seeing* Ted Williams hit. Once in a while they let me try to field some of them, which sort of dimmed my enthusiasm." Rocky's glove was mightier than his bat, but he could always handle a one-liner better than a line drive.

Rocky played (more or less) in the majors for 11 years and coached for two more. All told, he was on seven different teams: Brooklyn (1951-52), Cincinnati (1953-57), Washington (1957-58), Detroit (1959-60), Cleveland (1960), St. Louis (1960), and the Los Angeles Angels (1961-63). "I've had more numbers on my back than a bingo board," says Rocky. "My wife had to write to me care of Ford Frick. He was the only one who knew where I was. It's a good thing I stayed in Cincinnati for four years—it took me that long to learn how to spell it."

Rocky was a shortstop and second baseman by trade, a third baseman out of desperation and a left fielder for a third of an inning. "If I did anything funny on the ball field it was strictly accidental," he says. "Like the way I played third. Some people thought it was hilarious, but I was on the level all the time. When Charlie Dresson asked me if I could play third, I said, 'Hell, yes. I'll mow your lawn for you if you like. I want to stay up here.' "

Rocky endured in the majors because of his enthusiasm, his versatility and his hustle. "If I told him to go up and get hit on the head," Birdie Tebbetts once said, "he'd do it." For the most part, Rocky was a utility man, cheerfully accepting bit parts as a pinch-runner or late-inning defensive replacement. For instance, in 1956 he appeared in 71 games but had only 19 at bats. And hustle, he says, "is not running out of the dugout, as some of my troops at San Jose think."

Rocky's best year was 1958, when he was chosen for the All-Star team. "I was hitting .307 at the break," Rocky recalls, "but then I checked out Frank Lary's fastball on my jaw. The trouble with having a wired jaw is that you can never tell when you're sleepy—you can't yawn." Rocky didn't play in the All-Star Game, nor did he play in the 1952 World Series, when he was with the Dodgers. "I've been a paid spectator at some pretty interesting events," he says, "and I've always had a good seat. I guess they figured there was no point in carrying a good thing too far."

Rocky has a .247 lifetime average and hit 16 home runs during his career. In fact, about his only statistical distinction is that he started triple plays in both leagues.

"There use to be a rule against hitting me or walking me," Rocky says. "They had a lot going for them if I swung. I never figured myself an out man—I always swung, let it go wherever it wanted. Like I tell my troops, swing the bat. You never know what might happen. Two might get together." In 1961, after hitting his first homer in two seasons, Rocky said: "I'm still behind Babe Ruth's record, but I've been sick. It really wasn't very dramatic. No little boy in the hospital asked me to hit one. I didn't promise it to my kid for his birthday, and my wife will be too shocked to appreciate it. I hit it for me."

All of which adds up to the kind of record that leads a man whose life is baseball back to the California Leagues of the world, and Rocky is not crying in his Lucky Lager. He was asked the other day whether he thought he had reached his full potential as a baseball player. "I might have gone beyond it," he said.

Rocky finds that the league has changed a shade since he compiled an .884 fielding average in 39 games for Santa Barbara before being put out of his misery with a broken leg. "Reno wasn't in it," Rocky says. "That helped. The last time the Bees were in Reno, I lost the bus and two outfielders, but I won a shortstop and a bat."

The bus is leased from the Santa Cruz Transit Company. "It's not a brand new bus," says Jack Quinn, general manager and president of the Bees, "but it's not an antique. I don't want to put any laurels in my pocket, but it's as good as any bus in the league."

"The bus is air conditioned," says Rocky. "It is if you open the window. Every so often we have to tell the driver to throw another log on the air conditioner. We take a lot of interesting trips in our bus. Reno to Bakersfield—that's ten hours. We stay at a lot of interesting hotels, too. In one hotel lobby they have an artificial plant. Now, it wasn't always artificial. It's just that it's been there since the Stone Age. In another hotel they have television sets which only receive vertical lines. We play in some interesting ball parks, too. In one—well, I don't want to say the mound's too high, but when I pitch batting practice I got to chew gum.

"There are three things the average man thinks he can do better than anybody else," says Rocky Bridges, "build a fire, run a hotel and manage a baseball team." Managing in the California League is something else, however.

"In one game," Rocky recalls, "there is a man on first, one out and my pitcher is up. 'If you don't bunt him over on the first pitch,' I tell him, 'hit-and-run on the second.' He misses the bunt, takes the next pitch and the guy's thrown out. 'How can you blow a sign when I told it to you?' I ask him. 'Well,' he says, 'I forgot.' Four days later there's a man on first, one out and my pitcher is up. Different pitcher. 'If you don't bunt him over on the first pitch,' I tell him, 'hit-and-run on the second.' He misses the bunt, takes the next pitch and the guy's thrown out. 'How can you blow a sign when I told it to you?' I ask him. 'Well,' he says, 'I forgot.' Now, some guys might get teed off at that, but it halfway struck me as kind of funny. For the life of me, I couldn't see how they could do it twice within a week."

Rocky manages the Bees from the third-base coach's box. "I pick one of the older guys on the club, 22 or 23 —one thing that bothers me about this job is that I might come down with the croup—and put him on first base. I don't think anyone listens to him. I try to dream up strategy and things on third—like please hit the ball. The first game I managed good, but boy did they play bad.

"You got to treat the troops as pros but in the back of your mind remember they're novices. They do things you probably did and forgot. Of course, some of them it's safer to tell to go out and get an honest job. The other day my left fielder saw some guys rob a liquor store near the ball park and chased them until he got their license number. Afterwards, he told me that he'd always wanted to be a cop. 'Don't give up hope,' I said."

Rocky is an admirably patient and gentle manager. "I always said I'd never forget I was a player if I became a manager, but I wanted to see if I would. How many times you hear of a manager keeping the guys sitting in front of their lockers for an hour after the ball game? That's an insult to their intelligence. I can't see bringing out the tambourine and jumping up and down, either. You can be a good guy and still have their respect. Of course, if they start to goof off they can be handled in a different way."

"I know when Rock's mad at me," says Lon Morton, a San Jose pitcher, now *hors de combat* with a sore arm. He puts his arm around Lon Morton and says, "I'm mad at you." Morton alternately fascinates and exasperates Rocky. "There's a questionnaire all the players have to fill out," Rocky says. "One of the questions is what is your ambition. Every player but Morton put down 'big-league ballplayer.' Morton wrote, 'Hall of Fame.' Then there's Petraza, my left-handed pitcher who can also throw right, and Cotton Nash, the big Kentucky basketball star I got on first. Nash could be an interesting individual. I'm small, but I still like the big ones. Nash offers an interesting target for some of my infielders. Some of my infielders make interesting throws. It makes it very interesting, but then I was sent down here to learn the pitfalls of managing—not winning."

Rocky Bridges was born in Refugio, Texas, on August 7, 1927, under the name of Everett LaMar Bridges, Jr. When he was one, his maternal grandparents took him to Long Beach, Calif., where he has lived ever since. Rocky never learned to swim, however. "My uncle dumped me in the ocean when I was 6," he says. "I think I walked back underneath the water. I know I didn't walk on top." But then Bridges has always been a prodigious walker. He did not own a car until he got married. The day he signed with the Dodgers, he had previously signed with the Yankees, but walking home he thought it over and tore up the Yankee contract. He then took a bus to the Dodger scout's house and walked all the way home with that contract intact—a total of four miles.

Rocky has always had to scuffle. "When I was a

kid," he says, "I sold newspapers, delivered them, stole them." Even when he was a big leaguer, he was still making it the hard way. He worked winters for a foundry pouring centrifugal die castings, for Boraxo cleaning out furnaces and sacking soap, and for a pipeline outfit. "I drove a Mexican diesel," he says, "that's a wheelbarrow. I was on a jackhammer. I dug holes. It not only kept me in shape but, more important, it kept me in money." Since he has been with Los Angeles (the Bees have a working agreement with the Angels) life has been sweeter. Last winter, for instance, Rocky worked for Oscar Gregory, Paramount, Calif., Chevrolet dealer. "I do lip flappers [luncheon and banquet speeches]," he says. "I'm very big with the Elks."

Rocky is married to the former Mary Alway. "We're just like everybody else," he says, "cat, dog, four kids and debts. I used to lead the league in windows [the envelopes that bills come in]." His children are: Melinda, 11, Lance, 9, Cory, 6, and a baby, John Roland. Rocky cannot recall where the name Lance came from. "I don't remember a bar by that name," he says. "I married my wife on her birthday to cut down on expenses. One kid was born on December 30 so I could claim the deduction. We're a family of conveniences."

Rocky is not handy around the house. "I couldn't fix a track meet," he says. He does like to cook, however. He carries a recipe for veal parmigiana in his wallet that he clipped from a home magazine. Rocky's major diversion is golf. "I play at it," he says. "I know that people who have seen me out on the course find it mighty hard to believe that golf's my hobby. Actually, it's not a hobby. It's an ordeal. I'd do much better if they'd build golf courses in a circle. You see, I have this slice. . . ."

This season Rocky Bridges is living alone at a Holiday Inn in Sunnyvale, 11 miles from the Bees' ball park. "It's a more lonely life than I'm used to," he says. "You can't run around with the troops, and I miss my wife and kids. I write her, but she says I put more on the envelope than in the letter." Rocky sits by the motel pool with the papers until Larry Klaus, the team trainer, comes by to pick him up. In the majors, Rocky was always the first one in the clubhouse. He's still an early bird, getting to the park at 3 for an 8 P.M. game. "Rocky's lost away from a ball park," says Klaus.

At Municipal Stadium, Rocky puts on a pair of shorts and shower clogs, sticks a chaw of Beechnut in his cheek, sets up a chair in the sun behind third and reads *Better Homes & Gardens* or *House Beautiful*. His view is the outfield fence, which is decorated with ads for Berti's Bail Bonds, Robbie's Wheel Service and the Moderne Drug Co., and beyond it the Santa Cruz mountains.

"I started chewing in this league," Rocky says. "Guy got me chewing tobacco and smoking cigars the same night. I like a fat cigar. It's easier to chew. I used to have my trips measured by cigars. From Cincinnati to Long Beach was 40 cigars. It was 50 from Washington. I can't chew much around the house. I'm a closet chewer. I always liked to chew when I played ball. When you slide head first, you're liable to swallow a little juice, though. A lot of my troops be chewing lately, but not many be buying. I expect to get irate letters from their moms any day now. It's like a PTA meeting when the moms come around. I always manage to think of something good to tell them their sons are doing." The moms try to please Rocky, too. One day he got a note from a mother thanking him for letting her son off to go to his sister's high school graduation. Accompanying the note was a gift-wrapped five-pack of cigars.

One afternoon, as Rocky was climbing into his uniform, Al Coutts, an All-American second baseman from Los Angeles State, joined the team.

"Here's our new stooge, Larry," said Rocky.

"What size uniform you take?" asked Larry.

"Thirty-two," said Coutts.

"We got 38s and 40s," said Larry.

"You'll never make it on this club," said Rocky. "We go by sizes."

"Anyone we can option out wear a 32?" asked Larry.

"Don't be surprised by the umpires, Coutts," said Rocky. "I'm tired of complaining. What I'm really tired of is running. I pick my spots now. When they're close by. Another thing, you won't hear too much yelling out there. It's kind of a mutes' convention. As long as they play good, though, I don't care if they yell good."

"What time do I report here tomorrow?" asked Coutts.

"Around 6," said Rocky. "This is a kind of a do-it-yourself ball club."

"I don't have a sweat shirt," said Coutts.

"Here, take one of mine," said Rocky, reaching in his locker. "I hope you don't mind if it's a little damp."

Jack Quinn, the general manager, came in. Jack is the son of John Quinn, the general manager of the Phillies, and Rocky says Jack's so thin he could tread water in a test tube. Jack came to San Jose in 1962, the first year the franchise had been active since 1958. Jack won the pennant, drew 62,000 and was named minor-league executive of the year (lower division) for performing these feats "in the shadow of Candlestick Park." The Giants' park is only a 45-minute drive up 101 from San Jose. ("We ought to advertise that there's a good reception for all Giant games at Municipal Stadium," says Rocky.) Carried away, Jack bought the franchise and sold 300 season tickets. ("He ought to have a saliva test," says Rocky.) The Bees finished seventh in 1963, and last winter Jack could only sell 204 season tickets to such San Jose concerns as The Nite Kap, Ann Darling Bowl, Unicorn Pizza, Mid City Magnesite and O'Brien's Almaden Liquors. By mid-season Jack Quinn always seems to be looking forlornly over his shoulder. He gets that way watching foul balls vanish into the parking lot. "There goes another $1.50," he has been known to sigh many times a night.

"How'd you come out to the park, Coutts?" Jack asked.

"Cab," said Coutts.

"Stop by the office later and I'll reimburse you for

your cab fare," Jack said. "Unless you want it in stock certificates," he added hopefully.

"No game Monday, Jack?" Rocky asked.

"No."

"Roller derby?"

"Monday night's usually the roller derby," Jack explained. "It packs them in. No, Rock, it's an off night. The stadium's empty, but they're not used to us playing on Monday—or Tuesday, Wednesday, Thursday, Friday, Saturday and Sunday. But Monday's bad. Well, I better be off. I got to check the downtown ticket locations."

This was a joke. There are no downtown ticket locations in San Jose.

There was no batting practice that night for the Bees or their opponents, the Modesto Colts, as the field was being used first for a Pony League game and then for a Little League game. "You know what the Little League is?" Rocky said, watching the kids play. "Something to keep the parents off the street. I bet you don't know what's the first question Little Leaguers always ask me. 'How much money do you make?' "

After infield practice Rocky joined his troops for a supper of hot dogs and Cokes at a concession stand. Then the Bees went out and beat the Colts 18-0. The first man dressed was Vic LaRose, a utility infielder. Two nights before, when the Bees lost 1-0, LaRose had finally gotten into the game as a pinch-runner in the bottom of the ninth but had been stranded on first. He was the first man dressed then, too.

"He do get dressed remarkable quick," Larry had said when LaRose came in for his watch and wallet.

"It's amazing," said Rocky. "He ran all the way in from first."

"You better take a salt pill," Larry told LaRose. "You're bound to get dehydrated dressing so quick."

When he was dressed Rocky joined some of the fans, the two umpires and the Modesto manager in the Bee Hive. The Bee Hive is a club for box-seat holders which has been set up in an old trainer's room under the stand. Free whisky and beer are served for an hour before and an hour after each game.

"Eighteen to 0!" a fan said. "What happened, Rock?"

"I don't know," said Rocky, "but I'm for it."

Someone spilled a beer on the floor and asked the bartender for a sponge.

"Give me that sponge," said Rocky. "I'm the manager here." He bent down and mopped the floor.

An hour later, Larry was driving him back to the Holiday Inn.

"I haven't got it made yet," said Rocky. "You know when you know you got it made? When you get your name in the crossword puzzles. But I've gotten a big charge out of it. The troops don't come to you asking advice about getting married when you're coaching for the Big Club. I'm a white-knuckle artist when I fly, so I don't mind the bus. There's a good pinball machine in Modesto, too. I'm real lucky to be here. But, as Branch Rickey said, 'Luck is the residue of design.' "

John McGraw

COMMENTS

In the era of Ty Cobb and Christy Mathewson, the most dominant personality in baseball was a manager. But this was not your retiring, behind-the-scenes, self-effacing manager. This was John McGraw. For the almost 30 years that he managed the Giants in the early part of the century, he was the lightning rod: the smartest, winningest, most abusive, most respected, most hated man in baseball. The way he played the game then was the way the game had to be played. Christy Mathewson, who also did some pitching, tells just how McGraw played the game, circa 1912. But that's not the full reason this piece was selected. It's just as interesting for its style, for the fact that a ballplayer—probably—wrote it himself, for the insights it gives into the way ballplayers thought of their managers back then, for its picture of an era.

The first selection is a montage of short reminiscences by old ballplayers culled from *The Glory of Their Times*. It shows what time can do to memories and what John McGraw could do to ballplayers. It shows McGraw from several differing perspectives, not the somewhat limited one of his star pitcher at the height of his career.

Together, it's John McGraw, then and now, with and without warts, live and in remembrance. But always alive.

The Glory of His Time

by LAWRENCE RITTER

Rube Marquard: Take Mr. McGraw. What a great man he was! The finest and grandest man I ever met. He loved his players and his players loved him. Of course, he wouldn't stand for any nonsense. You had to live up to the rules and regulations of the New York Giants, and when he laid down the law you'd better abide by it.

I'll never forget one day we were playing Pittsburgh, and it was Red Murray's turn to bat, with the score tied in the ninth inning. There was a man on second with none out. Murray came over to McGraw—I was sitting next to McGraw on the bench—and he said, "What do you want me to do, Mac?"

"What do I want you to do?" McGraw said. "What are you doing in the National League? There's the winning run on second base and no one out. What would you do if you were the manager?"

"I'd sacrifice the man to third," Murray said.

"Well," McGraw said, "that's exactly what I want you to do."

So Murray went up to the plate to bunt. After he got to the batter's box, though, he backed out and looked over at McGraw again.

McGraw poked his elbow in my ribs. "Look at that so-and-so," he said. "He told me what he should do, and I told him what he should do, and now he's undecided. I bet he forgot from the bench to the plate."

Now, in those days—and I guess it's the same now—when a man was up there to bunt the pitcher would try to keep the ball high and tight. Well, it so happened that Red was a high-ball hitter. Howie Camnitz was pitching for Pittsburgh. He wound up and in came the ball, shoulder high. Murray took a terrific cut at it and the ball went over the leftfield fence. It was a home run and the game was over.

Back in the clubhouse Murray was happy as a lark. He was first into the showers, and out boomed his wonderful Irish tenor, singing "My Wild Irish Rose." When he came out of the shower, still singing, McGraw walked over and tapped him on the shoulder. All of us were watching out of the corners of our eyes, because we knew The Little Round Man—that's what we used to call McGraw—wouldn't let this one go by without saying *something*.

"Murray, what did I tell you to do?" McGraw asked him.

"You told me to bunt," Murray said, not looking quite so happy anymore. "But you know what happened, Mac. Camnitz put one right in my gut, so I cow-tailed it."

"Where did you say he put it?"

"Right in my gut," Murray says again.

"Well," McGraw said, "I'm fining you $100, and you can try putting that right in your gut, too!" And off he went.

Oh, God, I never laughed so much in my life. Murray never did live that down. Years later something would happen and we'd yell to Murray, "Hey Red, is that right in your gut?"

Fred Snodgrass: Of course, playing baseball was more than just fun. For a youngster, it was quite an education, too. Especially it was an education to play under John J. McGraw. He was a great man, really a wonderful fellow, and a great manager to play for.

Naturally, McGraw and I didn't always see things alike. I was a headstrong, quick-tempered, twenty-year-old kid when I joined the Giants in 1908. And sometimes Mr.

McGraw would bawl the dickens out of me, as he did everybody else. Any *mental error,* any failure to think, and McGraw would be all over you. And I do believe he had the most vicious tongue of any man who ever lived. Absolutely! Sometimes that wasn't very easy to take, you know.

However, he'd never get on you for a mechanical mistake, a fielding error or failure to get a hit. He was a very fair man, and it was only when you really had it coming to you that you got it. And once he'd bawled you out good and proper, and I do mean proper, then he'd forget it. He wouldn't ever mention it again, and in public he would always stand up for his players. It was really a lot of fun to play for McGraw.

As a matter of fact, it was because Mr. McGraw's favorite form of relaxation was watching the ponies that I became a professional ballplayer in the first place. He loved to follow the horses, you know, and in February of 1908 he came out here to Los Angeles to attend the races. He didn't bring his team, he was out here by himself. While he was here, he'd put on a uniform and work out to get himself in shape before spring training began, so he could sort of get the jump on all those old-timers who were on the Giants then.

At the time, the only contact I had with baseball was playing Sundays on a semipro team called the Hoegee Flags. (We were sponsored by a sporting goods house and on our backs we had flags of all nations.) We played teams all over Southern California, and I still remember the one that was toughest. It was a team down by Santa Ana, for which Walter Johnson pitched. If people think Walter was fast later on, they should have seen him then. Whew! Most of the time you couldn't even see the ball!

Anyway, one of my friends was helping Mr. McGraw work out at the ball park, shagging flies for him and things like that. McGraw asked a question about me, remembering I guess that the year before the Giants had played three exhibition games against St. Vincent's college in Los Angeles and that as a student there I had caught for St. Vincent's. Mr. McGraw had been the umpire and we had argued and quarreled constantly all through those three games.

"Oh, Snodgrass is the best catcher in semipro around here," my friend said.

"Well," McGraw said, "if you see him, tell him I would like to talk to him."

Word got to me, and I discussed it with my parents. There didn't seem any harm in talking to him, so I called him up at his hotel. He asked me to meet him in the lobby the next day, which I did.

"Are you thinking about playing baseball?" McGraw asked me.

"A little bit," I said, "but not too seriously. Although I did have an offer from Peoria in the Three-I League."

He reached into his pocket and said, "Here's a contract. Take it home and talk it over with your father and mother. If they think you ought to try baseball, our train leaves for spring training in four days. Let me know what you decide, will you?"

Well, as you can imagine, I was on that train four days later, going to Marlin, Texas.

You know, a lot of what I read in newspapers and books about baseball in the old days is absolutely 100 percent wrong. For instance, they seem to think that John McGraw directed every move we made on the field, that he was an absolute dictator who told us when to do this and when to do that, down to the last detail. Well, that's just not so, and it wasn't so for most other managers, either.

The fact of the matter is that thinking and alertness were crucial aspects of baseball then. Most of the time we were on our own. We used our own judgment. Nowadays they look at the manager or the coach for directions on almost everything. They aren't permitted to use their own judgment. They are told what to do on every darn pitch. But in our time we were supposed to *know* how to play baseball, and were expected to do the right thing at the right time.

McGraw allowed initiative to his men. We stole when we thought we had the jump and when the situation demanded it. We played hit-and-run when we felt that was what was called for. We bunted when we thought it was appropriate. Every player on the team was expected to know how to play baseball, and that was the kind of a game baseball was in those days. How many games do you see lost today just because they don't know how to bunt? That's a lost art, too. There was a lot of strategy in baseball then, and there isn't very much today. We played a game in which the two key words were "think" and "anticipate."

Of course, McGraw took charge sometimes. At certain points in a game he'd give instructions. But most of the time, as I say, the initiative was ours. The player of my day was allowed to think for himself, instead of having somebody do his thinking for him.

Why, do you know that we hardly ever had a pregame meeting on the Giants the whole eight years I was there? Hardly EVER! Today they always have a meeting before the game to discuss what they're going to do. We didn't *need* any meetings. Most of us spent all our waking hours talking baseball anyway, so it would have been silly to have a meeting. Just about the only meetings we ever had on the Giants while I was there were to divide up the World Series money.

And signs! McGraw hardly ever used signs. The belief that he signaled what was to be done on every play is ridiculous. We were supposed to do things on our own. For instance, we had a base-running club. In 1911, '12, and '13 we had six or seven men who would each average 40 or so stolen bases a season. In 1911 we stole 347 bases. Just the New York Giants—347 stolen bases in one season! Look it up if you don't believe it. And most of the time we ran on our own. We had signs among ourselves, so we could tell each other what we were planning to do.

Signs between the batter and a man on base, for instance. But those were *our* signs, not McGraw's.

On rare occasions, McGraw would indeed tell us to steal. Do you know how he'd do it? On his fingers, with the deaf-and-dumb sign language. A deaf mute, Dummy Taylor, was a pitcher on the club, so all of us knew the sign language. McGraw would sit there on the bench and spell out S-T-E-A-L so plain that anyone in the park who could read deaf-and-dumb language would know what was happening. We had no complicated signals. A nod of the head, or something in sign language; he might just as well have said "go on," like that, and off you'd go.

Intelligent as they were, most ballplayers were also superstitious in those days. Just as they are today, for that matter. There's an interesting true story about that. Hard to believe, but true. Early in the 1911 season we were playing in St. Louis, and in those days neither team had a dugout in that park. We had a bench under an awning, about halfway between the grandstand and the foul line. We—the Giants—were having batting practice, when out of the grandstand walked a tall, lanky individual in a dark suit, wearing a black derby hat. He walked across the grass from the grandstand to the bench, and said he wanted to talk to Mr. McGraw. So some of us pointed McGraw out, and he went over to him.

"Mr. McGraw," he said, "my name is Charles Victory Faust. I live over in Kansas, and a few weeks ago I went to a fortune-teller who told me that if I would join the New York Giants and pitch for them that they would win the pennant."

McGraw looked at him, being superstitious, as most ballplayers were—and are. "Well, that's interesting," he said. "Take off your hat and coat, and here's a glove. I'll get a catcher's mitt and warm you up, and we'll see what you have."

They got up in front of the bench and tossed a few balls back and forth. "I'd better give you my signals," Charles Victory Faust said. So they got their heads together, and he gave McGraw five or six signals. Mr. McGraw would give him a signal, and he would proceed to wind up. His windup was like a windmill. Both arms went around in circles for quite a little while, before Charlie finally let go of the ball. Well, regardless of the sign that McGraw would give, the ball would come up just the same. There was no difference in his pitches whatsoever. And there was no speed—probably enough to break a pane of glass, but that was about all. So McGraw finally threw his glove away and caught him bare-handed, thinking to himself that this guy must be a nut and he'd have a little fun with him.

"How's your hitting?" McGraw asked him.

"Oh," he said, "pretty good."

"Well," McGraw said, "we're having batting practice now, so get a bat and go up there. I want to see you run, too, so run it out and see if you can score."

Word was quickly passed around to the fellows who were shagging balls in the infield. Charlie Faust dribbled on down to the shortstop, who juggled it a minute as Charlie was turning first, and then they deliberately slid him into second, slid him into third, and slid him into home, all in his best Sunday suit—to the obvious enjoyment of everyone.

Well, that night we left for Chicago, and when we got down to the train and into our private Pullman car, who was there but Charles Victory Faust. Everybody looked at him in amazement.

"We're taking Charlie along to help us win the pennant," the superstitious Mr. McGraw announced.

So, believe it or not, every day from that day on, Charles Victory Faust was in uniform and he warmed up sincerely to pitch that game. He thought he was going to pitch that *particular* game. Every day this happened. To make a long story shorter, this was 1911, and although Charlie Faust warmed up every day to pitch, he never pitched a game.

He wasn't signed to a contract, but John J. McGraw gave him all the money that was necessary. He went to the barbershop almost every day for a massage and a haircut, he had plenty of money to tip the waiters—in the small amounts that we tipped in those days—and we *did* win the pennant.

Spring came around the next year and Charles Victory Faust appeared in the training camp. He warmed up every day in 1912, and *again* we won the pennant.

In 1913 he was again in the spring-training camp, and during the season he continued to warm up every day to pitch. By that time he had become a tremendous drawing card with the fans, who would clamor for McGraw to actually put him in to pitch. Finally, one day against Cincinnati they clamored so hard and so loud for McGraw to put him in to pitch that in a late inning McGraw *did* send him to the mound. He pitched one full inning, without being under contract to the Giants, and he didn't have enough stuff to hit. They didn't score on him. One of those nothing ball pitchers, you know.

Well, it was Charlie Faust's turn to come to bat when three outs were made, but the Cincinnati team stayed in the field for the *fourth* out to let Charlie come to bat. And the same thing happened then that happened the very first time that Charlie ever came on the field in St. Louis in his Sunday clothes: they slid him into second, third, and home.

He was such a drawing card at this point that a theatrical firm gave him a contract on Broadway in one of those six-a-day shows, starting in the afternoon and running through the evening, and he got four hundred dollars a week for it. He dressed in a baseball uniform and imitated Ty Cobb, Christy Mathewson, and Honus Wagner. In a very ridiculous way, of course, but *seriously* as far as Charlie was concerned. And the fans loved it and went to see Charlie on the stage. He was gone four days, and we lost four ball games!

The fifth day Charlie showed up in the dressing room at the Polo Grounds, and we all said to him, "Charlie, what are you doing here? What about your theatrical contract?"

"Oh," he said, "I've got to pitch today. You fellows need me."

So he went out there and warmed up, with that wind-mill warm-up he had that just tickled the fans so, and we won the game. And in 1913 we won the pennant *again*.

That fall I joined a group of Big Leaguers and we made a barnstorming trip, starting in Chicago and going through the Northwest and down the coast and over to Honolulu. In Seattle, who came down to the hotel to see me but Charlie Faust.

"Snow," he said to me, "I'm not very well. But I think if you could prevail on Mr. McGraw to send me to Hot Springs a month before spring training, I could get into shape and help the Giants win another pennant."

But, unfortunately, that never came to pass. Because Charlie Faust died that winter, and we did not win the pennant the next year. Believe it or not, that's the way it happened. It's a true story, from beginning to end.

Al Bridwell: We were both excited about playing for McGraw. At least I was, having heard so much about him. And it proved out, too. He was a wonderful man, a real fighter, that's what he was. He'd argue with the umpires, the opposing players, the people in the stands. Anybody wanted to argue, he was ready. I got along with him fine. He only suspended me once, for two weeks. It was on account of I socked him.

Well, I didn't really sock him. It was more of a push. I pushed him, sort of, and he fell down the dugout steps. Well, maybe it was a sock at that. I'm not sure now. After all, it took place about 60 years ago.

What happened was that I missed a sign. It wasn't my fault, it really wasn't. When I got back to the dugout he called me a lot of names and so I hit him. He suspended me for two weeks without pay, but once it was over he forgot about it completely. Never mentioned it again. He was a fighter, but he was also the kindest, best-hearted fellow you ever saw. I liked him and I liked playing for him.

The reason McGraw was a great manager—and he was the greatest—was because he knew how to handle men. Some players he rode, and others he didn't. He got the most out of each man. It wasn't so much knowing baseball. All of them know that. One manager knows about as much about the fundamentals of baseball as another. What makes the difference is knowing each player and how to handle him. And at that sort of thing nobody came anywhere close to McGraw.

Chief Meyers: Once a Giant, always a Giant. That's the truth. It was because of Mr. McGraw. What a great man he was! Oh, we held him in high esteem. We respected him in every way. According to Mr. McGraw, his ball team never lost a game; he lost it, not his players. He fought for his ballplayers and protected them. You couldn't come around and second-guess McGraw's players in his presence without having a fight on your hands right there. He stood up for us at all times.

Of course, errors of judgment—not thinking and not being alert—were taboo with him. He wouldn't stand for that. But regular errors—he often said errors are part of the game, and if there weren't any the game would be perfect and no one would come out and see us. "But don't make too many of them," he'd say, "or else you won't stay here very long!"

And how he hated lies. Don't ever come in with some alibi. That didn't go with him. No, he loved the truth, and you'd better come with the truth and nothing else. I remember one time a young player was on second base, and the next batter singled. This kid came tearing around third base and scored, but on the way around he missed the base. The third baseman shouted for the ball and touched the base, and the umpire called the youngster out.

"What's the matter, didn't you touch that base?" McGraw asked him.

"Yes, I did," the kid said. "I stepped right on it."

"You know something," McGraw said, "that'll cost you $100. For *stepping* on that base. Any time that umpire says you didn't touch the base, you didn't touch it. They never call that play any other way."

That was McGraw. What a wonderful man he was. Honest and forthright and charitable in the deepest sense of the word. We always called him *Mr.* McGraw. Never John or Mac. Always Mr. McGraw. And how he hated to be called "Muggsy!" That was a sore spot with him. Sometimes we'd call him that behind his back, but if he ever heard you, he wasn't your friend anymore.

From the Bench

by CHRISTY MATHEWSON

"The batteries for to-day's game," says the umpire, "will be Sallee and Bresnahan for St. Louis; Wiltse and Meyers for New York."

"Bunt," says McGraw as his players scatter to take their positions on the field. He repeats the order when they come to the bat for the first inning, because he knows that Sallee has two weaknesses, one being that he cannot field bunts and the other that a great deal of activity in the box tires him out so that he weakens. A bunting game hits at both these flaws. As soon as Bresnahan observes the plan of battle, he arranges his players to meet the attack; draws in his third baseman, shifts the shortstop more down the line toward third base, and is on the alert himself to gather in slow rollers just in front of the plate. The idea is to give Sallee the minimum opportunity to get at the ball and reduce his fielding responsibilities to nothing or less. There is one thing about Sallee's style known to every Big League manager. He is not half as effective with men on the bases, for he depends largely on his deceptive motion to fool the batters, and when he has to cut this down because runners are on the bases, his pitching ability evaporates.

After the old Polo Grounds had been burned down in the spring of 1911, we were playing St. Louis at American League Park one Saturday afternoon, and the final returns of the game were about 19 to 5 in our favor, as near as I can remember. We made thirteen runs in the first inning. Many spectators went away from the park talking about a slaughter and a runaway score and so on.

That game was won in the very first inning when Sallee went into the box to pitch, and McGraw had murmured that mystic word "Bunt!"

The first batters bunted, bunted, bunted in monotonous succession. Sallee, not yet in very good physical condition because it was early in the season, was stood upon his head by this form of attack. Bresnahan redraped his infield to try to stop this onslaught, and then McGraw switched.

"Hit it," he directed the next batter.

A line drive whistled past Mowrey's ears, the man who plays third base on the Cardinals. He was coming in to get a bunt. Another followed. The break had come. Bresnahan removed Sallee and put another pitcher into the box, but once a ball club starts to hit the ball, it is like a skidding automobile. It can't be stopped. The Giants kept on and piled up a ridiculous and laughable score, which McGraw had made possible in the first inning by directing his men to bunt.

The Giants won the championship of the National League in 1904 and the New York fans gave the team credit for the victory. It was a club of young players, and McGraw realized this fact when he started his campaign. Every play that season was made from the bench, made by John McGraw through his agents, his manikins, who moved according to the wires which he pulled. And by the end of the summer his hands were badly calloused from pulling wires, but the Giants had the pennant.

When the batter was at the plate in a critical stage, he would stall and look to the "bench" for orders to discover whether to hit the ball out or lay it down, whether to try the hit and run, or wait for the base runner to attempt to steal. By stalling I mean that he would tie his shoe or fix his belt, or find any little excuse to delay the game so that he could get a flash at the "bench" for orders. A shoe lace has played an important role in many a Big League battle, as I will try to show later on in this story. If it ever became the custom to wear button shoes, the game would have to be revised.

As the batter looked toward the bench, McGraw might reach for his handkerchief to blow his nose, and the batter knew it was up to him to hit the ball out. Some days in that season of 1904 I saw McGraw blow his nose during a game until it was red and sore on the end, and then another day, when he had a cold in his head, he had to do without his handkerchief because he wanted to play a bunting game. Until his cold got better, he had to switch to another system of signs.

During that season, each coacher would keep his eye on the bench for orders. Around McGraw revolved the game of the Giants. He was the game. And most of that summer he spent upon the bench, because from there he could get the best look at the diamond, and his observations were not confined to one place or to one base runner. He was able to discover whether an outfielder was playing too close for a batter, or too far out, and rearrange the men. He could perhaps catch a sign from the opposing catcher and pass it along to the batter. And he won the pennant from the bench. He was seldom seen on the coaching lines that year.

Many fans wonder why, when the Giants get behind in a game, McGraw takes to the bench, after having been out on the coaching lines inning after inning while the club was holding its own or winning. Time and again I have heard him criticized for this by spectators and even by players on other clubs.

"McGraw is 'yellow,'" players have said to me. "Just as soon as his club gets behind, he runs for cover."

The crime of being "yellow" is the worst in the Big Leagues. It means that a man is afraid, that he lacks the nerve to face the music. But McGraw and "yellow" are as far apart as the poles, or Alpha and Omega, or Fifth Avenue and the Bowery, or any two widely separated and distant things. I have seen McGraw go onto ball fields where he is as welcome as a man with the black smallpox and face the crowd alone that, in the heat of its excitement, would like to tear him apart. I have seen him take all sorts of personal chances. He doesn't know what fear is, and in his bright lexicon of baseball there is no such word as "fear." His success is partly due to his indomitable courage.

There is a real reason for his going to the bench when the team gets behind. It is because this increases the club's chances of winning. From the bench he can see the whole field, can note where his fielders are playing, can get a peek at the other bench, and perhaps pick up a tip as to what to expect. He can watch his own pitcher, or observe whether the opposing twirler drops his throwing arm as if weary. He is at the helm when "on the bench," and, noting any flaw in the opposition, he is in a position to take advantage of it at a moment's notice, or, catching some sign of faltering among his own men, he is immediately there to strengthen the weakness. Many a game he has pulled out of the fire by going back to the bench and watching. So the idea obtained by many spectators that he is quitting is the wrong one. He is only fighting harder.

The Giants were playing Pittsburgh one day in the season of 1909, and Clarke and McGraw had been having a great guessing match. It was one of those give-and-take games with plenty of batting, with one club forging ahead and then the other. Clarke had saved the game for Pittsburgh in the sixth inning by a shoe-string. Leifield had been pitching up to this point, and he wasn't there or even in the neighborhood. But still the Pirates were leading by two runs, having previously knocked Ames out of the box. Doyle and McCormick made hits with no one out in our half of the sixth.

It looked like the "break," and McGraw was urging his players on to even up the score, when Clarke suddenly took off his sun-glasses in left field and stooped down to tie his shoe. When he removes his sun-glasses that is a sign for a pitcher to warm up in a hurry, and "Babe" Adams sprinted to the outfield with a catcher and began to heat up. Clarke took all of five minutes to tie that shoe, McGraw violently protesting against the delay in the meantime. Fred Clarke has been known to wear out a

pair of shoe laces in one game tying and untying them.
After the shoe was fixed up, he jogged slowly to the
bench and took Leifield out of the box. In the interim,
Adams had had an opportunity to warm up, and Clarke
raised his arm and ordered him into the box. He fanned
the next two men, and the last batter hit an easy roller
to Wagner. We were still two runs to the bad after that
promising start in the sixth, and Clarke, for the time being, had saved the game by a shoe-string.

McGraw, who had been on the coaching lines up to
this point, retired to the bench after that, and I heard
one of those wise spectators, sitting just behind our coop,
who could tell Mr. Rockefeller how to run his business
but who spends his life working as a clerk at $18 a week,
remark to a friend:

"It's all off now. McGraw has laid down."

Watching the game through eyes half shut and drawn
to a focus, McGraw waited. In the seventh inning Clarke
came to bat with two men on the bases. A hit would have
won the game beyond any doubt. In a flash McGraw was
on his feet and ran out to Meyers, catching. He stopped
the game, and, with a wave of his arm, drew Harry Mc-
Cormick, playing left field, in close to third base. The
game went on, and Wiltse twisted a slow curve over the
outside corner of the plate to Clarke, a left-handed hitter.
He timed his swing and sent a low hit singing over third
base. McCormick dashed in and caught the ball off his
shoe tops. That made three outs. McGraw had saved
our chances of victory right there, for had McCormick
been playing where he originally intended before Mc-
Graw stopped the contest, the ball would have landed in
unguarded territory and two runs would have been scored.

But McGraw had yet the game to win. As his team
came to the bat for the seventh, he said:

"This fellow Adams is a youngster and liable to be
nervous and wild. Wait."

The batters waited with the patience of Job. Each man
let the first two balls pass him and made Adams pitch
himself to the limit to every batter. It got on Adams's

nerves. In the ninth he passed a couple of men, and a hit tied the score. Clarke left him in the box, for he was short of pitchers. On the game went to ten, eleven, twelve, thirteen innings. The score was still tied and Wiltse was pitching like a machine. McGraw was on the bench, leaving the coaching to his lieutenants. The club was still waiting for the youngster to weaken. At last, in the thirteenth, after one man had been put out, the eye of McGraw saw Adams drop his pitching arm to his side as if tired. It was only a minute motion. None of the spectators saw it, none of the players.

"Now hit it, boys," came the order from the "bench." The style was switched, and the game won when three hits were rattled out. McGraw alone observed that sign of weakening and took advantage of it at the opportune time. He won the game from the bench. That is what makes him a great manager, observing the little things. Anyone can see the big ones. If he had been on the coaching lines, he would not have had as good an opportunity to study the young pitcher, for he would have had to devote his attention to the base runners. He might have missed this sign of wilting.

McGraw is always studying a pitcher, particularly a new one in the League. The St. Louis club had a young pitcher last fall, named Laudermilk, who was being tried out. He had a brother on the team. In his first game against the Giants, played in St. Louis, he held us to a few scattered hits and gave us a terrific battle, only losing the game because one of his fielders made a costly error behind him. The papers of St. Louis boosted him as another "Rube" Waddell. He was left-handed. McGraw laughed.

"All I want," he said, "is another crack at that Buttermilk after what I learned about him this afternoon. He can't control his curve, and all you fellows have got to do is wait for his fast one. He gave you that fight today because he had you all swinging at bad curve balls."

Laudermilk made another appearance against the Giants later, and he made his disappearance in that game in the fourth inning, when only one was out to be exact, after we had scored five runs off him by waiting for his fast one, according to McGraw's orders.

After winning the pennant in 1904 by sitting on the bench, keeping away from the coaching lines, and making every play himself, McGraw decided that his men were older and knew the game and that he would give them more rein in 1905. He appeared oftener on the coaching lines and attended more to the base runners than to the game as a whole. But in the crises he was the man who decided what was to be done. The club won the pennant that year and the world's championship. The players got very chesty immediately thereafter, and the buttons on their vests had to be shifted back to make room for the new measure. They knew the game and had won two pennants, besides a championship of the world.

So in the season of 1906 McGraw started with a team of veterans, and it was predicted that he would repeat. But these men, who knew the game, were making decisions for themselves because McGraw was giving them more liberty. The runners went wild on the bases and tried things at the wrong stages. They lost game after game. At last, after a particularly disastrous defeat one day, McGraw called his men together in the clubhouse and addressed them in this wise:

"Because you fellows have won two championships and beaten the Athletics is no reason for you all to believe that you are fit to write a book on how to play baseball. You are just running wild on the bases. You might as well not have a manager. Now don't anyone try to pull anything without orders. We will begin all over again."

But it is hard to teach old ball-players new tricks, and several fines had to be imposed before the orders were obeyed. The club did not win the championship that year.

When McGraw won the pennant in 1911, he did it with a club of youngsters, many of them playing through their first whole season as regulars in the company. There were Snodgrass and Devore and Fletcher and Marquard. Every time a batter went to the plate, he had definite orders from the "bench" as to what he was to attempt—whether to take two, or lay the ball down, or swing, or work the hit and run. Each time that a man shot out from first base like a catapulted figure and slid into second, he had been ordered by McGraw to try to steal. If players protested against his judgment, his invariable answer was:

"Do what I tell you, and I'll take the blame for mistakes."

One of McGraw's laments is, "I wish I could be in three places at once."

I never heard him say it with such a ring to the words as after Snodgrass was touched out in the third game of the 1911 world's series, in the tenth inning, when his life might have meant victory in that game anyway. . . . Snodgrass was put out trying to get to third base on a short passed ball, after he had started back for second to recover some of the ground he had taken in too long a lead before the ball got to Lapp. McGraw's face took on an expression of agony as if he were watching his dearest friend die.

"If I could only have been there!" he said. "I wish I could be in three places at once."

He meant the bench, the first base coaching line, and the third base line. At this particular time he was giving the batters orders from the bench. It was one of those incidents which come up in a ball game and have to be decided in the drawing of a breath, so that a manager cannot give orders unless he is right on the spot.

It is my opinion that it is a big advantage to a team to have the manager on the bench rather than in the game. Frank Chance of the Chicago Cubs is a great leader, but I think he would be a greater one if he could find one of his mechanical ability to play first base, and he could sit on the bench as the director general. He is occupied with the duties of his position and often little things get by him. I believe that we beat the Cubs in two games in 1909 because Chance was playing first base instead of directing the game from the bench.

In the first contest Ames was pitching and Schlei catch-

ing. Now, Schlei was no three hundred hitter, but he was
a good man in a pinch and looked like Wagner when
compared to Ames as a swatter. Schlei came up to the
bat with men on second and third bases, two out, and a
chance to win or put us ahead if he could make a hit.
The first time it happened, McGraw unfolded his arms
and relaxed, which is a sign that he is conceding something for the time being.

"No use," he said. "All those runners are going to
waste. We'll have to make another try in the next inning.
They will surely pass Schlei to take a chance on Ames."

Then Overall, who was pitching, whistled a strike over
the plate and McGraw's body tightened and the old lines
around the mouth appeared. Here was a chance yet.

"They're going to let him hit," he cried joyfully.

Schlei made a base hit on the next pitch and scored
both men. Almost the same thing happened later on in
the season with men on second and third bases, and Ray-
mond, another feather-weight hitter, pitching. It struck
me as being an oversight on the part of Chance on both
occasions, probably because he was so busy with his own
position and watching the players on the field that he
didn't notice the pitcher was the next batter. He let
Schlei hit each time, which probably cost him two games.

The Giants were playing St. Louis at the Polo Grounds
in 1910, and I was pitching against Harmon. I held the
Cardinals to one hit up to the ninth inning, and we had
the game won by the score of 1 to 0, when their first batter in the ninth walked. Then, after two had been put
out, another scratched a hit. It looked as if we still had
the game won, since only one man was left to be put out
and the runners were on first and second bases. Mowrey,
the red-headed third baseman, came to the bat.

"Murray's playing too near centre field for this fellow,"
remarked McGraw to some of the players on the bench.

Hardly had he said it when Mowrey shoved a long fly
to right field, which soared away toward the stand. Murray started to run with the ball. For a minute it looked
as if he were going to get there, and then it just tipped

his outstretched hands as it fell to the ground. It amounted to a three-base hit and won the game for the Cardinals by the score of 2 to 1.

"I knew it," said McGraw, one of whose many roles is as a prophet of evil. "Didn't I call the turn? I ought to have gone out there and stopped the game and moved Murray over. I blame myself for that hit."

That was a game in which the St. Louis batters made three hits and won it. It isn't the number of hits, so much as when they come, that wins ball games.

Frequently, McGraw will stop a game—bring it to a dead standstill—by walking out from the bench as the pitcher is about to wind up.

"Stop it a minute, Meyers," he will shout. "Pull Snod-grass in a little bit for this fellow."

The man interested in statistics would be surprised at how many times little moves of this sort have saved games. But for the McGraw system to be effective, he must have working for him a set of players who are taking the old look around for orders all the time. He has a way of in-ducing the men to keep their heads up which has worked very well. If a player has been slow or has not taken all the distance McGraw believes is possible on a hit, he of-ten finds $10 less in his pay envelope at the end of the month. And the conversation on the bench at times, when men have made errors of omission, would not fit into any Sunday-school room.

During a game for the most part, McGraw is silent, concentrating his attention on the game, and the play-ers talk in low tones, as if in church, discussing the progress of the contest. But let a player make a bad break, and McGraw delivers a talk to him that would have to be written on asbestos paper.

Arthur Wilson was coaching at third base in one of the games in a series played in Philadelphia the first part of September, 1911. There were barely enough pitchers to go around at the time, and McGraw was very careful to take advantage of every little point, so that nothing would be wasted. He feels that if a game is lost because the other side is better, there is some excuse, but if it goes because some one's head should be used for furniture instead of thinking baseball, it is like losing money that might have been spent. Fletcher was on second base when Meyers came to bat. The Indian pushed the ball to right field along the line. Fletcher came steaming around third base and could have rolled home safely, but Wilson, misjudging the hit, rushed out, tackled him, and threw him back on the bag. Even the plodding Meyers reached second on the hit and McGraw was boiling. He promptly sent a coacher out to relieve Wilson, and his oratory to the young catcher would have made a Billingsgate fishwife sore. We eventually won the game, but at this time there was only a difference of something like one, and it would have been a big relief to have seen that run which Wilson interrupted across the plate.

McGraw is always on Devore's hip because he often feels that this brilliant young player does not get as much out of his natural ability as he might. He is frequently listless, and, often, after a good hit, he will feel satisfied with himself and fan out a couple of times. So McGraw does all that he can to discourage this self-satisfaction. "Josh" is a great man in a pinch, for he hangs on like a bulldog, and instead of getting nervous, works the harder. If the reader will consult past history, he will note that it was a pinch hit by Devore which won the first world-series game, and one of his wallops, combined with a timely bingle by Crandall, was largely instrumental in bringing the second victory to the Giants. McGraw has made Devore the ball-player that he is by skillful handling.

The Giants were having a nip and tuck game with the Cubs in the early part of last summer, when Devore came to the bat in one of those pinches and shot a three bagger over third base which won the game. As he slid into third and picked himself up, feeling like more or less of a hero because the crowd was announcing this fact to him by prolonged cheers, McGraw said:

"Gee, you're a lucky guy. I wish I had your luck. You

were shot full of horseshoes to get that one. When I saw you shut your eyes, I never thought you would hit it."

This was like pricking a bubble, and "Josh's" chest returned to its normal measure.

Marquard is another man whom McGraw constantly subjects to a conversational massage. Devore and Marquard room together on the road, and they got to talking about their suite at the hotel during a close game in Philadelphia one day. It annoys McGraw to hear his men discussing off-stage subjects during a critical contest, because it not only distracts their attention, but his and that of the other players.

"Ain't that room of ours a dandy, Rube?" asked Devore.

"Best in the lot," replied Marquard.

"It's got five windows and swell furniture," said Devore.

"Solid mahogany," said McGraw, who apparently had been paying no attention to the conversation. "That is, judging by some of the plays I have seen you two pull. Now can the conversation."

Devore went down into Cuba with the Giants, carrying quite a bank roll from the world's series, and the idea that he was on a picnic. He started a personally conducted tour of Havana on his first night there and we lost the game the next day, "Josh" overlooking several swell opportunities to make hits in pinches. In fact he didn't even get a foul.

"You are fined $25," said McGraw to him after the game.

"You can't fine me," said Devore. "I'm not under contract."

"Then you take the next boat home," replied the manager. "I didn't come down here to let a lot of coffee-colored Cubans show me up. You've got to either play ball or go home."

Devore made four hits the next day.

In giving his signs from the bench to the players, McGraw depends on a gesture or catch word. When "Dummy" Taylor, the deaf and dumb twirler, was with the club, all the players learned the deaf and dumb language. This medium was used for signing for a time, until smart ball-players, like Evers and Leach, took up the study of it and became so proficient they could converse fluently on their fingers. But they were also great "listeners," and we didn't discover for some time that this was how they were getting our signs. Thereafter we only used the language for social purposes.

Evers and McGraw got into a conversation one day in the deaf and dumb language at long range and "Johnny" Evers threw a finger out of joint replying to McGraw in a brilliant flash of repartee.

Every successful manager is a distinct type. Each plays the game from the bench. "Connie" Mack gives his men more liberty than most. Chance rules for the most part with an iron hand. Bresnahan is ever spurring his men on. Chance changes his seat on the bench, and there is a double steal. "Connie" Mack uncrosses his legs, and the hit and run is tried.

Most managers transmit their signs by movements or words. Jennings is supposed to have hidden in his jumble of jibes some catch words.

The manager on the bench must know just when to change pitchers. He has to decide the exact time to send in a substitute hitter, when to install another base runner. All these decisions must be made in the "batting" of an eye. It takes quick and accurate judgment, and the successful manager must be right usually. That's playing the game from the bench.

Casey   Stengel

Musings of a Dugout Socrates

by GILBERT MILLSTEIN

Any 72-year-old millionaire California banker—Casey Stengel, for example—who, having led one baseball team (the Yankees) to ten American League pennants and seven world championships in a dozen years, then elects to manage a professionally appalling, if humanly ingratiating, new National League team (the Mets) that he and everybody else know will finish a long last, and *then* shows himself capable of rising above it all, under such circumstances as the following—

Having concluded a doubleheader in Milwaukee (for some reason, the Mets won both games), the team boarded a plane for Houston at 1 in the morning, arriving at its hotel at 7, at which time Stengel ate breakfast and announced he was off to sleep for a couple of hours. (He was due at the ballpark at 11.) As he skittered out of the dining room in his usual way—crabwise—Stengel looked back over his shoulder and lobbed an epigram at his breakfast companions: "Anybody lookin' for me," he said, "tell 'em I'm being embalmed."

—is, by God, a man to conjure with, and, furthermore, one to find out from how it feels to be at the bottom after being on top for so long.

It feels awful, but is he downhearted? No, he's not; he's been with bum clubs before, the old Dodgers and the old Boston Braves; he's mad, but he had his mind made up when he took the job he wasn't going to just come in and jump on guys, except for lack of effort, and, remember, he could have gone other places; he'd had offers, said the indomitable, indefatigable, funny old man the other day in one of those long, chugging, tangential, peculiarly logical outer monologues for which he is as famous as he is for creating winning teams, winding up astonishingly by projecting the Mets to 1980 (but not committing himself for next year) and tying that in with a rousing recruiting speech for the Youth of America to come out for the Mets, a growth industry with rapid advancement and unlimited opportunity.

He sat stripped to the waist in his office at the Polo Grounds before a game, riding a swivel chair as though it were a light truck jolting down a corduroy road, flailing the air with his arms, jabbing a prescient finger and changing his face around whenever it suited him. He looked like a number of volcanic crags set for upheaval and it was an esthetic experience both to listen to and to watch him.

"I don't *like* bein' defeated," Stengel said. "I tear myself apart every one of them ninth inning one-run ball games we lose like that. How many we had like that could have gone the other way, but we're pluggin' five different holes every day. I tell you I don't *like* bein' defeated. I'd rather win, sure I would, who wouldn't?" He looked around the room for an argument, but the only other individual present was a visitor who kept quiet.

"I *expect* to win every day," Stengel trumpeted. He banged on the desk; an ashtray jumped up obediently and fell down again in a shower of cigarette ashes. *"An',* there's players on this club'd better feel that way, too," he went on. "I'll know everyone put out a hundred per cent by the end of the season, those who won't eliminate a weakness, those who can't."

He was clearly brimming with vital juices. One of the club's front office people, a man thirty-five years or so younger than Stengel, had driven him up to the Polo Grounds from his hotel. Stengel had bounced out of the car—literally—done some adroit broken-field running through a small group of fans bunched between the car and the clubhouse entrance; taken the flight of steps two at a time, all the while motioning behind him for the front office man to hurry up; waved a good morning and grunted at the doorman, and disappeared from view.

The front office man had seemed broken-winded and admitted as much. "I don't know how the hell he does it," he said, as he trudged slowly up the steps, at least forty-five seconds behind Stengel. "He's behaving like a highly paid college boy"—an illusion Stengel perpetuated even in his dress: he had on a navy blue blazer with brass buttons, gray flannel trousers, striped shirt and dark tie.

"Is there a contrast between here and there?" Stengel asked himself. He poked a crooked forefinger in the approximate direction of Yankee Stadium. He rummaged in his bag of tricks and plucked out an attitude of elaborate irony. "Certainly there's a contrast," he said. "They win with the Yanks over there and we don't with the Mets over here. R.B.I. You know what that means? Runs Batted In. That's the biggest thing wrong with this club, it needs more R.B.I. If you don't make the runs, you don't make the scoreboard and that's a mighty expensive scoreboard they got out there; seems a waste of money not keeping it goin'.

"*My* morale's good enough, but what'll do it? I'm gettin' mad in August. I'm gonna be good and damn mad if this club don't do better in the next two months. Are they tryin' for me? I don't know are they tryin' or is it inability to *execute*, but I go along with 'em and I try to make 'em play better. I don't want those weaknesses comin' up ten times in a row. They should be e-lim-i-nated. Say, I was young once and I did it eight or nine times myself, but I learned. Those other fellas, they got finished teams by now, but we're still experimenting in July and August. *And*, we're spasmodic. Other clubs, they're just havin' a bad day now and then when they have one, but we got it *every* day."

The seams on Stengel's face appeared to shift, the way crevasses on a mountain seem to when the sun is dodging clouds. "Spirit," he said. "It's not been lackin' in the public. *They've* come out. I didn't think they'd come out the way they did. I been with good clubs where they didn't

come out like this. But you got to be able to win to have
a following, whether you're a university team or a professional club. We're—ahem—like a university at the present time. But the people have been excited and enthusi-
astic and there's not a place they don't know *who* the
Mets are. I don't say *what*. Maybe they'll be something in
five, ten, fifteen years, 1980, only a lot of these fellas
here now won't be here that long. How long can this
club go without givin' people a run for their money? Can
we build this team and not lose fan appeal? There's people in this town sayin', 'I think maybe they'll do it later;
let's go along with 'em,' and then there's people sayin',
'Why haven't they improved?' "

Stengel stopped for a little to listen to an American
Legion band out on the field rehearsing for a concert. He
steamed slightly and pushed on. "With this club," he said,
"what you really got is a whole staff in Triple A ball
gainin' experience in the big leagues." There was an af-
fectionate rasp in his voice, not unlike that of a father
discussing a backward but not, he trusted, hopeless child.
"But will they find out up here?" he wanted to know.
"And what'll keep *their* morale up?"

The fact is that Stengel seems to have jacked up the
Mets' morale as much as anybody else, although they
were eliminated mathematically from the National League
race on the pitifully early date of August 7 by the
Dodgers in Los Angeles. For one thing, he has held more
post-game and pre-game team meetings than major league
managers are wont to. In his last few seasons with the
Yankees, there was a cutting edge to his voice when that
club lost a game he thought it should have won. Once,
when they were returning home after losing to the Athletics, the team got into a game of Twenty Questions in
the chair car. Stengel, who was sitting nearby, listening
in obvious irritation, got to his feet suddenly. "I'll ask you
a question," he said. "How many of you fellas think
you're earnin' your salary?"

By contrast, his tone with the Mets has been one of
gentle and sorrowful understanding and of remonstrance

without sarcasm because he has been reduced to teaching his men the fundamentals they should, in theory, have come equipped with. As a result, he has done a lot less office work than he did in other years and gotten out on the field much earlier to work with his coaches and the players directly. Daily, he can be seen scuttling around the batting cage, exhorting his hitters. Stengel has a theory that just about the most effective way of bunting is to hit directly downward—he calls it chopping wood—so that (1) the catcher will be the only man around to make a play and (2) will be able only to throw out the batter at first while other runners advance.

He is also a great advocate of catchers staying down as low as possible without going underground and is not loath to demonstrate. Not long ago, Richie Ashburn, an outfielder Stengel rehabilitated, even if only for the time being, in the bleak evening of his career, remarked that "I've been in big league baseball for fifteen years and I thought I knew a lot about the game, but this man knows more than anyone I ever ran up against."

Outside Stengel's office, the Legion band stopped. The silence had the effect of imposing some sort of compulsion on him to fill it and he proceeded—as minutely parochial as a time-study expert on an assembly line—to show why Ashburn thought what he did of him. He not only ran down every one of his general approaches to the game, but ticked off the statistics of every man currently on the roster and a good many who had departed, to say nothing of a scattering of the Mets' opponents.

"I'm not criticizin'" he explained. "I'm not here for that. But this thing's gotta be solved by *somebody*. One day, you're weak in fieldin'; one day, you're weak in thinkin'; one day, you're weak in hittin'; one day, you're weak in pitchin'; one day, you're weak in execution. How you gonna eliminate all that and get some R.B.I.?" He shook his head violently and snorted.

"Take fieldin'," he said, taking it. "You got carelessness. A fly ball goes out there and you got those two fellas in the outfield sayin' 'I don't want it; you get it,' and they bunk heads. I ain't seen no one die on a ball field chasin' balls." His mind moved to the infield. "Also," he said, "I bet I lost six games fieldin' by a pitcher. He's got an eighteen dollar glove, ain't he?" he demanded. "He ain't blind. He got good eyes, but he's a *pitcher*. Fieldin' ain't his job. So I lost six games fieldin' by a pitcher." He was grumpy about his infield situation. "I'm workin' every day for a double play combination. Why, do you know a double play is two-twenty-sevenths of the ball game? Us, we get one out, not two."

The thought of his pitchers then bemused him. He estimated he'd had possibly thirty-five since the beginning of the season. The staff was weak to begin with, but the schedule was murdering them, too—too many doubleheaders lasting as long as eight hours, too many plane jumps and not enough rest, too many in-and-outers.

"Them pitchers," he had nevertheless concluded, "got to get out there thinkin', 'I'm greater than those hitters, the majority of them, anyway,' but how long can they go on gettin' shell shocked and get out there with the spirit *and* attack *and* better control? If I tell you to pitch low and you pitch high, then what've you got? The brightest man in the world, maybe, but if you can't get that ball over, the umpire's gonna beat you if the batter don't. Throw those sinkers. Make 'em hit ground balls. Never heard anyone gettin' home runs on ground balls."

Stengel trotted in, so to speak, from the mound. "Go to the hitters," he adjured. "We got too many men strikin' out, too many men left on bases, too many one-run losses. If I can keep you from strikin' out twelve, fifteen times with men on third, I'd probably be more satisfied or near more satisfied. Can't platoon men if they don't hit against righthanded *and* lefthanded pitchin', sacrifice, bunt, beat the pitchers *and* the umpires.

"Take one of those young players. All he wants is home runs, say. He looks terrific out there. Lovely swing. So he strikes out and comes back to the bench and tears up the equipment when he doesn't get a home run. When what he wants is a hit. I tell him, 'Oh, that pitcher, he's a good one all right, but hit him *easy*—not too hard, not too soft—the ball'll move; otherwise you're a strikeout king, not a home run king.' "

Having exhausted all nine positions, Stengel set himself to belt out a few moral fungoes. "Then, there's the slipshod man," he roared, "or, I'd-be-better-if-I-had-better-teammates fella." He permitted himself a falsetto mimicking of the slipshod man. *"That* man," he swore, "he's got false confidence he's gonna talk his way through the big leagues. Well, he ain't. Here, you gotta work a little harder. I wouldn't play ball just for fun. Find out what you *can't* do. Come to the park early and eliminate it. Help *yourself*." Suiting action to word, he rose from his swivel chair, made his way to his locker and started pulling off the rest of his clothes and putting on his uniform.

"That's what bein' in the big leagues means," he said. "Can a man hit, run and slide three ways, and, don't let up 'til the ninth inning is over?" He yanked on a pants leg in affirmation. "Then, he's a player and a team'll have good luck. Don't come around and tell me, 'I'm not in physical shape.' When you got a good job and a plant to work in, what's to stop you from comin' around ahead of time and running, say. Ask yourself, 'Can I run? Did I prepare myself all winter in my line of business?' "

He stuffed his shirt into his pants and a wistful note crept into his voice. "Another thing," Stengel said. "Money has no value here now. I can't *buy* a player for five hundred thousand dollars. I'd like to buy *five* for two hundred and fifty *million*, but I'll tell you something, that's what I'd like, not what the owners'll let me do. Then I wouldn't be behind one run and I'd get over *that* hill." Finally, he plunged into his recruiting speech, and his tone became very nearly lyrical.

"I'd like to get some of these Youths of America," he said. "Now if I wanted to be a big leaguer, I'd say to myself, 'This is a team can give me the experience.' No doubt about it, it's a terrific opportunity for the Young Men of America. I'd think to myself, 'If I went to any other club, it'd take me longer to become a pitcher or an outfielder or an infielder, whatever.' On *this* one, if you can outplay another player, there's a possibility that in one or two years of hard work you can become a major leaguer. Other clubs, the other fella has got to get older or get injured before there's a job open or it's five years waitin'.

"Why won't everyone listen?

"Look up the record of every player on this club. He's played more with us than he did the year before with anybody else. We need about ten more players and that could be the Youth of America. Look at all the prospects this club's had. There's good pay, a good annuity plan, live first class, go everywhere, the best hotels. *An'*, if I was one of those prospects, I'd say to myself, 'I won't let that other fella take *this* job away from me. I'll just play so good, the manager and the coaches and the owners have *got* to like me and I've got a regular job.' "

Outside his office, the Mets had, by this time, begun to take batting practice, which reminded Stengel that it was time to get out onto the field, which, in turn, provoked a last thought. "We got," he concluded, almost pleadingly, "clean uniforms if you get 'em dirty. Why, the owners is just *dyin'* to have you get 'em dirty; *I like to see 'em dirty*. There's laundries. You tear a uniform, they're just waitin' to take it right off you and give you another one.

"There's never been," he said, slamming his locker shut with an emphatic bang, "such an opportunity."

The Last Angry Old Man

by EDWARD LINN

When the New York Yankees came back from a 3-1 deficit in the 1958 World Series to win the last three games, Casey Stengel mounted the baggage trunk to deliver the customary victory address to the writers and the television cameras. "I couldn't have done it," he said, "without the players"—a proposition he quite obviously hoped would not be taken too seriously. Casey always wanted as much credit as he could get.

Certainly he deserved a good deal of it. In his first five years as manager of the Yankees, the man once ridiculed as a clown won an unprecedented five straight pennants and World Series. Overall, he won 10 pennants and seven World Series before the Yankees fired him for growing old.

These days Casey wants to take credit for the Mets' incredible success, even though it is financial rather than artistic. They have finished a solid last each year, and their name has become synonymous with ineptitude, but they outdrew the Yankees at home by close to half a million fans last season, and this year's attendance is running even farther ahead.

"Now they say," Stengel goes on, " 'if you ever win you won't draw.' That's a lot of bull. We *sold* this team. I get more mail than anybody in the country. I have friends all over this city from playing with Brooklyn and New York and the Yankees."

He is somewhat more modest about accepting the responsibility for their record. He deflects it, very nicely, by ridiculing the players and by blaming the team for the total ills of mankind. Is Casey's arm in a cast as a result of tripping over a doorway at West Point? "I got this broken arm from watching my team," he'll tell a visitor. "We're improving magnificently. All they gave me last year was a head cold."

Casey Stengel, as you can see, is a remarkable man. On July 30, 1965, a date to be noted by all serious students of geriatrics, he will be 75 years old. To realize how old that is, you have to remember that when Stengel played his first game in Brooklyn in 1912, the team was known as the Superbas and the opposing shortstop was Honus Wagner.

The most remarkable thing of all about Stengel, though, is that at the age of 57 he was a minor-league manager with no more reputation for wizardry or clairvoyance than one might expect of a man who had managed in the major leagues for nine years without ever getting out of the second division. If you really want to get technical he had a 10th year in there. The Brooklyn Dodgers thought so much of him that in 1937 they paid him a full year's salary *not* to manage.

At the age of 58, when most men are beginning to study the tides and the Social Security tables, Stengel became manager of the Yankees, an appointment which startled the baseball world. After 21 years of working with inferior—and infuriating—ballplayers, the old man finally had players who could (to use his favorite word) execute. The game of baseball has not been the same since. With a full squad to work with, Stengel showed that the bench and the bullpen were just as important as the starting lineup. He demonstrated, almost daily, how games could be won by protecting even the good hitters from their one weakness, and choosing the one best spot to exploit a weaker hitter's strength. It was Stengel who showed them that your top pinch hitter should be wheeled in at the first opportunity to break the game open, instead of being husbanded until the late innings. And it was Stengel who showed everybody that, in the age of the lively ball, the relief pitcher was the most valuable man on any squad.

The man he showed it with was a fast-balling left-hander named Joe Page. Page came in 60 times for Stengel that first season, winning the championship for him and, undoubtedly, saving his job. When Page left two years later with a dead arm, Casey didn't even thank him. "Shake my hand?" Page has said. "He wasn't even there to say good-bye."

Although it has become customary to talk about the great satisfaction it must have given Casey to come back and take charge of a profession that had written him off as a clown, that is not quite the whole story. When you are 58 years old, you already know who you are and what you are. Success which arrives so late can be more embittering than satisfying.

What does it do to a man to know that he can do his job better than anybody else in the world—to know in his heart that he *knows* how it should be done—and not only be denied his opportunity but to be looked upon as a garrulous fool?

Consider the field of politics. Gen. Charles de Gaulle was not summoned back to lead his country until the age of 68, and he has spent his best efforts ever since trying to settle old scores with his former allies. Konrad Adenauer had to wait until he was 72 before he became chancellor of Germany, and Syngman Rhee was 73 before he finally became president of South Korea. Once in power, they proved to be vain, imperious, stubborn old men, jealous of their authority and, in the end, unwilling to depart.

Casey Stengel is nothing if not a leader of men, and he has his full share of the great leader's vanities. But for a 75-year-old man who has always been a heavy drinker and smoker, his physical condition is incredible. All of his wrinkles are in his face. Casey has a broad chest—far broader than it appears to be in uniform—and he has the clear, smooth skin of a young man.

Casey Stengel has two faces. There is the face the public has come to know and laugh at, the gimpy, dog-eared old man winking, grimacing and babbling on in what is taken, on faith, to be profound—if not always decipherable—wisdom. The public Stengel is no myth. He is a wonderfully funny and engaging man—a wit and a comic both. He can be loyal, too, although he has generally been more loyal to his writers than to his players. His writers are his best friends, his drinking companions and, most important of all, his best and most available audience. He feeds them material daily, and he protects them by giving outsiders—particularly radio and television people—little cooperation and less information. ("Where are they," Casey likes to ask, "on a Wednesday afternoon in Houston?")

There is, of course, another side to that friendship. The writers are the people who help develop his image and who reflect it to the public. When Casey calls them "my newspapermen" and lets them see how he protects them, he is putting a rather subtle pressure on them to look upon him as "their" manager and protect him too.

But beneath the public face there is the face the underlings have come to know and resent. Casey is a strong leader, the kind of leader who not only has to run the entire show but has to know that everyone else knows he's running it. There has always been the strong suspicion that Solly Hemus, one of his original coaches with the Mets, was fired because he ignored Stengel's admonition that coaches should be seldom seen and never heard, and more particularly because he ignored it so frequently on the television show conducted by Howard Cosell, an abrasive critic who has got under Casey's skin.

The most surprising part of it all, at first glance, is that anybody who has lived as long as Stengel and enjoyed so much success should be that sensitive to criticism. "They think I never won anything before I came to the Yankees," Casey will say. "They forget I won four years earlier at Oakland." (Casey's memory is legendary. It is also inaccurate. Actually he won his pennant at

Oakland the year before he came to the Yankees. He had won at Milwaukee five years earlier.)

During the height of Stengel's success with the Yankees, a reporter asked him if he had patterned his managing style after John McGraw, a natural-enough question since he had just finished telling a dozen stories about how McGraw had platooned him. "You don't copy another manager," Casey growled, "unless you want to get fired." He was so insulted that he strode up the dugout stairs, turned around and proclaimed, "He was a great man in this town, McGraw, and he won a lot of pennants. But Stengel is in town now, and he's won a lot of pennants too."

By the time Casey came to town the great name was Joe DiMaggio, and Casey—who makes few public-relations mistakes—was always very careful to bow down before the shrine. Casey will still volunteer the information that DiMaggio was the greatest player he ever managed, although the DiMaggio who was playing out his final three years under Stengel was far from the incomparable ballplayer he had been before the war.

But if Casey had to bow down before DiMaggio, he went to heroic lengths to avoid paying any similar homage to his next superstar, Mickey Mantle. Stengel handled Mantle by turning his back to him. When he spoke about him to the press, in the later years, it was usually to criticize him. The most puzzling incident came during the course of the luncheon that was held to announce what turned out to be Stengel's final two-year contract with the Yankees. To Casey, it was a fitting occasion to list the greatest players of his 10-year tenure. DiMaggio was the obligatory choice as the all-time champion, of course, but from there Stengel went on to name almost every Yankee who had ever made an All-Star team—except Mickey Mantle.

Casey's coldness toward Mantle bewildered the other Yankees, because Mickey, who is a remarkably good-natured, self-effacing man, has always been enormously popular with his teammates. The players not only like him, they admire him. With all that has been written about his bad legs, only the players knew how often Mantle would go back to the trainer's room, before the game, and all but faint from the sheer pain he was enduring.

Even here, Mantle received not the slightest sympathy —let alone consideration—from the master. Casey took the attitude that if Mickey wanted to sit out a game, it was up to Mickey to come and tell him so. Once it was put to him that way, Mantle made it a point of honor never to beg off.

It was no accident that when Ralph Houk took over, he immediately appointed Mantle captain and held forth whenever possible on Mickey's value to the team. Nor was it an accident that Houk told the writers, in his first press conference, that if they ever put him in the position where he had to rap a player or lie to them, he would unhesitatingly lie to them.

The most persistent criticism of Stengel has always been that he would rip his players apart to his friends, the newspapermen, for an item or a laugh. Clete Boyer, for one, never made any great secret of his distaste for Stengel. "You open the paper in the morning," Clete would say, "and you read how lousy you are."

You didn't always have to wait for the paper. Casey once conducted a visitor to the batting cage while Jerry Lumpe, a good, all-round infielder, was spraying line drives to all fields. "That's Lumpe," Casey said loudly. "He's a great hitter until I play him."

There was never very much to be gained, though, in criticizing anything Stengel ever did with the Yankees. You kept running up against that record. With the Mets he is far more vulnerable. While it is true enough that New York's great romance with the Mets seems to be based upon the ball club's lovable incompetence, you do have the feeling that *somebody* should defend the players. Stengel defends his bullpen pitchers by saying, "What am I supposed to do with the plumbers I got down there?"

He can get considerably more specific. The only good

defensive catcher the Mets have ever had is Chris Cannizzaro (whom Casey always calls Canzoneri). When
Cannizzaro made two errors in one game, Casey told his
writers, "He's a remarkable catcher, that Canzoneri. He's
the only defensive catcher in baseball who can't catch."

Everybody laughed heartily, except possibly Cannizzaro.

Tim Harkness (whom Casey always called Harshman)
found nothing at all to laugh about in his year plus with
the Mets, unless he was able to find something riotously
funny in being constantly belittled and debased. In Harkness's first game—the opening game of 1963—the Mets
were shut out, 7-0. All Casey seemed concerned about
afterward was Harkness's failure to handle a hot shot hit
down to him by Bill White, a play so difficult that it was
judged a hit, not an error. "I'll give him a week to play
himself off the club," Casey snorted.

No matter how strenuously Stengel ridicules his players, however, the manager of a team that has set previously undreamed of marks for losing ("They've shown
me ways to lose I never knew existed") is open to some
mild criticism himself. Casey is a remarkable old man,
all right, but he is still an old man, given to an old man's
wanderings.

Jimmy Piersall, who left the Mets in some acrimony,
sums up the rising criticism in his usual puckish way.
"Everybody knows that Casey has forgotten more baseball than I'll ever know," Jimmy says. "That's the trouble,
he's forgotten it."

Somewhat less puckishly, Piersall says, "Casey isn't a
manager anymore, he's just on display."

Jackie Robinson, never a fan of Stengel's, observed
last May that Casey had grown so old that he had lost
his mental alertness, and reporters have written that he
has even been known to drop off to sleep on the bench
during a game. The Mets were playing a night game in
Los Angeles when the story hit the papers, and while
Casey has occasionally been caught without a pinch hitter he has never been caught without a line. "I don't

want to get involved with Robinson," he told his writers. "He was a great ballplayer once. But everyone knows," Casey said, referring to the firm Robinson once worked for, "that he's now Chock Full o'Nuts."

The Mets were catching a chartered plane to Houston after the game, a trip that took six and a half hours. Casey very quickly gathered a full contingent of writers around him and began one of those nonstop discussions (read *monologue*) which he so enjoys and so completely dominates.

The writers came and went in shifts, and Casey kept talking.

The moment the plane hit the runway, he bounced up and was off and talking again. On the bus to the hotel he announced that he wanted all his newspapermen to have breakfast with him. He talked on through breakfast, holding the writers to his table as long as possible. When the last writer had escaped, Casey went out to the lobby, collected a crowd of strangers around him and continued his marathon talk until he was ready to leave for the park late in the afternoon.

After the game, he took some of his newspapermen to the Coachman's Club, which normally closes at one A.M. Out of deference to Stengel, it remained open for an extra hour that night.

Casey Stengel had remained in view for something like 36 hours, chattering away. The subject of Robinson's criticism never came up, and yet everybody was fully aware that the old man was demonstrating that he was not quite in need of a warm cup of milk and a long night's sleep.

Casey Stengel will not go softly into that good-night; he will expire either drinking Scotch or ridiculing the Mets.

As everybody who covers the team knows, however, Casey *has* dozed off occasionally during a game. It would be astonishing if he didn't. On the road, where he loves to sit up and drink with his writers, his normal schedule seems to call for him to retire at two A.M. and rise at four A.M.

When the Mets are at bat these days, he is almost always standing up, not only to make sure that he remains alert but, it seems, to let everybody see that he is alert. He was surprisingly sensitive about the broken wrist too. When he first came to the dugout on his return to Shea Stadium, he posed only a few minutes for his friends, the photographers. Then he took off the sling, flung it away and snapped, "Why don't you go take some pictures of the Yankee manager? I hear he's having troubles too."

For the next few days he found occasion to show the out-of-town writers the street shoes that had indirectly caused all his troubles by not being worn, a not very subtle way of making it clear that he had not fallen but had caught his spikes. For who, after all, falls and breaks his bones? Why, old men fall and break their bones.

If you want to see a 75-year-old man bristle, just hint to Casey Stengel that it is hard to see how the Mets could have lost any more games under any manager than they have lost under him. "Who would *you* have played that I haven't?" he shouts. "We're still trying to get ten or twelve men who are *big*-league players in the *second division*. If the man is gonna strike out, you can't call a hit-and-run, can you? So they say you got a bad manager."

It is easy enough to understand why Casey absolves himself of all blame once he is kind enough to point out all the other candidates. There is, first and foremost, the league itself.

Casey has always been bitter about the poor crop of players that was put into the expansion pool. "They forgot us in this league," he says, "even more than in the other." He has become increasingly bitter about the established teams' disinclination to help him even when his need is desperate. Casey knows that money can't buy ballplayers anymore, but he did feel he was entitled to a little consideration when second baseman Ron Hunt, his best player, broke his shoulder early in the year. "They wanted $150,000 for a player they can't use themselves," he said, "twice as much as they'd ask from anybody else. They say they don't. They're fibbing."

He also blames his own front office, not too surprising when you consider that the three other expansion clubs have all improved so much more rapidly than the Mets. He blames the front office particularly for their original player selections. "We took too many *names*. Excellent names. High-salaried names. Wonderful fellows, but at the end of their string."

Stengel's greatest disappointment, his great disillusionment really, came when he discovered that neither his name nor his charm could induce the better young prospects to sign with the Mets. In the Mets' first year, Casey even left the team for a day to try to exert the power of Mrs. Payson's money and his own personality upon that season's hottest young prospect, pitcher Bob Garibaldi. Garibaldi listened patiently, but eventually signed with San Francisco. The experience was so unsettling that Casey has never laid his prestige on the line like that again.

"Why shouldn't they want to play in New York?" Casey was saying earlier this season, as he was changing into his uniform. "Why shouldn't they want to play in the best field in baseball? Our uniform is as good as theirs. We live as good as anybody. They can play here fast if they have the ability. They can *make* this team if they put in the time. They can play in the *big* leagues in the *big* city and if they were in baseball for twelve years that would be something tremendous."

But before long the recruiting speech gives way to an old man's perpetual bewilderment at youth's perpetual lack of wisdom.

"The Youth of America," he snorted. "You say, 'Here is the opportunity,' and the Youth of America says, 'How much are you going to pay me?'

"It's like going to the university," he said. "They want

the biggest, the best, the most. All of them twisting around. If necessary, we'll pay the bonuses but they should *earn* it." All at once the old man was shouting angrily, "All right, go make the mistake, but quit making eight or nine of them!"

Then, suddenly, the anger passed. He began to chortle, and he was the lovable Casey Stengel again, serving up a small portion of Stengelese. "They're young enough to field the ball. Are they smart enough to make the play?" He had stripped down to his flaming-red shorts—a sort of trademark by now—and he began to make sweeping motions with his good arm. You could all but hear the fandango music in the background. "They protect you in the field," he said, "with the *appliances*. They give them *appliances* that are like a net. The first baseman used to carry a postage stamp, now they carry fishing nets. They used to say 'Two hands for the beginners,' but it counts just as much if he catches it with one hand, don't it?"

Casey was beginning to enjoy himself, and he knew that his visitor was enjoying him too. "They can protect you in the field," he said, in a singsong mocking voice, "but they can't protect you with the bat. These old pitchers are too smart for them and"—a note of satisfaction, close to malice, had crept into his voice—"they're going to *stay* too smart."

He was swinging an imaginary bat now, one-handed. "The Youth of America," he said. "You bring them in and they swing as hard as they can and you tell them to just me-e-e-t the ball and they look at you. They don't know their hitting area, so they swing at balls they can't hit, and when you try to protect 'em they say"—mincing tone—"'The fellow isn't playing me.' If they'll put in the time instead of saying 'I didn't get a chance,' they can *make* this team. They're lucky. They can find out in two years whether they can make this team instead of five years. I'll stay with them. I'm interested in building this team. That's why I took the job."

That made it sound as if he were planning on staying around for another epoch or two. "That's *my* business," he says. Has he no plans for quitting? "I don't have to tell anybody my personal business. My job is to get this team rolling. I'll tell you one thing; whoever manages this club next will have better players."

And then Casey was saying, "I have to ask what is wrong with myself and say, 'It ought to be done faster.' We held players too long and some were too independent and not too serious. They didn't progress every year. Things happen and you say, 'Maybe I ought to be in another line of business.' "

But the mood passes quickly. The Old Man did not suffer through all those years of undeserved ridicule in order to discover, here at the end, that he was only a poor clown after all. Fully dressed now except for his shoes, he pointed a finger into his visitor's face. "I should get more help here. I got to do it all myself." He looked down challengingly, then added abruptly, *"And,"* he said, *"I can do it too!"*

COMMENTS

I never got a chance to play under Casey Stengel—my bad luck, I was born too late—but I've heard enough stories about him, I've observed him enough, I've talked to enough other ballplayers about him to know he was neither a clown nor a mean old man. He must've been some kind of combination of both. I think he was a clown when it called for being a clown and he was a very shrewd guy when it called for being very shrewd.

This is how shrewd he was. It was spring training of 1960, Casey's last year with the Yankees. Hal Stowe was a rookie pitcher trying to make the club. Except he wasn't trying very hard. Stowe figured that the best way to become a big-leaguer was to act like one. That meant bullshitting around the batting cage, screwing around the outfield instead of doing wind sprints and hanging around with the Big Guys. The Big Guys, like Mickey Mantle and Whitey Ford, wouldn't shag flies because that was demeaning, that was something only rookies did. Hal Stowe felt the same way.

Instead of doing all the little things—like busting your ass—that a rookie is supposed to do to make the big club, Hal Stowe was too busy hanging out with Mantle and Ford, going to dinner with them, making sure that nobody thought he was a rookie.

He was just trying to slide through. Everybody knows that spring training is a vacation for the established players, so Hal Stowe thought that if he acted like he was on vacation, maybe everyone would think he was an established player.

He was trying to snow 'em. Ol' Hal Snow.

Now it's the end of spring training, and Hal Stowe doesn't make the team. So one of the writers, who had been snowed, goes up to Casey Stengel and says, "How come Hal Stowe isn't going north? He had a pretty good spring." Casey, the Casey Stengel who everybody thought was sleeping all the time, the Casey who was supposed to be so old and out of it that he didn't know what was going on, *that* Casey knew very well what was going on every minute of the day. He answers, "It's true, Hal Stowe pitched pretty good this spring, but I noticed in the outfield that he never ran, that he never did all the things he was supposed to, that he never really hustled, he never really worked at it."

Stengel saw through the bullshit.

Not all managers do. Not even all Yankee managers.

Two years later, Hal Stowe was doing the same routine all over again for the next Yankee manager. All during spring training, Stowe hung out with Mantle and Maris and Ford and all the other Big Guys. He'd have drinks with them, go out to dinner with them, he tried to arrange his locker next to theirs.

Meanwhile, the guy Stowe was competing with for the last spot on the team was spending most of his time working his ass off. I knew I had to do something. I didn't have the knuckle ball then. I would run extra, do extra exercizes, all the little additional things you hoped some coach would notice and it would go on your file and maybe you'd get extra brownie points or something. I thought that was the way you made the big leagues. What'd I know? So I worried. I thought Stowe would be more believable to them as a big-league ballplayer because he looked and acted like one, and I would be less believable because I didn't look like one and I didn't act like one. I haven't changed very much.

Looking and acting like a big-leaguer is very important to baseball people. If Jerry Rubin could hit .400, he'd still have trouble making the cut.

So the Yankees, under Ralph Houk, took Hal Stowe

north that spring. And if it wasn't for some clutch, bull-dog-style pitching by a 23-year-old fast-baller who was too in awe of Mickey and Whitey to even speak to them, Hal Stowe would've made the club. You see, Houk *wanted* him to make the club. He was ready to accept a guy who looked like a big leaguer, a guy who would fit in, a guy who would please Mantle. Houk didn't see. Stengel, even when he was winking, did.

And Casey did wink a lot. I'd see him at a dinner, the hall of fame, or somewhere, and there he'd be, holding court, doing his act. He knew what people wanted from him and he was going to give it to them. If the writers needed something for their stories, Casey provided. Maybe that's why a lot of ballplayers didn't like Casey. No ballplayer likes to see another ballplayer get ink. That's a baseball fact of life. Particularly when the other ballplayer doesn't even play ball. They don't like to see another guy getting a lot of ink for something other than raw talent.

It pissed off a lot of the Yankees to have writers come into the clubhouse and, while you were sitting in front of your locker after going 3-for-4, pass you right by. And then, in the paper the next day, you read a story about Casey Stengel.

I think this is called jealousy.

The Yankees were also pissed off at Stengel because he would criticize them to the writers. Houk would never criticize publicly. Stengel would, but only if he could get off a good line.

Like his line about Greg Goossen. "I got a kid, Greg Goossen, he's 19 years old and in ten years he's got a chance to be 29."

Greg Goossen probably wasn't ready to laugh at that for at least six years, when he was in the minor leagues and realized that Stengel was right.

Stengel was right a lot. So maybe the ballplayers were in a constant state of agitation and being pissed off, but sometimes that's a good state for a ball club to be in.

I know I wouldn't have been pissed off if I could have played for Casey. I knew I was his kind of ballplayer. I wanted to play for him. Just one year. I was the Rod Kanehl type. I'd try to tip the catcher's mit with my bat to get a free pass to first base. I'd get my uniform all dirty. And how many managers would appreciate a guy doing extra laps in the outfield? I knew running the extra laps wouldn't hurt if anybody saw me, and I knew that Stengel was the kind of manager who would see. I could run in the outfield knowing it wasn't in vain if he was my manager.

I can just hear Casey talking in spring training. "Well, I'm taking this kid Bouton. He had a couple of bad outings, but he works hard, and I may need a pinch-runner."

Stengel may have been one of the last of the breed of his kind of manager, the manager as star. If he wasn't the last, he was definitely the best. Best of breed in the sheer-force-of-personality division.

As I said before, the people in baseball—the people with money, the ones who own the clubs—don't like strong personalities as their managers anymore. They choose their managers on what shows in the guy's file, on his efficiency ratio. Did he ever rock any boats? Did he ever piss anybody off? Can we count on him at a press conference? Is he reliable, trustworthy? Will he sell Boy Scout cookies?

Casey, of course, fails every one of those tests.

But if I owned a baseball team, if I could hire a manager, I'd hire Casey. If Rocky Bridges wasn't available.

Ralph Houk, Yogi Berra, Johnny Keane

Which of Us
Took the Greater Fall?

by BILL VEECK

What about Johnny Keane? Here is the most out-of-character figure of them all. Keane is normally the guy you see hanging around the lobby during any baseball meeting hoping to catch on with somebody. That isn't meant to downgrade his abilities. Sure, he's a good baseball man, much traveled and widely experienced. Do you know how many good, solid baseball men—much traveled and widely experienced—are hanging around lobbies looking for jobs in today's shrinking market?

But Johnny Keane, the man who normally gets fired, wasn't hanging around any lobbies. Johnny Keane was sitting there with his choice between the two pennant winners. Johnny Keane, the man who gets fired, ended up as manager of the New York Yankees, the number-one job in baseball.

And the reversal of character holds even here. The Yankees, who are accustomed to standing back haughtily and letting the applicants come to them, hat in hand, needed him at the time of the official signing almost as badly as Busch did.

When the Yankees won the pennant in 1964, the most astonished person in the country was Ralph Houk. Houk, like Gussie Busch and Branch Rickey did with St. Louis, had quit on his team, and he had quit on them with far less reason. The Cardinals didn't really have any right to win the pennant, and when they did Busch had already taken steps that were irretrievable. Houk decided in August that 1) the Yankees were going to lose; 2) that it was all Yogi Berra's fault and 3) that Yogi would therefore have to go. When they fooled him and won, he went ahead with his plan just as if they hadn't. Ralph Houk's ability to adjust his thinking is so slight that he could not bring himself to admit that having been wrong in August, he might do well to draw up a new set of plans in October.

Houk shares two qualities with Busch: a firm sense of purpose and a too often nonexistent sense of humor, although they are qualities that stem from entirely different sources. Busch's is the rigidity of the aristocrat that tells him he can do no wrong. Houk's is the rigidity of the combat leader which tells him that the mission must be accomplished whatever the opposition, whatever the odds.

As a combat leader, Houk would study the terrain, absorb the intelligence reports, map out the battle plan and attack. If the battle plan called for him to take a machine-gun nest, you could be confident that he would either take it or go down moving toward it. You could be equally confident that his men would follow him every step of the way.

If it turned out that the intelligence report was wrong, that the terrain was rougher than he had been told, that there was a machine gun hitting them from an unknown angle, he would still follow the battle plan and he would still either take his objective or go down moving toward it.

Which makes him a whale of a combat leader and a disastrous general.

As a manager, Houk had an absolute horror of being accused of pushing the panic button (there's the military background again and maybe even the secret fear). By his definition any change in plans is a sign of panic. Houk, for instance, has usually been most reluctant to bring up any player during the season. As far as he was concerned, he had very carefully picked his squad during spring training, considering every angle, filling every hole, and to call up some other player to fill some spot that was not being adequately covered was an admission that he had been wrong.

It worked for him as a manager. Of course, it helps a little to have a squad with the ability of the Yankees, but it also helps if you have the ability, which Ralph Houk does have in abundance, to convince the players that they can do anything you tell them they can do.

Unfortunately for Houk, the promotion to the front office brought out his worst quality, that total inability to improvise, and negated his greatest virtue, his ability to lead men.

To adjust one's plans to changing conditions is not, of course, a sign of panic at all. It is a sign of balance, of intelligence, of real leadership. Freezing to an outdated situation, that *is* a sign of panic.

When Houk wrote off the Yankees as early as he did, he was pushing the panic button, plain and simple. When he went ahead with the plans that had been made in anticipation of losing, he was not only pushing the panic button again, he was indulging in the most obvious kind of self-justification.

The decision to make Yogi Berra, of all people, the manager of the Yankees was admittedly one of the more moonstruck episodes in baseball. So moonstruck that no one will ever be able to convince me that Yogi was ever anything more than a handy stopgap Houk latched onto in order to boost himself up in the front office.

Ralph has the kind of background and personality that makes it relatively easy for him to handle Dan Topping. Topping is a guy who once ran a football franchise with Shipwreck Kelly so that he could hang around with all those great football players. He is no longer that kind of a hero-worshiper. He has won all the pennants anybody needs, and he has grown cynical and weary. As a matter of fact, Topping wants out of baseball. He is hanging on, now that the Yankees have been sold to CBS, only because he wants to get Dan Topping, Jr., established with the club. He is so fed up with it all that he may not even hang around long enough to do that. Still, Houk is the kind of man Dan always wanted to be, and it is most difficult to look into the mirror of your own secret self and fight back. As a millionaire sportsman you'd have to rank him about halfway between Busch, the aristocrat, and Jim Norris, the well-known collector of fight characters.

Houk has come a long way from the bullpen, and he did not make that trip because he has no capacity to learn. With that passion of his for detail—which is really, again, the platoon leader's concern about keeping his rear guarded—he had kept his hand very firmly in the farm system during his days as a manager. He was at least as aware as anybody else that the Yankee system, which had once been more fertile than the banks of the Nile, had dried up and turned to dust.

With Mantle's legs always chancy, and Ford fighting off new injuries year by year, Houk could see very plainly that the years of easy Yankee domination were coming to an end. Since the manager is, as we have said, always the fall guy, Houk's ambition became to move himself up to the front office so that he could be the man to assess the blame rather than the man who takes it.

While he has no capacity for public relations and even less interest in it, Ralph was also very well aware, if only from reading the papers, that he was no match for Casey Stengel of the Mets in the battle for newspaper space which everybody had become so concerned about. When the opportunity arose, Houk was there either to suggest or to quickly agree that Berra was just the man to compete with Stengel. Actually, Houk couldn't have cared less who became manager, just so long as there was a logical reason for removing himself from the line of fire.

Now, pitting Yogi against Stengel was the worst mismatch in history. No boxing commission would have allowed it. Yogi is a completely manufactured product. He is a case study of this country's unlimited ability to gull itself and be gulled. Yogi had become a figure of fun originally because with his corrugated face and squat body he looked as if he should be funny, and because when he turned out to be a great ballplayer in spite of his odd appearance a natural feeling of warmth went out to him, as to the ugly duckling who makes it big in a world of swans. It pleased the public to think that this odd-looking little man with the great natural ability had a knack for mouthing humorous truths with the sort of primitive peasant wisdom we rather expect of our sports heroes.

Besides, there was that marvelous nickname. You say "Yogi" at a banquet and everybody automatically laughs, something Joe Garagiola discovered to his profit many years ago.

Casey Stengel, an earlier prospector in those fields, had made this discovery long before Garagiola. Casey had always bounced his best lines off Yogi, and the newspapermen and magazine writers, picking it up, were happy enough to go along with the act, since it made their own jobs that much easier and also because, I suppose, enough of them eventually came to believe it themselves.

Not that Yogi had ever been heard to say anything funny. But by then he didn't have to. Every time Yogi hiccupped, he was answered by gales of laughter. Boy, you said to yourself, nobody can hiccup as funny as that Yogi.

I had first come to know Yogi during the time I was operating the St. Louis Browns, a charitable organization formed to provide work for the otherwise unemployable. Yogi was working in New York for a far more profitable organization, but he was still returning to St. Louis in those days to spend his World Series check in his native city.

I used to play cards with him regularly in the St. Louis firehouse, and although you didn't have to put a gun in his ribs to get him to talk, he had little enough to say. He certainly didn't deal in malaprops or basic peasant wisdom. He talked just about the way any guy would talk while he was involved in a friendly game of chance, like you or me or Adlai Stevenson. He was, to sum him up, a friendly guy, a regular guy, a neighborhood guy without sham or pretension.

His real talent was that he was a good audience, a natural enough legacy from a boyhood spent with Garagiola.

He would sit there, relaxed, until the phone rang and a call from his wife, Carmine, ended the game for the day. Carmine always saw something special in Yogi, she was always aware that he had it in him to go further than anyone else thought. She was ambitious for Yogi. And her ambitions didn't include a daily card game with the boys at the firehouse.

It wasn't until I hit the banquet circuit with Garagiola that I started to hear the Yogi gags. While I would be sitting there waiting to go to work myself, it would often cross my mind that I had heard the same stories credited to Babe Herman or Rube Waddell or some other athlete of rough-hewn reputation. I had even used a few of them myself to embellish my own banquet character, Satchel Paige.

The malaprops, witticisms and naïvetés attributed to the Yogi-man got the Yankees a lot of ink over the years. They were never malicious, never really unkind. It was more as if the writers were collaborating in a gigantic "bright sayings of clever children" contest, a department in which the quality of the contributions doesn't have to be very high because everybody knows that the children themselves are so endearing.

All right, you ask, if the newspapermen who covered him regularly knew he was neither a humorist nor a leader of men, then Houk and Topping must certainly have known it too. How then could they have gone ahead and named him manager?

That's what makes this such an illuminating little episode and illustrates so beautifully the way the business of baseball is conducted even on the club that is widely heralded to be the most efficiently run of them all.

Because the whole thing began as just another Yogi Berra joke.

It began in the major league meetings at the end of 1960 when three of the more pixieish sportswriters, disgusted by the increasingly ridiculous names that were being put forth as the new manager of the San Francisco Giants, decided to conduct an experiment to determine the speed of communication (rumor division) and the gullibility of the *genus* sportswriter in search of something—*anything*—to justify the expense account.

The three writers were Stan Isaacs of Long Island *Newsday*, Leonard Shecter of the New York *Post* and Larry Merchant of the Philadelphia *Inquirer*, all famed as twisters of the Establishment's tail. They concocted the evil little design of circulating the name of the unlikeliest prospect that it was within the powers of the human mind to conceive, and then sitting back over their drinks to clock the length of time it took for their own rumor to come floating back to them adorned by all sorts of authoritative, unimpeachable sponsors.

The unlikeliest candidate they could think of was Yogi Berra.

The rumor bounced back to its parents so fast that it wasn't even fun. But since Yogi was now a bona fide candidate, reporters called him for his comment. No, Yogi told them, he hadn't been contacted yet but yes, he would most certainly welcome the challenge and the opportunity—which, I will wager, had never occurred to him before. Yogi was on his way.

The following year, the Red Sox found themselves looking for a manager too. The Red Sox were a magnificently run organization, as a quick glance at their lineup could have told you. With that left-field wall casting its foreboding shadow over the shortstop, the Red Sox had, by dint of long-range planning that staggers the imagination, come up with a lineup composed entirely of left-handed line-drive hitters. Because of that lineup the Red Sox found themselves looking, for a manager. As might be expected, they remembered reading that Berra's name had been added to the managerial lists and decided that he was just the man they wanted—presumably on the grounds that he couldn't be a worse manager than Pinky Higgins and, since Yogi was still swinging his big bat, he could certainly outhit him.

The Yankees weren't about to give Yogi up, but he already had a legitimate offer under his belt.

A year later, Baltimore was in fairly desperate search for not only a manager but for a manager who might even create a little interest in the team. Lee MacPhail decided that Yogi was just the attraction they needed, and he went so far as to offer him a contract. That was Houk's chance to step in and suggest that Yogi might be the answer to New York's own problems.

Yogi did get the Yankees more space in the papers which was, when you come right down to it, what he was hired for, although he still didn't come close to the Grand Old Gnome of Shea Stadium. But then, Stengel had something going for him. Casey is a legitimately funny man.

There is, however, one point that should be added here, irrelevant though it might be. Yogi did do one thing that Stengel didn't. Yogi won the pennant, and Casey finished last. He cut it close, winning by only one game, but the pennant was really pretty much locked up through the entire final week. And whatever their protestations, a close race was exactly what the Yankees wanted.

Did he make mistakes? Of course he did. Stengel had spent a lifetime managing before he came to the Yankees. Houk had served a four-year apprenticeship in the minors and three more years coaching under Stengel. Berra had spent one year as a player-coach. When he was hired, it was obviously with the tacit understanding that he was going to be permitted to make his mistakes right out there in the open where everybody could see them. It didn't seem quite fair to tell him, at the end of the year, that he had been on probation all the time.

How much help did they give him? As a freshman manager he needed, above all else, a wise old head as pitching coach. Houk's first move as general manager was to dump his wise old head, Johnny Sain—although that seems to have been because Sain and Berra had never seen eye-to-eye. To replace him, Houk and Berra picked Whitey Ford, giving the freshman manager a freshman pitching coach, and a part-time one at that.

The pitching got messed up, no question about it. And Yogi was at least partly to blame. He was using his long relievers short and his short relievers long, and like all new managers he was waiting too long before he got his starting pitcher out of there.

Still, he was operating under a major handicap. The relief pitcher who can come in over the last two innings and get the other side out can cover up a multitude of sins. Yogi didn't have him. Except for one brief period early in the season when Steve Hamilton was stopping them, and the final month of the season when they had Pete Ramos, the Yankee bullpen was useless.

The Yankee relief pitching didn't stop the other team at the end of the game, and the Yankee hitters became lambs over the last couple of innings, a complete reversal of their history.

But then the hitting fell apart during the early part of the game too. For once, the Yankee long-ball was conspicuously absent. Mantle was out with injuries. Maris was a rally-killer until the last month of the season. Only Howard, among the big hitters, was consistent.

The first baseman ran hot and cold. The second baseman had a very mediocre year. The shortstop had a terrible year. The third baseman had an impossible year. The other outfielder, Tresh, was a major disappointment. Normally, you win a pennant when all your players have good years together. The Yankees won it with all their players having bad years together.

Admittedly, there are intangibles here. Maybe, under Houk, the pitching staff would have been better; probably it would have been. Possibly Richardson, Kubek and Boyer would have hit better under Houk. Possibly balls would have flown out of the park just like in the good

old days. That we'll never know. All we do know is that
they sure didn't hit any better for Ralph while they were
losing those four straight games to the Dodgers in his
farewell appearance.

I know something else, too. With all their difficulties,
the Yankees did come on with that rush down the stretch.
Unless I have been sadly misinformed by all those sensa-
tion-seeking columnists, the manager during that stretch
run was Yogi Berra.

And now something else. Seldom in my experience has
a manager of a pennant-contending team been more
shabbily served by his general manager, during his time
of trouble, than Berra was served by Houk. During the
entire year, Houk made only one move. He brought up
Mel Stottlemyre, who was widely acknowledged to be the
best pitcher in the minor leagues.

Ramos, you say? Oh no. Ramos wasn't Houk's idea,
although he has shown no particular reluctance to accept
the credit. Ramos was *sold* to the Yankees by Gabe
Paul, and even here he was sold to Dan Topping. When
Houk was consulted he argued that they weren't close
enough for Ramos to make that much difference. Houk's
solution wasn't to go out and get a relief pitcher, it was
to fire Berra. When CBS bought the club, Ralph told
them that the Yankees weren't going to win the pennant
because Berra had butchered the job, but that everything
was going to be fine again next year when Yogi was
gone. After all, if it wasn't Yogi's fault, somebody just
might have gone home with the ridiculous idea that it
was Ralph's.

Nor did Ralph stand by his manager, like an oak, when
the players came to his office to cry that Yogi was a poor
manager and notably lacking in the essential qualities of
gentlemanly behavior and inspiring leadership as enunci-
ated by the YMCA. It would seem far more probable
that they departed with the distinct impression that they
wouldn't have to put up with Yogi's crudities for another year since, as the season progressed, the players felt

increasingly free to express their complaints to newspapermen.

To be fair about it, though, I could be doing both Houk and the players an injustice. These were players who had become accustomed over a period of years to bringing their troubles to Houk. Ralph himself is accustomed, by background and by nature, to listening to the troops and distrusting everyone else. It was natural enough, perhaps, that the players would influence him all out of proportion to their intent. It was perhaps inevitable that he would see massive indictment in what they only meant as mild complaint.

After that has been said, however, it is still clear enough that it was hardly any service to Berra to permit the players to come around behind the manager's back and weep on his ready shoulder.

When you sum up Berra's year as manager, then, you have to say that he was thrown into the job cold, that his team fell apart on him, that there was an absolute minimum of help from the front office and that he was being undercut by some of his players.

And still he won. I wouldn't award him a gold star for the year, but I wouldn't give him a failing mark either. Not by a long shot.

Berra is gone from the Yankees and Houk remains to chart the future course. To me, this is ample cause for everybody in the American League to take heart. I tell you that with Houk's rigid hand at the controls, the Yankees can be had. As they are.

In a time of swift change, the Yankees are in the hands of a man who cannot and will not change. They were able to squeak by in the American League, in a dogfight, for a couple of years only because they were the only team in the league that *knew how* to win a pennant. Even here, they looked so bad in two straight World Series that the other American League clubs could not help but get the message that the mighty Yankees are ready to be taken.

The Yankees can no longer trade minor-league averages for major-league players, because they don't have the minor-league averages to work with anymore. And that means they have to trade man for man. I haven't noticed Houk out there on the battle lines pitting himself and his judgment against his colleagues. If a trade can help you it can also hurt you, and Houk is not a man to leave himself that vulnerable to criticism. The Major still keeps his rear well protected.

I'll tell you something. I was sulking around the house for awhile, kicking the dogs and frightening the children, because with Del (The Yankee Clipper) Webb gone, Ford (A Legend in His Own Time) Frick going, and George (What's So Funny?) Weiss on the brink of retirement, I was losing all of my targets.

No longer do I look upon myself as a hardship case. I have the wild and gladsome feeling that Ralph Houk is going to develop into a target worthy of his distinguished predecessors.

He's a natural target right out of the starting gate because he fancies himself a strong man, and like most self-anointed strong men, he has the habit of confusing strength with weakness. He met the challenge of his first serious holdout in the spring of 1964 by threatening Jim Bouton with a $100-a-day fine for every day he failed to sign. Now, this is out-and-out blackmail, and while it is perhaps not worthy of mention, it is also against the rules of baseball. Owners used to be able to indulge their instinct for this kind of petty tyranny back in the thirties before the players had any kind of representation, and you can just see little Ralphie Houk lapping it up in the hometown newspaper and dreaming of the day when he would grow up and be a feudal baron too.

This kind of thing demonstrates quite clearly that the Major still carries a shotgun where his sense of public relations is supposed to be. I tell you, Ralphie baby, you keep pulling that kind of rock and CBS is going to blow you right out of the chair with its own well-notched shotgun.

Sheer bookkeeping screams out that the Yankees must change their image in order to compete with the image of the bumbling, stumbling but lovable little Metsies. At bottom, all this "image" talk mystifies and bewilders Houk. His natural habitat is the field of action, not the executive suite and certainly not the marketplace. Sure, he will put on his gray suit and hold his press conferences and smile his broad empty smile, because he has been assured that this is all part of the job. But he doesn't believe a word of it. You take the hill, you smash the gun emplacement, you win the pennant, there's solid accomplishment! There's something you can plan and blueprint and come to grips with.

So Houk continued to go to the press conferences determined to put forth the warm and colorful image the bosses desire, and before he was halfway through, the old inflexibility would take hold and he would be saying, almost plaintively, "But we still win on the field and that's all that really counts, isn't it? Well, isn't it . . . ? Isn't it . . . ?"

Show me a man who operates on what his logic, his morality and all his nerve ends tell him *should* be true, instead of what *is* transparently true, and I'll show you a man who is not only going to fail miserably but who is going to wear his failure as proof of his own basic worth and integrity.

The Mets, who finished last, outdrew you in 1964 by almost half a million fans, Ralph. Why *can't* you remember?

Houk sets himself up as a natural target, too, because he is devoid of a sense of humor. Unlike Weiss, whose face clearly shows at all times that life is a grim business out of which only fools could take any pleasure, Houk usually has a big smile pasted on his face. It takes a little while before you see that the smile comes automatically whether you've said anything funny or not. He is going to smile at the suspicion of humor, just to make sure you don't catch on that he has none.

In one way you have to sympathize with him. Tough

as he is, feared as he is, he is suddenly playing in a league he knows nothing about. He will find that these faceless CBS people who smile and cozen him, just like any other fawning, faceless fans, will have a ruthlessness such as he's never faced before. He is in there with the mechanical men of our time, with men who are activated solely by the figures being fed them from a machine. These are the combat soldiers of our time; we have achieved the age of the robot. If the ratings (i.e., the attendance) continue to go down they will chop him down, effortlessly, routinely, almost thoughtlessly. Just as they chopped down Judy Garland, Phil Silvers and others too numerous to remember.

And there won't even be anybody to hit back.

If Ralph does go, he will be replaced by about a dozen CBS vice-presidents. And won't *that* be fun? If there is anything more ridiculous than a corporate vice-president trying to run a ball club, it is a committee of corporate vice-presidents trying to run a ball club. Comedians, sportswriters and other opportunists should be able to have a field day with them.

The Yankees image was badly scarred and tarnished by the World Series and its aftermath. Where it had previously been cold, austere and chillingly efficient, it became cold, austere and clumsy. In the Series, they kicked all four losing games away, something not even the most visionary Yankee-haters ever expected to see.

In the managerial exodus that followed, the Yankees came off far worse than the Cardinals, image-wise. Keane, offered the world and all, won the admiration of the pure of heart by spurning Gussie Busch's gold. Berra, fired, signed on happily as roving something or other, with duties so vague that you had to conclude that he was expected to earn his money by staying away. The best measure of Houk's sure sense of public relations is that the reaction to the firing of the old Yankee hero seemed to surprise him. To show their goodwill, the Yankees let it be known that they were giving Yogi a clause guaranteeing him severance pay of $25,000 above and beyond his salary, which only made it seem as if the Yankees would be only too happy to pay him the $25,000 to get him out of their hair. If it also seemed as if Yogi didn't care how badly he was treated just so long as he was well paid, that bitter lesson rubbed off on the Yankees in an odd way, too. The fans, grown accustomed to loving good old Yogi, didn't want to feel that way about him and so whatever feeling of distaste they may have felt was very quickly transferred to the Yankees.

The Mets were still to be heard from. This guy Grant, or whoever is calling the shots over there, is a really good operator. The hiring of Stengel and Weiss was originally nothing more than an easy way to integrate the club into the sports history of the city. With the hiring of Berra it was converted into a calculated plan to raid the Yankees, the easiest possible way of bringing the Yankee fans into Shea Stadium and, more fun still, of keeping the Yankees permanently embarrassed and permanently on the defensive.

With the Mets, Yogi will be the space-catcher the Yankees hoped he would be for them, because while Yogi can't play the comic lead, he makes an excellent second banana. With Stengel there to bounce his jokes off him, Yogi will seem to be funny again. And don't think the Old Man doesn't know how to do it. Casey could give public-relations lessons to B.B.D.& O.—and all the rest of the alphabet too. Casey's decade of unparalleled success with the Yankees seduced us all into forgetting where his real talents lie. Casey doesn't really care whether he wins or loses, just so long as the turnstiles keep moving.

For Berra, it might be a foolish move. Unless he had a sudden and highly unlikely feeling of revulsion at the way he had permitted the Yankees to treat him, he would have been far better off staying right where he was. The Yankees, to put it baldly, were stuck with him. Yogi could have sat there for ten or fifteen years, drawing down an annual $35,000 or so for playing golf.

Yogi apparently thought he had a chance to become the manager of the Mets after Stengel departs. His chances aren't that hot. He apparently thinks that with Weiss and Stengel around, he can draw on past associations and loyalties to take care of him. Unhappily for Yogi, Stengel and Weiss will both be gone very soon, and neither Grant nor Mrs. Payson nor Bing Devine owes Yogi Berra a thing. He was a public-relations coup for them, nothing more.

Notice, once again, the reversal of form that has become almost obligatory through this whole strange interlude. Yogi Berra, accustomed throughout his career to undeserved praise, is suddenly hit with undeserved criticism. The man whom everybody had always protected and coddled was the man who became the patsy.

A Locker Room View

by JIM BOUTON

Ralph Houk's promotion from manager to general manager was a classic example of the Peter Principle in operation. As general manager, Houk arrived at his level of incompetence. Mike Burke eventually recognized the Peter Principle, applied the Peter Prescription and demoted Houk back to manager, where he belonged.

Houk tried hard to be a general manager. He took to wearing $200 suits with color-coordinated ties, and he spent 50 cents more for his cigars. And when he'd join the team for an occasional road trip, I'd see him at the airport newsstand buying yachting magazines instead of PLAYBOY. Houk tried to look comfortable in his new role, but mostly he looked out of place, or as one player said, "like a whore in church."

Houk's biggest mistake, after he and Berra were promoted, was losing Johnny Sain as pitching coach. The Yankees are still hurting from that.

Sain and Yogi (how can you call him Berra?) had differences that went all the way back to when they both played for the Yankees and Sain, the pitcher, wanted to throw curves, while Yogi, the catcher, kept calling for fast balls because they were easier to catch. So when Yogi became manager, Sain asked for a two-year contract (coaches normally have one-year contracts) to find out if the Yankees really wanted him and to provide them with an excuse if they didn't.

They didn't. There were the obvious reasons why Houk did not hang on to Sain. Yogi didn't want him, Houk didn't care too much how Yogi's pitchers did and Houk didn't want to become the first general manager to give a two-year contract to a coach. But there were other, more important, reasons. For one, Sain had a quiet way of seeing through people, and after a few years Sain's presence began to make Houk feel uncomfortable. Also Sain had been known to give helpful advice to players in their contract disputes. Most coaches and managers will hint, or come right out and say, that if you don't sign for management's figure you won't make the ball club. Sain refused to be used like that. His favorite saying was, "Don't be afraid to climb those golden stairs." Houk was now sitting at the top of those golden stairs and for him Sain meant problems.

The Yankees should have kept Sain and let Houk go. While the Yankees have been losing eight pennants in a row, Sain has been coaching Minnesota, Detroit and almost Chicago into the World Series.

Whitey Ford was the best available pitching coach on short notice. He was also his own best pupil, and since he pitched in rotation every four days, it meant that Yogi's pitching coach was only 75 percent effective. Add that to the players complaining and you realize that Yogi was not a bad manager. He may have been a great manager considering how poorly the Yankees played after Yogi left.

Veeck is right about the players complaining to Houk. The biggest gripers were Elston Howard, Clete Boyer and, surprisingly, Tony Kubek, who also spoke for Bobby Richardson. Mantle and Ford kidded about Yogi, but I don't remember them ever complaining. It was beneath them.

And I never heard of Houk kicking the whiners out of his office, either.

Yogi's problem was not himself, but the players. Houk, the master psychologist, the smoke blower, was our pacifier, and when he was taken away we reacted like babies. The players never respected Yogi. He was always "good old Yog," who was thought to be in over his head even as a coach.

I think Veeck is wrong when he says Yogi was a completely manufactured product. He was only partly manufactured. And Yogi actually did say some funny things.

One time we were all on the team bus which would take us to the airport where we'd fly to St. Louis for the 1964 World Series. We were waiting for Bob Fishel, the PR man, who had gone back to the office to see if he could get me an extra World Series ticket. Finally, he came running onto the bus, handed me a manila envelope with the ticket inside and said, "Boy are you lucky, this was the last one."

Yogi, sitting across the aisle, said, seriously, "Are they all out of them manila envelopes already?"

Another time, a sportswriter asked Yogi what time it was, and Yogi said, "Right now?"

Once some players invited Yogi to come along and watch a stag movie, and Yogi said, "Who's starring in it?"

Most of the time, though, Yogi didn't say funny things. There was the time toward the end of the 1964 season, when we were in a three-team pennant race with Chicago and Baltimore. We were in Chicago and had just blown a doubleheader—to make it five straight—and during the long, slow, hot bus ride from the ball park to the airport, the bus was like a morgue. No false sorrow here. We were slipping into a poor third and with about 30 games to go we needed every game. It was genuine depression. For most of us anyway.

During the ride, Phil Linz decided to play the harmonica he had just purchased that morning. He got out the little instruction book and began to play "Mary Had a Little Lamb." Yogi, sitting up front, couldn't believe his ears. He screamed back at Linz to shove that harmonica up his pocket. Or somewhere. Personally, I don't know why Yogi got so upset. The way Phil was playing, it sounded like a sad song.

Since Linz had just spent good money for that harmonica, and since he hadn't been getting into many games even though he'd been hitting well, and since the five straight losses weren't his fault, and since he loved music, he continued playing. It's not true that Linz turned to ask Mantle what Yogi had said and that Mantle reported, "Play it louder."

Anyway, when Phil got to the part about the lamb's fleece being white as snow, Yogi came charging to the back of the bus and in a loud voice reiterated what he had said earlier about the most appropriate place to put the harmonica. Whereupon Linz flipped the harmonica toward Yogi and said, "Do it yourself."

Yogi, a notoriously bad harmonica hitter, swatted at it and lined it cleanly off Joe Pepitone's knee. This brought Pepi up into the aisle doing his number entitled, "Oooh, You Hurt My Little Knee." Everyone began stifling giggles except for Frank Crosetti, who stood up and hollered that it was the worst thing that had ever happened to the Yankees. Cro was only slightly wrong. It may have been the best thing that ever happened. From that point on, the club got hot, we moved back into first place, Yogi and Linz began posing regularly for pictures with prop harmonicas, and sportswriters were calling the harmonica incident the turning point.

Of course, if we had stayed in third and lost the pennant it would still have been called the turning point. Sportswriters love to write about turning points. What had seemed like a bad scene turned into a good break. Those who knew Yogi were not surprised.

The players used to always kid about how lucky Yogi was, and it seemed true. When Yogi bought stock, the market went up. When he sold, it went down. Yogi got into the bowling business just before the boom and got out just before the crash. While ballplayers were spending the off-season inventing new ways to lose money, Yogi was becoming a major stockholder and corporate executive of the Yoo Hoo soft-drink company just by investing his name. One of the players once said that if God had to make someone to look like Yogi, the least he could do was make him lucky.

The players also felt that having Yogi around was like

having a good-luck charm. Once we were on a plane that was bouncing through a thunderstorm. Lightning was dancing off the wings. Everyone was afraid, of course, but it was nothing like the chill we all felt when some wise guy remembered that Yogi had stayed back a few hours and taken a later flight. We said we could all see the picture of Yogi the next day with a sad look on his face as he was reading a newspaper headline that said, "YANKEE TEAM KILLED IN PLANE CRASH. BERRA LIVES—CATCHES LATER FLIGHT."

Whitey Ford said no, the headline would read, "MICKEY MANTLE, 29 OTHERS KILLED."

Of course, Yogi is still alive, and living now in Shea Stadium. Even the observant Veeck didn't realize that it was inevitable that Yogi would be in the number-one spot again. I think Yogi should do well with the Mets. He knows the game. He doesn't have the handicap of having been buddies with half the team. And even if the Mets should lose, Yogi's luck will get him into the front office or some nice place.

At least the job of managing the Mets won't kill Yogi like managing the Yankees killed Johnny Keane. Literally. I watched Johnny Keane age 20 years in the year and a little he managed the Yankees.

Johnny Keane, Houk's personal choice, was the perfect example of the wrong man for the wrong team at the wrong time. Where the Yankee players had become annoyed and uncomfortable with Yogi, they actually became angry with Keane. As they did with Yogi, the players were always comparing Keane with Houk. "He doesn't pat anybody on the back. He doesn't kick anybody in the butt. He's so cold he won't even talk to anybody." Not like Ralph.

Johnny Keane was a very religious man who at one point in his life had thought of becoming a priest. So he couldn't believe the training rules on the Yankees. There were none. We always had such a good team that we could stay out till all hours and still beat anybody. When we began losing for Keane he thought late hours was the reason. But since we had always won before, we knew it wasn't. I'll never forget when Keane first confronted us with our debauchery. It was late in his first spring training with us, and we had been playing ho-hum baseball and keeping atrocious hours as was our custom in the spring. During the season we only altered our ballplaying.

So Keane called us together and had difficulty beginning his first sentence. Because this was so new to him, he had trouble finding the words for just what it was we were guilty of. He finally said he thought that about 10 or 12 of us had become a little "careless in our habits" this spring. That brought smiles to all our faces. Then he said he had been in baseball a long time and we weren't going to be able to show him anything he hadn't already seen. He was wrong. About two weeks into the season, he had another meeting that started off with, "I thought I'd seen everything, but . . ." Those meetings became such regular events he could have put them on tape and saved his breath.

Our attitude was to make fun of Keane. We'd be sitting in a bar somewhere at three in the morning and one of the guys would tell the bartender that we knew it was "careless," but we all wanted another round. Or the players would call him "Squeaky." Not because of his voice, which was a strong baritone, but because he was short and thin and we compared him to a mouse. If Keane had been six-foot-two and 200 pounds, he could have done everything the same and gotten lots more respect. Houk, who was strong and acted tough, would ask a slightly injured player if he needed a rest, and the guy would say, hell no, and hit two homers. Keane would tell the same guy that he wasn't hurt bad enough to sit out, and the guy would go up and take three halfhearted swings. Houk would tell one of the Big Guys to bunt, and the players would all say, "Hey, great idea, surprise 'em with a bunt." And the guy would lay one down perfectly. Keane would tell the same guy to bunt, and all the players would say, "Him bunt? What's going on?

Houk would've let him hit away, you bet your ass."

Size and strength are important to baseball players. They'll say in awe of somebody, "That sonofabitch will break your arms," or so-and-so will "pinch your head off." Around the dugouts no one says, "That sonofabitch sure is intelligent."

Houk was our kind of guy, a tobacco-chewer, a beer drinker, a carouser. Maybe the reason Houk never had a curfew was because he felt that would mean he would have to come in, too. Ralph might threaten to knock a guy off his barstool, but at least that meant he was in the bar.

He had that reputation for being a tough guy; except the only fights I ever remember him getting into were one-punch affairs with a drunk pitcher and a dancing singer. Ryne Duren, the pitcher, was also blind. He wore glasses that looked like the bottom of Coke bottles, which enabled him to distinguish mounds but not home plates. During a victory celebration on a train, Duren playfully tried to push Houk's cigar further into Houk's mouth, and Houk belted Duren with the back of his hand. At the time Houk happened to be wearing a World Series ring (12 oz.) on the back of his hand. Duren landed on the back of his seat.

The other punch I know of came at Toots Shor's, when Gordon MacRae asked Ralph's wife Betty to dance. Ralph wanted to leave and another dance probably meant ten more minutes of listening to Toots Shor. No *wonder* Houk decked MacRae when he insisted on dancing. One punch and it was "I'll see you in my dreams" for Gordon MacRae.

Usually Houk does not pick on someone with the pugilistic background of a Duren or a MacRae. What he likes to do is rough up chipmunks. Not the kind that gather acorns, but the kind who report sports for some newspapers.

One spring Maury Allen of the *New York Post* wrote that Ralph Houk had lost control of the team or something like that. The next day I saw Houk pick up Maury

Allen by the lapels of his Banlon shirt and bang his (Maury's) head against the cinder-block wall of his (Houk's) office. Houk did this with the door open in case any players wanted to watch. This was important. Because aside from the pleasure of watching Maury's head bouncing off the wall, and intimidating Maury and other writers into writing good things about the Yankees, the main reason he did it was to unite the Yankees against a common enemy. Someone besides ourselves to blame for defeat. Chances are good that Houk apologized to Maury Allen. Houk would always apologize. Quietly. The next day. In private.

Another time Houk berated New York *Daily News* reporter Joe Trimble in a loud voice on the team bus, and the players applauded. The next day Houk apologized to Trimble. In a soft voice. When they weren't on the team bus. Houk would humiliate in public and apologize in private. This way he felt he could keep friendships, without diminishing the effect it had on players and other writers.

Yogi wasn't a tough guy and the players didn't respect him, but at least they liked him. I think the Yankee players didn't like or respect Johnny Keane.

Oh, we all said we did. We said we respected him so much we were trying *too* hard. But deep down we thought we lost under Keane because he wasn't our kind of guy, and if only we could get Houk back, we'd win. In fact, right after Houk replaced Keane, we got hot, and like everyone else, I felt we were going to win and that it really was Keane's fault that we had been losing. After a few weeks reality reared its ugly head, and we couldn't win even with Houk. What a shock. Was losing really our fault? Couldn't be. Keane must have gotten us into bad habits. We probably just forgot how to win. Next year Houk would pull us out.

Of course he never did. Not because he didn't try. He still blew his smoke and did the little things his players always liked. For instance, players like to know exactly where they stand. Or sit. Houk usually told them. Most managers, and Johnny Keane was no different, don't even discuss the subject, but Houk calls you right in and says, "You're going to be sitting on the bench for the next month." Managers are afraid to tell that to a player, but it's really a lot better getting it that way than checking out the lineup card every day in anticipation.

And Houk made the scrubeenies feel like part of the team. Before a game he'd say to a guy, "You're going to win this with a pinch-hit in the ninth." Or he'd say to a pitcher, "I'm glad to see you still running your sprints— we'll need you in about two weeks." Most managers make the mistake of ignoring the marginal players. Not Houk who is a master psychologist.

More recently he's even been learning how to master the press. Or maybe he's mellowing with old age. Writers who follow the Yankees today say Houk has become a pussycat. He'll sit in his office after a game and try to help the writers out with a funny line or an anecdote. The walls of the office may even be padded now. Or he'll send a drink over to their table in a restaurant. Maybe this is because the Yankees are no longer a power-house. Maybe if they get back on top Houk will become his old self again. C'mon, Baltimore.

It was because the Yankees had been such a power-house, with all that tradition and those big names, that Keane was reticent with us at first. He seemed slightly in awe of the Yankees, and didn't want to give the impression of coming in to take over. Then, as that first summer wore on, his quietness became a coolness as he heard the rumblings, and he became more certain every day that we were conspiring against him. As he did with Yogi, Houk listened to the complainers, who were becoming even more numerous. Houk never kicked anybody out of his office or called a meeting to shape us up. By the end of '65 and the beginning of '66, Keane would only spend time with his trusted coach, Vern Benson, whom we all called "Radar," because he always seemed to want to listen in on our conversations. And the players would stand around in groups of five and six and *have* conversations, usually about how much longer Johnny Keane would remain as manager. I remember one time Keane walked into a hotel lobby where a bunch of us were talking, and as he walked by we all said, "Hi, John." John, smiling and nodding, said, "Gentlemen of the jury."

I'm sure those are all unhappy memories for all the Yankee players, especially considering Johnny Keane's death and the certainty that his ordeal with the Yankees took its toll on the man. Johnny Keane was a good manager, maybe even a great one for the right team. Like the 1964 St. Louis Cardinals. I'll never forget what Keane said that year about pitcher Bob Gibson. It was the finest thing I've ever heard a manager say about a player and it's the way I want to remember Johnny Keane. Gibson had just beaten us in the seventh game of the World Series, but not before running into trouble in the ninth when two home runs were hit off him. Gibson had already beaten us twice and when he had trouble in the ninth Keane never even came out to the mound to talk things over with him.

Afterwards, in the clubhouse, one of the sportswriters asked Keane if he had thought of taking Gibson out at that point, and Keane said, "I never considered taking him out. I had a commitment to his heart."

As this book was going to press, Ralph Houk said one of the finest things I've ever heard *him* say. (The *finest* thing I ever heard him say was, "Congratulations, Jim, you've made the ball club.") It was March 5, 1973, and Yankee pitchers Fritz Peterson and Mike Kekich were explaining about their family trade at a press conference. You remember that was the deal where Peterson traded his wife, their youngest child and their dog to Kekich, for his wife, their youngest child and their dog. They each kept their eldest child and their own house. The latest word was that Peterson's wife, child and dog refused to report and Kekich was demanding the return of his players.

The situation was both humorous and sad, but some

members of the press thought Peterson and Kekich should be punished for violating, as Dick Young of the New York *Daily News* said, "society's rules." Young did not insist that they be branded with an "A" on their foreheads, but he did expect the Yankees, or the commissioner, to do something. The commissioner read his mail for two weeks and then decided it was "deplorable." But Ralph Houk was at his all-time best. Said Houk, "The players' lives are their own. We all have problems. You only go through this world once and everyone has a right to go through it happy." This may indicate that Houk the manager is changing with the times, or it may be manager Houk's way of minimizing the effect on his team while he waits to trade one of them. But it may also be a truer insight into Ralph Houk the person. C'mon Yankees.

Connie Mack

COMMENTS

Go through a photo library's file on Connie Mack. There's a shot of Connie, face unlined and eyes bright, in the formal uniforms of the 1880s. There's a shot of him, dignified and respectably middle-aged, shaking hands with John McGraw, both of them wearing their homburgs, a few years after the century had turned. There's one—Connie now starting to gray—with Babe Ruth. With Joe DiMaggio. With Bob Feller. There are shots of him with presidents from Taft to Truman. There are pictures with Thomas Edison and General Eisenhower. With everyone of importance from 1900 through 1950.

If you were important, you posed with Connie Mack. He was the GOM (grand old man) of the GOG (great old game). He was involved in baseball for almost 70 years. He managed for over 50. He managed until he was past 90. Bob Considine has him here, still managing, still active, at the age of 86. Baseball was his whole life. Four years after he stopped managing, one year after his team—the Philadelphia A's—was taken from him, he died.

Cornelius McGillicuddy
—Mr. Mack

by BOB CONSIDINE

Cornelius McGillicuddy, who was given the enduring alias of Connie Mack by an unsung newspaperman in 1884 —because his full name could not fit in the small space of a newspaper box score—must be one of the oldest truly active businessmen in the U.S.

As president-treasurer-manager of the Philadelphia Athletics baseball club he works seven days a week, 365 days a year and pays himself a salary comparable to that of the President of the U.S. But Mr. Mack, as his countless associates, friends and acquaintances call him religiously and with a certain awe, is not a rich man. He has, among other responsibilities, 15 great-grandchildren and a small army of personal pensioners dependent on his earning capacity. In 1946 he reported an income of $79,000, which made him perhaps the highest-paid-84-year-old employee in the country, but he was unable to buy the Buick he had on order. Minor stockholders in the Athletics, which Mister Mack has managed since 1901, chipped in, bought him the car and provided a chauffeur —one of the rare concessions made to Mr. Mack's incredible age.

Mister Mack, who will be 86 years old next December, might almost ask for patent rights to the game of baseball if he had not signed away such claims by lending himself to the pretty fable that the sport was the handiwork of the late General Abner Doubleday. He did much to fashion its rules, pioneered in developing the torturous art of catching, was a major manipulator in the rape of the National League at the turn of the century (which produced the American League and made big-league baseball big) and he introduced the modern style of pitching.

This occurred one day in Waterbury, Conn., when Mister Mack, crouching 15 feet behind home plate and catching the ball on its first bounce with the aid of a fingerless kid glove, decided that there must be a better way for his pitcher to deliver the ball. He felt it was essentially unfair for his thrower to hop, skip and run through his cramped little 6 x 4 pitching box and to throw underhanded to a batter who not only was given seven balls and four strikes but could also demand that the ball be delivered to him at a favored height. So he walked out to the marked-off box in which his hurler stood and said, "Try throwing the ball overhand."

The man looked up at him as if he had gone mad, but followed his advice. The ball shot over the plate at a lively clip, and the batter—as startled as a batter of today might be if Bob Feller suddenly delivered a through-the-legs pitch—missed it vaguely. It took the fans three more pitches to realize that Waterbury was being cruelly had. Then they rose and made as if to come out on the field and attack the pitcher.

But Connie reached him first. "Don't listen to those fellows," he ordered. "Just pitch your own game." The man did, and his daring new delivery produced a considerable vogue; so considerable, in fact, that the pitcher's box was moved back from 45 feet to its present 60 feet 6 inches from the plate. And pitchers have been throwing like that ever since.

Mack was one of the first catchers to move up to a position just behind the batter and catch the ball before it bounced. His proximity to the batters of that dimly distant era stimulated in him the devil which is part of his kindly nature. It occurred to him that if he was that close to a man who was bent upon bringing ruin to him and the Mack team he might as well trip him or "tip" his bat—to interfere with his swing—or in other ways militate against the man's getting a hit.

"Don't ever say I was a great catchaw," he told this reporter recently. "But," he added with a bit of glitter in his slightly watery blue eyes, "I was kinda tricky. We got away with a lot back in the days when we played with only one umpire. The only time I ever really got caught was by an old ballplayer named Weaver. I must have been with Washington. Anyway, this Weaver—a fine fellow—he got angry with me after I had tipped his bat a few times, and he used to say that he'd get even with me.

"Well, Mr. Constantine, he did. By gosh, the next time he had two strikes on him he just stepped back from the plate and instead of swinging at the ball he brought his bat down on my wrists. I dropped like a shot. Let me tell you it hurt.

"But I figured out a way to get back at him. I waited until our last game of the year against Weaver's team, and Weaver's last time at bat, and when he had two strikes on him I tipped his bat again, just to show him I could still do it."

Except that each passing decade gives him more and more the appearance of a stately and well-plucked gobbler, Mister Mack has not changed much in the last 50 years. He was born in East Brookfield, Massachusetts, either just before or just after the midnight which separated December 22, 1862, from December 23, 1862. His brother Mike, who lived to be 90 by sticking steadfastly to a daily glass of whisky (Connie gave up his own modest drinking and golf when he was 76), liked to cackle that Mister Mack, who preferred the December 23 date, was a pretty smart fellow but just didn't know what day he was born on. Mike always said he saw the birth on December 22.

Whatever the date, the son of Michael McGillicuddy—who was at that moment fighting against the South with the Massachusetts Regiment—was christened Cornelius. At the end of the Civil War, Michael McGillicuddy returned to his job in an East Brookfield cotton mill, and when Cornelius was nine years old he also got a job

there, working summers. He was given an hour for lunch
but never used more than 15 minutes of it to eat. The
remaining 45 were given to games involving a bat and
ball, variously called one o'cat, four o'cat, roundball and
baseball.

When he was 15 Connie presented himself to the keep-
er of a general store in his neighborhood and asked to be
measured. He blanched a bit when the man announced
that he stood six feet one. This confirmed his secret fear
that there was something freakish about him. He began
suffering claustrophobia at his cramped little desk in the
local public school, and so, shortly after his sixteenth
birthday, he abruptly quit. There was no furor in the
McGillicuddy family. His schooling seemed adequate for
the job he had in mind—that of a general hand in the
Green and Twitchell shoe factory in East Brookfield.

Connie could pay more attention to his baseball now
and by 1882 was the regular catcher on East Brookfield's
best ball club. In 1883 his imagination was irrevocably
fired by the appearance in East Brookfield for an exhibition game of the Worcester team, then in the National
League. Later that year Cap Anson brought his mustached
and mighty Chicago Colts to East Brookfield and Connie rubbed shoulders with these gods from another world
and knew that nothing must stop him from trying to be
one with them.

Early in March 1884 Connie received a telegram
prompted by his East Brookfield battery mate, Billy Hogan, who had plunged onward to the comparatively lofty
position of pitcher for the Meriden club of the Connecti-
cut League. The telegram offered him a job with the club.
Connie went straight to his foreman and told him he was
quitting. "You'd better stay," said the foreman, a man
named Morris (he is still alive today, at 100). "No, Saturday night's my last night in the boot shop," Connie insisted, a statement which he sometimes now regrets having made. "I hope Mr. Morris didn't think I was rude," he
mused not long ago, as if he had been mulling it over for
64 years.

There was still the matter of proving to the manager of the Meriden club that he was able as well as willing. This Connie did in a game against Yale in which he handled his pitcher so well that the man struck out 21 Yales, including a vigorous young New Haven star named Amos Alonzo Stagg, who was later to make something of a name for himself in football. The lanky young catcher from East Brookfield was promptly offered $60 a month, held out and got $80, and became so popular with Meriden fans that at the close of the season they presented him with a gold watch.

Mister Mack was to become an almost starchy upholder of baseball ethics in the generations to come. But the game was unhampered by niceties in the '80s. With no twinge of conscience he deserted his loving fans in 1885 and jumped to the Hartford team of the same league because the Hartford management offered him $125 a month. By 1886 he was earning $200 a month, and in September of that year he and four other members of the club were sold to Washington of the National League for $3,500. It was a heady burst of good fortune, but Mister Mack was not dazzled out of his wits. He insisted on being paid $800 to catch the final month of the season at Washington. He also got a contract for $2,750 for the 1887 season and once again was so well received in a town whose ball park's grandstands then seated 1,800 (and whose White House incumbent was Grover Cleveland) that the fans presented him with a silver tea set.

Two years later, happily married to his childhood sweetheart, Margaret Hogan, and father of a growing family, Mister Mack jumped his job with Washington to join the ill-started Brotherhood, a league which the players themselves hoped to operate as a co-op in opposition to the entrenched National. He jumped for the same salary as was paid to him by the Washington team and became so warmly attached to the prospects of the new organization—especially those of his new club, Buffalo —that he invested all the money he had saved and all that he could borrow. The league folded after its first

year and with it went everything the little family pos-
sessed. The gaunt young man of the house hooked on to
the Pittsburgh Pirates in '91, however, and was well on
his way to becoming the National League's outstanding
catcher in '93 when his left ankle was fractured in a game
with Boston. His uselessness as a player, plus his keen
baseball mind, prompted the Pittsburgh owners to appoint
Connie manager of the club at the end of the 1894 season.

Mister Mack was 32 and considered, in those days,
rather elderly for freshman manager. But the owners,
perhaps tolerant of his years, maintained their patience.
When the Pirates finished sixth in 1896, however, he was
discharged.

The man who was to be hailed 47 years later as perhaps the best manager in the American League was saved
from complete obscurity by Ban Johnson, president of the
Western League. Johnson, a ruthless dreamer who lived
and died believing that baseball was perfected in order
to serve him as a gigantic chess board on which to move
his living pieces, lifted Mister Mack out of reluctant retirement and set him up as manager and one-fourth owner
of the Milwaukee club. Johnson changed the name of his
league to the American in 1900 and laid plans to invade
the big time monopolized by the National. He ordered his
friend Charles Comiskey, owner of the St. Paul franchise,
to move his club to Chicago. He set up other clubs in
Cleveland and Buffalo, and took over Detroit and Kansas
City. He dispatched Mister Mack to Philadelphia one cold
December day in 1900 to raise money for a ball park and
to find a club which could successfully compete with the
well-established Phillies.

Mister Mack found the needed money in the pocket of
a dour and crusty baseball manufacturer named Ben
Shibe, who spent enough of it to build a small park at
29th and Columbia Avenue, named Columbia Park. With
$500 of a bankroll supplied by a willing but naive Cleve-
lander named Somers, Mister Mack persuaded the Phillies'
greatest star, Nap Lajoie, to jump to the new Philadelphia
club. Then he talked another Phillies star, Lave Cross,

into switching his allegiance. He also kept his eyes open for young men who showed promise. One of the young players he found before the curtain went up on American League baseball history in Philadelphia was a pitcher at Gettysburg College named Eddie Plank, who was later to enter baseball's Hall of Fame.

John McGraw, sharp-tongued critic of every club except his New York Giants, inadvertently gave the new Philadelphia American League team its nickname. Asked by a reporter to comment on the new club, Muggsy barked, "Looks like the American League's got a white elephant on its hands in Philadelphia." Mack read the interview and placidly selected the name "White Elephants" for his club. They finished fourth in 1901 and were on their way to winning the pennant in 1902 when the Supreme Court of Pennsylvania ruled that Mister Mack could no longer use Lajoie and other appropriated stars. He was forced to break up his team and the experts immediately wrote off the chances of the club—which had by now been given the additional nickname of Athletics.

But Mister Mack was not defeated. He remembered an eccentric southpaw named Rube Waddell who had played in the Western League and whose major ambition in life was to become a bartender. He found Waddell pitching in a California league and had him shipped East. With the Rube's help the Athletics, or A's, won the pennant, their first of nine under Mister Mack, who also has the appalling record of finishing last in his league 16 times.

From that time through the season of 1914 Mister Mack won five pennants and three World Series and produced in 1911 one of the two or three greatest ball clubs of all time, a team whose infield was made up of Stuffy McInnis at first, Eddie Collins at second, Jack Barry at short and Frank (Home Run) Baker at third. It was given the greatest plaudit that could be contrived in the minds of the sportswriters of that uninflated day. They called it "the $100,000 infield."

When the Athletics lost the 1914 Series to the some-what talentless Braves, Mister Mack smashed the club like an expensive china vase. His players had cupped attentive ears to the offers of the newly created Federal League, a rival to the American League which Mister Mack had so successfully built up, and several of them did make the jump. With this and a general housecleaning, the greatest reversal of fortunes in the history of any city's club got underway. His 1914 team had outdistanced its competitors by winning 99 games and losing 53. The 1915 relics won only 43 games and lost 109. The 1916 A's won 36 and lost 117. They finished eighth for seven consecutive seasons.

After a decade in the environs of the cellar Mister Mack came up again. By astute outbidding of his rivals he assembled a superb combination of ballplayers. With this crew, built around Al Simmons, now his rough and adoring third-base coach, Lefty Grove, who was to win more than 300 games, Jimmy Foxx, Mickey Cochrane, George Earnshaw, Jimmy Dykes and others, the A's jumped from fifth in 1924 to second in 1925, and when the great Yankees declined after 1928 forged on to win the pennants of 1929, 1930 and 1931.

Mister Mack sometimes gets a little sentimental about that club. Recalling it recently, he remembered the seventh inning of the fourth game of the 1929 Series against the Cubs. The Cubs were leading 8 to 0.

"It was my intention at that stage of the game to send in substitutes for all the regulars at the start of the eighth inning," he said. "But when we came to bat in the seventh some odd things began happening. Al Simmons, the first man up for us, hit a home run which landed on the roof of the left-field stands, fair by just inches. If it had been foul—well, that doesn't matter now.

"Foxx then singled. So did Bing Miller. Dykes singled. It was his fourth straight hit of the day and I got the feeling that we had something special on the fire. Dykes's single scored Foxx, and now Joe Boley singled, scoring

Miller. Burns batted for Rommel and flied out to English for the first out. But Bishop singled, scoring Dykes. The score was now 8 to 4.

"Joe McCarthy, a fine manager, took out Charles Root, his pitcher, and put in Artie Nehf. Mule Haas then hit a long fly to center which Hack Wilson lost and it went for a home run, making the score 8 to 7 in favor of the Cubs. When Cochrane walked, Joe McCarthy, a fine manager, replaced Nehf with Sheriff Blake. But Simmons singled to left. Foxx singled to center scoring Cochrane with the tying run. Big Malone started pitching then. He hit Miller with a pitched ball. Dykes then doubled for his fifth hit, scoring Simmons and Foxx with the ninth and tenth runs of the inning, and Burns and Boley—they struck out.

"You know, Mr. Constantine," said Mister Mack with a slight cough, "there was talk that I danced with joy during that big inning. It's not true. I just sat there, and when we won the game I walked off with hardly a word to the boys. It doesn't help any to appear to be too pleased before such an important series is won. Such an attitude might lead to overconfidence, and that's fatal."

These wondrous years of the A's lasted until 1933. Financially they represented a high tide in the fortunes of the ball club. With the possible exception of the New York Yankees, the Athletics had the fattest payroll in any league. Shibe Park had been renovated and with that and other expenses the club's overhead mounted. By 1933 the crash, which had already cut Philadelphia's ability to support a high-class ball team, hit Mister Mack; his club was $500,000 in debt. Simmons, Haas and Dykes had been sold to the White Sox for $150,000. Now pressed to the limit by financial stringency, Mister Mack sold Grove, Foxx, Bishop and Rube Walberg, leaving himself with only tattered remnants of his former starring team. When the massacre was over he was told that if he dared come out of the dugout and show himself in the opening-day ceremonies of 1934 he would be booed as no man in the history of the city had ever been blasted. In the face of the threat Mister Mack stalked gingerly off his barren bench on opening day and walked, head up, to the center-field flagpole. The old man dared them to howl him down, and no one took the challenge. Suddenly a whole city seemed to agree with him that he had been forced to sell in order to survive.

From 1934 through 1947 Mister Mack's hapless teams never finished in the first division. But by late 1940 Mister Mack, who had bought out the shares of John Shibe, owned 58 per cent of the stock in the A's. He was now the Mr. Chips of baseball. The fans delighted in his gentle whimsy. There was the story of the Philadelphia cab driver, apparently new to the town because he did not recognize his passenger, who carried Mack to the North Philadelphia Station one night. The old gentleman, lost in thought, mechanically paid the sum recorded on the meter, picked up his bag and wandered off.

"Hey, pop," the driver snarled, "what about a tip?"

Connie stopped, lost in thought. "A tip?" he asked in a voice that sometimes spurts up an octave.

"Yeah, pop, a tip. How about one?"

"Certainly," Connie answered. "Don't bet on the A's."

By June of 1947 any outside observer might have been forgiven for assuming that Mister Mack's long career in baseball was drawing to a rather weary close. He had assembled a club of nobodies whose strength he estimated at the start of the season by telling Art Morrow of the Philadelphia *Inquirer*, "We can promise our patrons good baseball and nothing more." But to everyone's surprise he began getting excellent pitching from the likes of Phil Marchildon, who still bore the scars of his months of captivity by the Germans; Dick Fowler, a young man seemingly crushed by family troubles; Bill McCahan, whose uncle had played in the outfield for Mister Mack in 1905 (McCahan went on to pitch a no-hitter for him before the season was over); Joe Coleman, given to Connie by his friend, the late Brother Gilbert (who had discovered an incipient young tailor named George Herman Ruth at St. Mary's Industrial School in Baltimore 33 years before); Bob Savage, first big-leaguer wounded in World War

II, and a 20-year-old Pennsylvania Dutchman named Carl Scheib who had been pestering him for a job for the previous five years. He shaped these earnest young men around a resurrected second-rater named Bill Dietrich, who had been in and out of the league since 1930, and the A's began winning games.

Mister Mack decided about 70 years ago that pitching is 75 per cent of a team's worth, and nothing in the interim has changed his mind. By the end of the 1947 season he had added one or two other willing young hands, including the staff's only southpaw, Lou Brissie, a big courageous fellow who must play with a clumsy plastic guard over his shell-riddled left leg, part of which he left in Italy. He built a new infield around a revitalized veteran shortstop named Eddie Joost, put Hank Majeski, a Yankee castoff, on third base and unveiled an excellent young infielder in Ferris Fain, for whom he was subsequently offered a reported $100,000 by the Yanks. He inspired a phlegmatic young Czech named Elmer Valo with the energies of a human dynamo and breathed new life into a Detroit outfielder named Barney McCosky. In the other outfield position he placed Sam Chapman, a muscular former All-American gridman. The A's made a race of it and looked better than their fifth-place finish would indicate.

Mister Mack began to live all over again and the undercurrent of sincere wishes that he retire melted away. This year, more than ever, he is the grand old man of baseball, and though most of the seasoned observers feel that it would be too good to be true if Mister Mack in his fantastic antiquity came home in front, players, managers and owners throughout the league like to say that if they themselves cannot win the banner they want the old man to cop it.

Prosperity has returned to the Athletics. The 1947 spurt attracted 900,000 paid admissions to Shibe Park and the A's drew a million customers on the road, sharing the money those outlanders deposited at the box offices. This year the Athletics, contenders from the opening gong, will draw more than a million clients at home—the biggest attendance in the tremendous history of the team—and perhaps a million and a half on the road, though they have one of the smallest payrolls in either big league.

The highest-paid men on the team—Marchildon and Joost—make $17,500 a year or less, and the sweatful young Valo probably does not make more than $8,500. Mister Mack just does not believe in the kind of salaries paid by the rich owners of the Yankees, Red Sox, Indians and Tigers. Nor does he believe in paying a lot of money and trying to buy a ready-made winner. Except for the cost of helping half a dozen of his players through their colleges—Mister Mack's first advice to any teen-ager who wants to play for him is, "You'd better let me send you to school first"—he paid only $20,000 for his present pitching staff.

But seldom in the history of baseball has there been a closer affinity between labor and management than there is with the 1948 Athletics—otherwise a typically soulless baseball corporation. Mister Mack is a fabulously beloved figure, as such love is measured in baseball. There is no cow-eyed infatuation for him among his players. That would be asking too much of the average big-leaguer, who is fundamentally a mercenary. But the warmth of the player for Mister Mack is readily apparent. "I love that old guy," one said recently, "but what a shrewd old goat he is!"

Except for a new and sometimes alarming trembling of his classic scorecard, with which he wigwags signals to his boys from his vantage point in the dugout, Mister Mack has shown few outward indications this year of the suffocating excitement that is in him. He still wears the high, starched collars that have been his trademark for half a century; when the style went out in Teddy Roosevelt's day, Mister Mack persuaded the firm to keep making them for him. His 150 pounds are smoothed out tautly over his six-foot one-inch frame. The story that his strongest exclamation is "Fudge!" is as hardy a fairy tale as the never-dying report that Babe Ruth was an orphan. A historic outburst of his temper will always be remembered in the dugouts of America: his chronically griping pitching ace, Lefty Grove, trudged into the dugout one day after Mister Mack had pulled him out of a game, threw down his glove in disgust, and growled, "Nuts!" Mister Mack stood up quickly and walked over to him. He pushed his face close to Grove's. "And nuts to you, too!" he shouted, then marched back to his place in his spindly way and sat down.

To Mister Mack this 1948 club is something special, and in his comparatively rare bursts of loquaciousness he likes to say it is his favorite team because it is his fightingest. It could be, too. By the July 4 turning point of the season, when it was only half a game out of first place, it had won 17 of its games by one-run margins; had snapped back to win after the Red Sox had annihilated it in an early July game with a 14-run rally in one inning, and had otherwise paid dividends on his enormous affection. At the end of July the A's were still only half a game behind the Red Sox.

In his excitement these days Mister Mack sometimes makes plainly discernible mistakes in simple strategy, and if these cost him a game he is distraught as he goes home after a contest. He is beginning to shake like a great angular twig whenever the team loses, and he finds it hard to sleep those nights until he has reviewed each move of the game in his mind. When he signals for an obviously wrong move these days Al Simmons turns his back a bit sadly on the old man, as if he did not detect the signal, and calls for the right move. But this never fools Mister Mack. When Al comes back to the bench at the end of the inning Mister Mack usually speaks up.

"You used better judgment than I did, Al," he will say quietly, and then go about his timeless task of wagging his scorecard at his fielders.

It is not good taste on the Philadelphia bench to second-guess Mister Mack openly, but it has been done even in this year of dizzying success. Not long ago he ordered his leading run-producer, Majeski, to lay down a bunt. One man was out at the time and the A's were behind. Majeski reluctantly did as he was bidden and sacrificed the runner to second. But the next hitter popped up futilely and Majeski said with warm sincerity, "That was lousy baseball, Mister Mack."

Mister Mack thought for a time and said, "You're right, Mr. Majeski!"

Mister Mack calls a lot of his players "Mister." In his relations with them he reveals many other niceties which another manager might scorn as a show of weakness. If one of his pitchers works himself out of a tight hole, or a player makes a timely hit or a fine defensive play, Mister Mack often will stand up as the player returns. He will shake hands with him and say with voice-cracking warmth, "Thank you," then sit down and go on with the business of running the game.

The A's bench is perhaps the quietest in baseball. Remarkably few obscenities are heard and the razzing of the other team is always kept above the belt. When a newcomer violates one of the unwritten laws of bench conduct he soon learns that he has blundered. Bobo Newsom, a garrulous soul who loves Mister Mack with a vociferous affection, showed up at Philadelphia a few years ago in the course of his endless march through the majors. "Hello, Connie!" he roared at their first meeting. Just before the start of his second game with the A's, Bo was called upon by six rather grim young A's. "We call him Mister Mack, see?" their spokesman growled. So did Bobo after that.

Mister Mack is handed a new scorecard before every game, and in warm weather a fresh bath towel is placed behind his back by any of a half dozen roughly adoring coaches, clubhouse attendants, players and the like. He makes impatient sounds like "stop babying me" when minor homages are being paid to him, but it is the belief of those very close to him that the old man would feel hurt if he were not thus pampered. Certainly what he gets in this line is precious little compared to the still enormous physical energies he alone must expend each day.

The old gentleman seldom sees his players after a game, unless one has made some catastrophic blunder. But, perhaps once a month, he does pop into the locker room, usually to have a concerned word with a coach or his son. Now and then it is a simple ceremonial call. Not long ago, pleased with the way in which his hard-working young team had just won another, Mister Mack poked in his head, patted his long knuckly hands together in polite applause, looking around the room as he did. "This is for you," he said with quiet warmth.

Mister Mack doesn't go in for that newfangled nonsense of a telephone line running between the A's dugout at Shibe Park and the bullpen at the far end of the field. To call in a relief pitcher he uses a system that went out of style in most other big-league ball parks years ago. To get in Joe Coleman from the distant reaches of the pen Mister Mack orders a coach to stand out in front of the dugout—in view of the pen—and to pantomime a man shoveling coal. If the call is for Carl Scheib, the coach stands up and beats his fists against the nearest wall. Consulting briefly with himself, the bullpen coach interprets this act as "man pounding on Shibe Park—Shibe—Scheib." But only a group well versed in the gentle wanderings of Mister Mack's mind could piece together his signal which calls in Dick Fowler. He orders the coach to stand out in front and make a stooping motion as if he were picking flowers. Mister Mack is extremely fond of Fowler and with unfailing courtliness always addresses him as "Mr. Flowers."

Mister Mack has possibly had more personal friends than any American now alive, for he has outlived several crops of them and is still enormously popular. A devout Catholic who never misses a Sunday Mass or a holy day of obligation, Mister Mack seems to attract waves of sportsminded priests at each stop along the big-league circuit. Considering the wideness of his circle of friends and those who feel friendly toward him, Mister Mack's memory is phenomenal. At Connie Mack Day in Meriden in 1947 an old fellow was helped to the microphone at home plate and recalled, "Con, you remember when we played against each other right here in '83? And remember I got a hit in the ninth and knocked in a run?"

Mister Mack took the microphone. "I certainly do!" he exclaimed, then added, "And I also remember that we won the game, 2 to 1."

Off and on since 1915 there have been reports that Mister Mack was ready to retire. He did quit once, without public knowledge. It happened a few years ago when he decided to hire Al Horwits, former Philadelphia baseball writer, as publicity man for the team. To show his sons, who hold various executive offices in the organization, that he was open-minded about the appointment he submitted it to them for approval. Two of them voted against Horwits and Mister Mack waxed indignant. "You have my resignation," he told his glum sons, and stalked out of his office. His retirement lasted for as long as it took the boys to run after him, telling him that on more sober thought they had decided that Horwits was just about the finest public-relations man obtainable—which he is. Mister Mack cocked his head like a reflective crane for a moment and relented.

The old gentleman has no thought of retiring, not even if by some dazzling and dramatic accident he wins the 1948 pennant to crown gloriously his sixty-fourth year in professional baseball. He has gone beyond the stage when a man can lay down his chores of his own volition. The sheer weight of his experience precludes a decision to call it a day. "People ask me if I'm tired of baseball," he said not long ago. "I can only give one answer. There is nothing in baseball I dislike. I'll stay in the game as long as my mind is clear. When I reach the stage when I don't know my business, or trade a .300 hitter for a .200 hitter, then you'll know I'm unfit."

But to his closest associates—his boys, his wife, his traveling secretary and chief minority stockholder, Benjamin Shibe Macfarland, and one or two others—the old man willingly gives the true reason why he'll never quit of his own accord.

"If I did," he says, and his old eyes mist up as he looks around helplessly, "I'd die in two weeks."

Walter Alston

COMMENTS

Walter Alston is this generation's Connie Mack. He endures. The selection on him was written ten years ago. The writer, Mel Durslag, marveled then that Alston had managed to stay around. Ten years later, everybody can still marvel. This season he will be beginning his 20th consecutive year as manager of the Dodgers. Only two managers—Mack and McGraw—had longer tenures with one club. And ten years later, things haven't changed much with Alston. He is still quiet, reasonable, reserved, a homebody, the very model of the modern manager. And he still gets those one-year contracts, one at a time. He still lives, as Durslag pointed out, on the edge of doubt. It hasn't seemed to hurt him for the first 19 years, though.

Manager with a Hair Shirt

by MELVIN DURSLAG

It is a harsh statistic that National League baseball managers from 1940 to the present have lasted an average of only 2.8 years. As manager of the Los Angeles Dodgers, Walter Emmons Alston is now well into his 10th year. In the eyes of his colleagues, this makes him a sort of miracle worker.

If Alston's seniority is unusual, the conditions under which he attained it are unenviable. He happens to be baseball's most harassed field leader. Harpooned by critics, hissed by fans and second-guessed by members of his own organization, he teeters almost daily on the ledge of disaster. A stranger can readily identify Alston. He is the one in the hair shirt.

Rarely does a season open without predictions that Alston will be fired unless he wins the pennant. His employers do little to assuage his pain. On the contrary, they aggravate it. This year, they again put him on the spot, even before the first game. A report got out that a few players on the team were complaining about the manager. The griping was garden variety. Yet the general manager of the Dodgers, E. J. (Buzzie) Bavasi, flew immediately from Los Angeles to Chicago to deliver a dramatic harmony talk in the locker room.

The gesture was unappreciated by Alston. For one thing, the embarrassed manager felt capable of handling his players. For another, he envisioned the headlines that inevitably came. "End Nearing for Alston?" asked one. "Alston On Hot Seat Again!" blared another.

The story had about faded from the sports pages when

Dodger president Walter O'Malley stepped forth with a gratuitous "vote of confidence" for his manager. Since nothing in sports is more suspect than a vote of confidence, speculation about Alston spurted anew.

Nor was the standing of the Los Angeles skipper strengthened a week later when Bob Kennedy, "head coach" of the Cubs, was quoted by a San Francisco paper as having remarked in the dressing room, "If the Dodgers lose today, Durocher will be manager tomorrow." Red-faced, Kennedy telephoned Alston to apologize, explaining that his words had been misinterpreted.

The Dodger front office may not offer Alston much peace of mind on the field, but it makes up for it by giving him only a one-year contract.

"Anything longer would make me nervous," he once observed.

Alston never has discussed salary with the management. He signs a blank contract in the fall and often doesn't discover how much he is earning until he meets the general manager at spring training in Florida. His present pay, however, is a respectable $45,000, commensurate with his outstanding record as a big-league manager.

He has finished out of the first division only once. He has delivered three pennants and two world's championships. His work the last five years has been judged by baseball people as especially good, since he has stayed pretty much on top while making the transition from a veteran team to a young team. This is rarely accomplished without a dizzy drop in the standings. Alston's success, baseball men feel, has been all the more remarkable because of the Dodger front office's grand tendency to overrate rookie players, with a view to the Chavez Ravine box office or possible deals.

Now 51, Walter is a quiet, usually unruffled grandfather who stands 6 feet 2 and weighs a solid 210 pounds. An Ohioan from a family of farmers, he is a graduate of Miami University of Ohio and lives in Darrtown. His speech is plain but articulate. His answers are never devious. He is a patient and a tolerant man, but, in his own way, a tough leader.

Alston can erupt. Displeased with a call in a game against Cincinnati last year, he summoned all four umpires and bombarded them with language not recommended for a convocation of Brownies. He wound up his speech by pointing his finger firmly at each ump and announcing: ". . . And that goes for you and for you and for you, and especially for you!" He was thrown out.

Alston can also become violent. At spring camp one year, he spotted pitchers Larry Sherry and Sandy Koufax coming in after curfew. When the boys ran to their room and locked the door, the aroused Alston followed. He smashed in the door, breaking his World Series ring.

Some students of human behavior feel that Walter's occasional explosions may stem from the underdog status he has had since coming to the Dodgers in 1954. He was less than a popular choice. The man he succeeded was Charlie Dressen, who in three years with the club won two pennants and barely lost a third in a play-off. In 1953, Dressen's championship team took 105 games, an all-time high for the Dodgers.

Fans resented the uncoupling of Charlie by President O'Malley. Refusing to yield to Dressen's demand for a three-year contract, O'Malley dumped him and brought in Alston, who had been managing in the Dodger farm system since 1944.

To the New York press, it was inconceivable that the high-flying Dodgers would hire such an obscure man, especially one so devoid of color. Would Alston ever call a pitcher of his "gutless," as Dressen had? Would he ever say of his third baseman, "He should be taken behind the barn and shot," as ex-Dodger skipper Leo Durocher had? Plainly, Alston was no manager in the jungle tradition.

His popularity in Brooklyn was hardly enhanced when the club finished second in the 1954 pennant race. It was almost as if Alston had committed a crime. At the start of the '55 season, a New York baseball columnist wrote:

"The honeymoon is over. This year the burden of proof is on Walt."

O'Malley came through with an unresounding vote of confidence, announcing at spring camp that Alston wasn't necessarily playing for his job. But it was generally accepted that he was.

The manager's response to the crisis was to take the pennant and give Brooklyn its first world's championship. When the Dodgers trimmed the almighty Yankees in a seven-game World Series, Alston was hailed as a conquering hero. He won the pennant again in 1956, but this time lost the Series to the Yanks.

Late in the 1957 season, with the Dodgers mired in third place, a report spread that Alston would be replaced at the end of the year by his shortstop, Pee Wee Reese. Asked about the rumor, General Manager Bavasi replied, "We don't discuss next year's manager until December. I haven't talked to Alston, and he hasn't talked to me." By Christmas, Walter had received word that he was forgiven for not winning the pennant and could return in 1958.

The '58 season turned into a calamity. O'Malley had departed the friendly borough of Brooklyn and moved his franchise to Los Angeles, where he was committed to build a superstadium, at a cost of $18 million or more. Faced with this obligation, the Dodger owner was understandably concerned with ticket sales in his new home.

The Dodgers had a team that was old by baseball standards. Such stars as Duke Snyder, Gil Hodges, Pee Wee Reese, Carl Furillo, Don Newcombe and Carl Erskine were pretty much over the hill. Yet, for commercial reasons, it behooved O'Malley to go into Los Angeles with "name" players who were guaranteed box office. The shift to the promising young performers the Dodgers had been grooming was delayed.

"We needed young blood desperately," says Alston. "But we didn't dare make changes at that time."

Meanwhile, the front office brought back Charlie Dressen as coach, favoring Alston thoughtfully with the first of several possible successors by whom he was ultimately to be surrounded. Before the Dodgers even got to spring camp, stories were out that it was only a matter of time until Dressen took back his old job.

Financially, the 1958 season was successful; the Dodgers drew more than 1,800,000 in home attendance. But they finished a staggering seventh, and O'Malley didn't conceal his disappointment. From all quarters of the organization came complicated explanations. Alston said simply, "We played lousy ball. We were a bust, fielding-wise, hitting-wise, pitching-wise—and probably managing-wise too. We all had a part in it."

The following May, when the Dodgers lost five straight at home, the gossip had it that Dressen would take over by midseason. Luckily for the Dodgers, he didn't. Alston won the pennant, then flattened the favored Chicago White Sox in the World Series. Never in the National League had a team come from as far away as seventh the previous year to win a flag.

Asked if he would have resigned if his club hadn't made a reputable showing, Walter smiled thinly. "Managers don't resign," he answered. "They get fired."

Alston, however, couldn't resist telephoning Bavasi after he wrapped up the Series. Walter began softly, "What do I do now, Buzz?"

When Dressen left the Dodgers in 1960 to become manager at Milwaukee, the front office replaced him with another potential successor to Alston, Bobby Bragan. He stayed only a year, before moving to Houston as a scout and later a coach. A slot on the Dodgers' field staff once again was open.

On a December morning in 1960, I received a telephone call from Leo Durocher, who just had been rejected as a candidate for manager by the fledgling Los Angeles Angels. Leo thought it was more than coincidence that, in the previous six months, four other clubs had also passed him over. He said he suspected a blackball and wanted a story printed as "an explanation to my friends." He added:

"People I know have been calling me and asking, 'Why are you turning down these jobs, Leo? Are you crazy?' I want to make it clear I'm not turning down anything. I would like to come back to baseball. I'm not asking for the world with a fence around it. I feel I have a right to earn a living in baseball, and I don't want to be knocked out of the box by unwritten agreements."

When the story appeared, Leo's insinuations were hotly denied by major-league owners. Significantly, however, none volunteered to employ him—except O'Malley. The American League was moving into Los Angeles at the time and threatened to cut into the Dodgers' market. With his genius for crashing into the news, Durocher unmistakably was box office. As a baseball man, he also had O'Malley's respect. The Dodger owner decided to hire him as a coach.

Though Alston had nothing to do with Leo's appointment, he was solicited to make the official announcement. After a flight from Darrtown to California, he had the privilege of revealing to the world the newest candidate for his job.

As individuals, Alston and Durocher are perhaps as opposite as men can be. Walter is quiet; Leo is boisterous. Walter drives a Mercury; Leo drives a Cadillac. Walter buys his suits off the rack at a store in Hamilton, Ohio. Leo's clothes are made fastidiously by one of Hollywood's most exclusive tailors. His wardrobe includes six tuxedoes.

Walter occupies a comfortable but modest home, for which he made most of the furniture. (His hobby is woodworking.) Leo's $150,000 home, in the fashionable Trousdale Estates of Beverly Hills, was decorated exclusively by a designer who has done the mansions of millionaires.

Alston and Durocher readily acknowledge their differences. Shortly after hiring Leo, Walter observed, "We have to face facts. Leo is a colorful figure and a bold and amusing talker. I would be a damn fool if I tried to outdo him. We must live our own way and respect each other."

On the field, Durocher admits that his theory of handling personnel differs from Alston's.

"Walt's idea," says Leo, "is to carry over a beef until the next day, when heads are clear. As a manager, I never did this. When something went wrong, I preferred to sound off on the bench or in the clubhouse, while the beef was still fresh. I always wanted to leave the park with the trouble off my chest. If I ever tried to carry over a beef, I wouldn't sleep all night."

Does Durocher feel that the players respect his method as much as they do Alston's?

"I must admit the players respect Alston. Whether they respected me didn't matter, just as long as they played for me. I never posed as a choirboy. I was just a guy who wanted to win, and I would have taken your teeth to do it."

The two men spent their first year together in blissful harmony. When the team finished second, four games behind Cincinnati, the Dodger front office was, of course, unhappy. Asked if Alston would be coming back, Bavasi replied, "I think Alston did a good job this year. We finished second, which is no disgrace."

"Then Alston will be back next season," an interviewer hinted.

"I didn't say that," answered Bavasi. "We haven't made up our mind yet. There are certain reservations. It is our custom never to divulge what we're going to do about managers until December."

"Does it look good for Alston?" he was asked.

"You can say that anyone could be manager," he answered. "We have not decided for sure."

This less-than-thunderous endorsement for the Dodger skipper led to the first serious report that Durocher would take over the team. Two weeks later, the Dodgers called a press conference. Nonchalantly, as if there never had been reason for doubt, the club announced that Walter had been rehired for 1962. Said one observer, "The Dodgers never plan to fire Alston. They prefer to torment him."

Christy Mathewson, the author, researching his subject, manager-cum-pitcher John McGraw.
—*Brown Brothers*

Connie Mack moved players around with his scorecard. Today they use coaches.—*Wide World*

This is John McGraw, not W. C. Fields, choosing up sides with Connie Mack. A tough way to make out a lineup.
—*Brown Brothers*

Casey at the bat. The face that launched a thousand quips.
—*Wide World*

Joe Schultz, my manager the summer I tried to hang on in the big leagues. Joe's idea of attention to detail was to make sure we all wore the same color sweat shirts.—*Wide World*

Ralph Houk and Leo Durocher doing their thing. If they ever start a baseball manager's school, "kicking" will be a required course.—*Wide World*

"I'm a handsome, debonair, easygoing six-footer," says manager Rocky Bridges. "Anyway, that's what I told them at the Braille Institute."—*Wide World*

Dick Williams, flat head. Dick Williams, the dry look.—*Wide World*

Yogi picks up some spare change between innings selling ice cream to young Yankee fans. — *Wide World*

SERVICE

ICE CREAM DISHES

Cone or Cup	10¢
Large Cone or Cup	20¢
Floats	25¢
Sundaes	30¢
Thick Shakes	30¢
Pints	45¢
Banana three Dip	45¢

The 1962 season began smoothly. In early June, the Dodgers took the lead, lost it to the Giants, then regained it quickly. They were still in front in mid-August, when a major explosion rocked the club. During a game at Pittsburgh, one Los Angeles player missed a sign and another got hit by his own bunt for an automatic out. Seated in the dugout, Durocher barked that the miscreants should be fined. Alston turned on Leo viciously and told him that fining was the function of the manager. A carbonated exchange followed, the details of which made glaring headlines in the newspapers.

The following day, Alston was kicked out of the game for arguing with an umpire. To the amazement of the players, he put Durocher in charge. Walter was applauded for his bigness, and many concluded that all wounds had healed. But they hadn't entirely. Several days later, Alston called me aside to contest a stand my paper had taken on the dugout commotion. It was our feeling that Walter was wrong in berating his coach in front of the players; a rebuke in private appeared to have been more in order.

"You're pretty sensitive about Durocher's feelings," said the angry Alston, "but you don't seem to care much about mine. What about the times he has shown *me* up in front of the players? How much of this do I have to take?"

For all their crises, the Dodgers continued to show the way in the race. Still four games on top with only seven to play, they prepared for their first World Series in Dodger Stadium. All the tickets were sold. The players, dry-washing their hands, figured that the winners' share of a Series with the Yankees would run a record $12,000 per man.

Busy counting their money, the Dodgers dropped their bats. They were carried to a play-off by the Giants and were wiped out in the third game. The loss devastated them. They locked themselves in the dressing room and wouldn't see newsmen. O'Malley and Bavasi vanished.

Only Alston would own up to the shocking defeat. He met the press and answered questions politely. He offered no excuses, blamed no players, did not second-guess himself. The pennant, he said, wasn't lost that afternoon; it was kicked away during a previous week by a team that unaccountably had gone flat.

O'Malley departed for Wyoming the next day to hunt bighorn sheep, and Bavasi didn't come out of seclusion until a story leaked that Durocher, dining in a Sunset Strip restaurant, had passed a remark that maybe the Dodgers wouldn't have lost if he had been manager.

"If Durocher really said that," exploded Bavasi, "he's fired! And I mean fired on the spot!" Durocher, by his own admission, *had* said something to that effect.

A New York paper, meanwhile, carried an exclusive story that Alston was out—and Durocher in. In San Francisco, Del Webb, co-owner of the Yankees, confided to reporters, "I hear the Dodgers will be making an announcement tomorrow. Pete Reiser is the new manager." (Reiser was the Dodger batting coach.) An Associated Press story began:

"The Los Angeles Dodgers will probably take their time about announcing whether manager Walter Alston has been rehired or retired. But one thing already seems apparent: If Alston is back next season, coach Leo Durocher won't be. And vice versa."

Those who thought O'Malley would fire Alston after that season believe he retained the patient manager for two reasons.

First, the press had clobbered the Dodger front office for the unknightly way it let Alston take the rap for the pennant loss. O'Malley was doubtless embarrassed.

Second, the firing of Alston at that time would have been a move too obvious for one with O'Malley's keen sense of showmanship. He saw a story far more dramatic. He not only would rehire Alston, but Durocher too. And to spice the managerial picture even further, he would bring back Charlie Dressen.

As a special assistant to the general manager, Charlie went on the payroll again. A robust 64, he made it plain that he was not too old to manage. This was borne out on June 18, when the Detroit Tigers tapped him to succeed Bob Scheffing.

O'Malley admits frankly it is no accident that his field leader has been surrounded for the last few years by coaches of proved managerial caliber.

"It has been done deliberately," says the Dodger president, "on the ground that we don't want bridge partners or cronies for assistants. It is our job to get the most knowledgeable men, and it is the manager's place to solicit their advice and accept it or reject it. I admit that, in Durocher's case, he sometimes gives advice that isn't solicited, but that's Leo. We knew the nature of the man when we hired him."

The Dodgers drew 2,775,184 in home attendance in 1962, a major-league record. O'Malley insists that he requires many more dollars than other clubs do because of his enormous financial obligation with the new stadium.

"To pay off our facility and keep our operation going smoothly," he says, "we must draw 2,000,000 fans a year for the next several years. To accomplish this, we need a team that stays in contention. Our manager's responsibility isn't small."

At their present pace, the Dodgers will continue to hit 2,000,000 or more, but Alston remains in his hair shirt. It is a popular game in Los Angeles to seed the candidates for his job. Many rate Durocher first, in the belief that his daring and color appeal to the owner. Others argue that O'Malley won't gamble his future on a manager as extreme as Durocher, but would prefer a man like Dressen, no paragon of modesty, but a more conservative leader on the field. Still others rank Reiser first, pointing to his age (only 43) and vigor. It even has been reported that the Dodgers would like to swipe Freddie Hutchinson from Cincinnati.

Calmly, Alston sits in the eye of this hurricane, managing his team, with the steadiness that has characterized his work for the last ten years.

"I would be a liar if I denied that all this heat bothered me," Walt admits, "but my philosophy is simple. I merely say that a man must do the best he can—and the hell with everything else."

Leo Durocher

COMMENTS

In my mind there have always been two Leo Durochers:
Leo the Good and Leo the Bad. I always thought that I
would have enjoyed playing for Leo the Good. That was
the Leo they called "the Lip," who led the '51 Giants
from 13½ games back to win the pennant, the Leo who
adopted the rookie Willie Mays, the Leo who used to holler "stick it in his ear." I would've been one of Leo the
Good's favorites, because I was always doing things like
banging into catchers to knock the ball loose. I can almost hear Leo hollering about me in the dugout. "Look
at that, boys, a pitcher breaking up a double play. That's
what I like to see." I was always Leo's kind of ballplayer,
and it would have been fun to be one of his favorites.

To hear the players tell it, with Leo the only thing to
be was a favorite. There was no middle ground. The al-
ternative was to be in Leo's doghouse, which is where the
other Leo, Leo the Bad, would have kept the other me.
The other me talked politics in the clubhouse, was a
friend of writers and supported the Players Association.

Leo the Bad would've called me a clubhouse lawyer, or
one of the other names he used to belittle players he
didn't like. I wouldn't have liked the Leo who lost the ability to communicate with players in his later years. After
my book *Ball Four* came out, Durocher, who hadn't read
it ("I don't have to read that kind of stuff. I know what
it's all about"), said he never would have me on his team.
This saddened me and blew my image of Durocher. I had
always felt that Leo would play a convicted rapist if he
could turn the double play.

I sometimes wonder if it's the passing years that have made Durocher bitter or whether he was that way all the time and no one noticed. He was always abrasive, but only in the last few years has he seemed particularly sour. Maybe he hasn't changed. Maybe men don't change, but their abilities do. Durocher has failed in recent years because *as a manager* he didn't change with the times. He didn't adjust to the new ballplayer, the one interested in things other than baseball, the one concerned about the future, the one involved in union activities.

For example, in the spring of 1967 Marvin Miller and Dick Moss of the Players Association were going around to the teams to explain the new pension benefits that had been won. At the meeting with the Cubs, Durocher, a strong management supporter, was belittling the progress and heckling Miller and Moss. Then Miller pointed out that Durocher's own pension benefits had been increased from $8,000 to $18,000, or $10,000 per year. And then Durocher did something that embarrassed and antagonized his players and put just a little more distance between them. The manager waved his arms disdainfully and said, "I tip more than that in the shithouse." The players just moaned.

Actually, at least once, Durocher has tried to adjust. Prior to the 1972 season with the Cubs, Leo decided to do something to improve his communications with the press and his players. What he did was to appoint Hank Aguirre, an ex-pitcher, as a communications coach, a special liaison between the warring factions (the warring factions being Durocher and everybody else). This way, instead of Durocher hollering at the writers through a closed door, he could holler at Aguirre through a closed door, and Aguirre could relay the message. And instead of Durocher screaming at Joe Pepitone, he could have Aguirre scream at Pepitone. I don't know if the idea worked or not, but Durocher is now managing Houston.

Other than that, the only changes in Durocher have been subtle personality ones. And it may have nothing to do with anything, but I've noticed the same sort of meta-

morphosis taking place in Willie Mays. The passing years
have made him bitter. When Mays came up to the major
leagues, he was excited, he played stickball in the streets
of Harlem, he was happy, open, cooperative. A lot of
good things have happened to Mays since then, and yet today Willie Mays is angry. (And his anger has nothing to
do with the plight of black stickball players.) And he's
suspicious. And uptight. And very uncooperative. I sometimes wonder if Leo Durocher contributed to that. Roger
Kahn, who wrote the first of the two pieces we've selected on Durocher, says that Leo "reared" Mays. It did
seem like Durocher was a help to Mays when he first came
up. But maybe it was bad over the long run to have a
promoter like Durocher for a friend. I have the feeling
that Durocher never cared about Willie Mays the person,
only Willie Mays the star ballplayer. Maybe somewhere
along the line Willie realized that Durocher was just being nice to him so he could use him, and Mays thought
this was what friendship was all about. Perhaps Mays then
began to collect friends the way Durocher did, friends
like Frank Sinatra and Dean Martin, who could make you
look like a big shot. Of course, when Durocher needed
them it turned out they'd been bullshitting him just like
he'd bullshitted Mays.

Maybe Durocher is an angry man today because he built
his life around fake friends. Possibly Mays learned from
his manager and built his life the same way. It's easy for
ballplayers to fall into that trap, because there's no end
to the people who want to be seen with you, use your
name and are willing to make you feel like an instant big
shot. If you want to be a big shot, it's irresistible. Time
eventually exposes the big shots, the con artists, the pro-
moters. That's why Durocher is most effective as a manager over the short run, before people find out about him,
before he "wears out his welcome."

I don't know Durocher personally, so I guess I could
be wrong about him. But I've had a chance to observe
him from across the field and hear about him in the dugouts, as well as read about him. (I don't have to *know*

that kind of guy. I know what he's all about.)

The second piece, by William Furlong, seems to be closer to what Durocher is like today. That doesn't mean the article by Kahn, the gentler one, isn't accurate, although it's always Roger's style to emphasize the good in his sport heroes, to make everything seem sweetly nostalgic.

Furlong's story, on the other hand, is much tougher. Len Shecter was the sports editor of *Look* who gave Furlong the assignment on Durocher. It wouldn't have been unlike Len to tell Furlong he didn't want sweet nostalgia.

Rather than update the pieces, we thought it would be of added interest to compare the points of view of the writers as they saw things at the time. It tells something about sportswriting as well as about Durocher. It's amusing, for example, to see how both Kahn and Furlong have used the same statistic to make opposite points. Kahn says Durocher "is one of the very best of all baseball managers. In 16 seasons . . . Durocher teams have won three pennants, one World Series and had an overall percentage of .560." Meanwhile, Furlong says Durocher "began managing in the big leagues over 30 years ago and he *did* win a world championship. But only one."

I think both Durocher pieces make excellent reading, particularly set against each other, and together they convey my dual feelings about the man.

Leo is still being Leo after these chapters were put together. On March 12, 1973, before a spring-training game in Pompano, Florida, Durocher interrupted a Players Association meeting with Marvin Miller and ordered his players to take batting practice. The Houston players didn't moan, not out loud anyway, probably because they were mostly rookies. The veterans had been encouraged by Durocher not to attend. The players were embarrassed for Durocher and thought he should have shown more class.

Durocher's idea of class is still the same. He's still bigshotting it. A Houston player told me, "It's always Frank Sinatra this, and Frank Sinatra that. The other day someone asked Leo if he wanted to play golf and Leo said, 'Gee, [*Gee?*] I haven't shot golf since I played with Frank.' " That's when third baseman Doug Rader said, "Who the hell cares about *Frank?*"

The Astros may be good enough to win the pennant in spite of Durocher, but that's not stopping Leo from going for a new world's record for wearing out a welcome. Even at Durocher's pace this may take time, since the Astros have almost become comfortable not liking their manager. "Nobody particularly likes Leo, but at least he's not pestering us all the time like Harry Walker."

And the spring-training games don't even count.

"They Ain't Getting No Maiden"

by ROGER KAHN

Cornered by acquaintances, Leo Ernest Durocher of West Springfield, Mass., Brooklyn and Beverly Hills, Calif., concedes that his life story would make an excellent movie. It has everything, Durocher suggests. Existentialism. Good clean sex. Pathos. Pride. Prejudice. "And besides," he adds, superseding all other considerations, "Sinatra would like to play me."

As this season of 1966 was entering its hard, hot summer, Durocher was approaching his 61st birthday head on. Recently he confided to an interviewer that he was 59 years old, although sometime earlier he had confided to the *Official Encyclopedia of Baseball, Revised Edition,* that he was born on July 27, 1905. He has outworn his welcome in many towns, and he was 59 going on 61. By any standards that is an unsettling situation.

What cheers the man and nourishes his ego is that he is working at what he believes The Guy Upstairs—his favorite term for the divinity—intends him to do. After ten years of other employment, Durocher had returned to managing in the major leagues. The Chicago Cubs, the team Durocher returned to, may have been the worst of 20. Their organization was sterile, their owner, P. K. Wrigley (*Hi, Ho, Hey, Hey, Chew your little troubles away*), was remote, and the team, which broke last that season, hadn't finished in the first division since the second year of Harry Truman's presidency. But he is happy in his new job, Durocher insists. "As long as I can walk out there," he says, "managing is what I want to do."

There is no question that Durocher wanted the Cub job. A larger question before the house of the North Side of Chicago is how long he will continue to want it. No fewer than nine of Durocher's former players were managing alongside him in the major leagues, and the four in the National League beat his brains out more often than not. That burns a man, particularly after he has built his career on total victory, particularly after he has built himself the highest house in the most expensive subdivision in America, particularly when he is 59 going on 61 and impatient.

A few years ago, when he was married to Laraine Day, the Mormon actress, Durocher believed The Guy Upstairs had larger plans for him, including capital gains. The Cleveland Indians asked him to manage for a $35,000 salary plus $10,000 expenses, plus a lucrative complex stock deal. "Better up the stock deal a little," said Durocher, the capital gainsman. When the Indians did not, he was disappointed and at liberty.

Yet he was all but offended later when Charles O. Finley offered him a job managing Kansas City in the American League. "I'll pay you fifty thousand on a two- or three-year contract to come to Kansas City," said Finley, misjudging his man.

"Mr. Finley," said Leo, at ease in Beverly Hills, "if I want a steak I'll send for it."

So, with some second thoughts on hubris, Durocher found himself working from 1961 through 1964 as a coach under Walter Alston, manager of the Dodgers and a stolid bucolic. One thing Durocher knew about The Guy Upstairs. He did not intend Leo to end up as a coach under a farmer. But, Leo reasoned, Alston might just get fired, and he might just be hired to replace him. Tension between Alston and Durocher did not all by itself cause the Dodgers to blow the 1962 pennant, but the club was sharply divided between Durocher men and Alston men. And the team didn't win.

After a rousing comeback in 1963, the year the Dodgers took the World Series in four straight, the team collapsed to sixth and the Dodger front office collectively concluded that someone had to go. Leo was dismissed, and Alston was retained. To make sure Durocher would not charge persecution, the Dodgers fired all their other coaches, too, including Joe Becker, a friend of Alston's and a man Alston very much wanted to keep with the ball club.

"I have no feud with Leo," Emil J. (Buzzy) Bavasi, the Dodger general manager, says. "But you know how he is, and how he wears out welcomes. He'd paid back the money we lent him—well, actually we withheld it from his salary—and then we let him go."

Within weeks the Chicago Cubs joyously announced the engagement of Leo Durocher. "But we have no immediate announcement as to Durocher's title," an official said. "We have found from long experience that it doesn't make any difference what title a team leader has as long as he has the ability to take charge."

Durocher considered the remark and the Cubs' long experience with a series of rotating "head coaches." "I just gave myself a title," he said. "I'm not the head coach here. I'm the manager."

He is indeed. He is one of the very best of all baseball managers. In 16 seasons with the Brooklyn Dodgers and the New York Giants, Durocher teams won three pennants, one World Series and had an overall percentage of .560. True, teams managed by Casey Stengel won three times as many pennants, and teams managed by Al Lopez had a better winning percentage, .588. But in baseball, numbers seldom provide a full measure of a team or of a man.

The special genius of Durocher is not only in the victory but in the manner. He is, all by himself and at once, innovator, symbol and creator. Those nine managers who once played for him view him variously with idolatry, admiration and dislike. None ignores him or his influence. He is that strong a man among strong men.

"My kind of team," Durocher says of clubs he built at Brooklyn and New York, and knowledgeable baseball men perceive a combative image. Both time he started with uncertain material, although better than what he started with at Chicago, and produced arrogant and exciting champions. (Indeed there may never have been a more exciting team than Durocher's 1951 Giants, who started poorly, were 13½ games behind in August, and won the pennant when Bobby Thomson hit a home run in the ninth inning of the third playoff game against Brooklyn.)

He makes phrases, strong, memorable ones, although lately it has pleased his fancy to protest that he never actually said, or anyway didn't actually mean, the one that may yet get him into Bartlett: "Nice guys finish last." Mostly he fights. Mostly, if his interest does not flag, he'll stay up late nights and get up early mornings to win. He'll bellow, beg, intimidate, curse, bless, to win. He'll kick and scratch and brawl and charm to win, and these are some of the things Durocher says:

"I'd bench my brother. I come to kill ya. Anybody can finish second, but I got to win. If we're spittin' at a—crack in the wall for pennies, I got to beat ya. Maybe I don't understand that word 'sportsmanship,' but this is professional. What are we out at the park for except to win? I'd trip my mother. I'll help her up, brush her off, tell her I'm sorry. *But mother don't make it to third.*"

To an extent, Durocher is a prisoner of his own glibness. With the essentially docile Cubs he had to labor for viciousness, seeking out words and phrases that prove he is just as mean as ever, as though the discovery of some ballfield kindness would undo it all, the revelation that he suffered bouts of civility and compassion would end the dream and transform him suddenly into Mary Poppins.

He could not be rough with the players who had no self-confidence anymore. Nor could he be rough with his employers. He had learned that lesson. Thirty-seven years ago, while arguing about his salary, he cursed at an employer, the general manager of the Yankees, and never was allowed to play for the Yankees again. That left, as an outlet for hostility and a proving ground that he had not gone soft, the sportswriters who covered the team. Durocher did not win many games for the Cubs in April and early May, but he cursed more sportswriters than any manager in either league.

The rules, he explained to the press, were simple but absolute. "I don't answer none of your double-barreled questions," Durocher said. "If you're wondering what a double-barreled question is, it's one you can't answer right either way, like how long you been beating your wife. Now, boys, there's no sense in asking me those questions because I'm not going to answer them, and anybody who says I will or ever did is a liar."

A New York newspaperman who wanted to interview him on opening day in San Francisco approached softly as Durocher slouched in the front seat of the team bus.

"Nah," said Durocher. "I ain't giving any—interviews. I got enough—troubles now."

He had a cold. Well, he didn't know whether it was a cold or a virus or what, but when the Cubs got to L.A., he was going to see his doc and get fixed up. "Damn," he said. "I don't know what it is."

He might still have been the Giants' manager if he had not outworn his welcome with them too, and it was a hard thing for him at Candlestick Park, looking out at the two teams, his and theirs. The Cubs have a fine third baseman in Ron Santo and a good outfielder in Billy Williams. Both hit with power. But the club professional, Ernie Banks, now 35, seems suddenly old when he swings. The other talent is a long way from competence.

"You had one of those great springs," Durocher said on the field at Candlestick to Willie Mays. He had brought Mays into the majors, reared him, so to speak, and here was Willie playing for the other club. The other club had all the talent, even his own.

"Not too bad, Leo. Not too bad," Willie said.

"You hit .383 with nine home runs," Durocher said.

"I didn't see no figures," Mays said.

"Willie," Leo said, "this is me you're talking to. Me. I

know ya, Willie. You got the figures written on the inside of your shoes."

It was an unpleasant afternoon for Durocher. In the fourth inning Mays hit a home run, and the Giants scored six times. Later, after Len Gabrielson hit another homer, a Chicago pitcher named Bill Faul threw the next two pitches close to Mays' head.

Willie took three steps toward Faul and shouted something. That was all. The Giants won, as the wind came shrilly up the bay, by 9 to 1.

Afterward, a portly, elderly baseball writer said to Durocher in the clubhouse, "I guess when you were quoted telling Willie to stay loose at the plate you meant it, eh, Leo?"

Durocher was still weak from the virus, or whatever it was. He couldn't get warm, he said. The press felt sorry for this new old manager who had lost big on opening day.

"Quoted where?" Durocher said, clearing hoarseness from his throat as his voice rose.

"In a spring training story," the baseball writer said.

"You're not asking the right question," Durocher said. "Why don't you ask me if I said it?" He called the writer by name, schoolteacherly. Then he shouted, "Why don't you ask me if I said it?" Suddenly Durocher did not feel weak any longer. "Because if you ask me if I said it, I'm going to tell you I didn't. Never. Never did. And any man who says I did is a liar. You are a—liar, friend."

The press was gathered in disordered rows around Durocher and his victim. Before the fury of the blast reporters swayed like evening corn. No one said much after that. No one felt sorry for Durocher anymore, but no one persisted. Had Bill Faul meant to throw at Mays, or had successive pitches slipped? If they were knockdowns, who had ordered them? Durocher? Then what about Leo's self-proclaimed love for Mays? Was that something he now forgot at game time? These were good questions, but the blast had cowed the press. Nobody asked them.

He lost two out of three in San Francisco, where he could have managed a fine team, and took his club into Los Angeles, where he might have managed last season's pennant winner. "A little two'sie-out-of-threesie," he said, was what he hoped for, what he wanted his Cubs to bring him.

His health improved and when General William Eckert, the trim, quiet man who was the new Commissioner of Baseball, appeared on the field of Dodger Stadium, Durocher burst into the free flight of a Hollywood master of ceremonies.

"Mr. Commissioner," he said, "I'd like you to meet my shortstop, Mr. Kessinger. Don, boy, say hello to the Commissioner."

"Hello," Don Kessinger said.

"Abbie, come over here," Durocher ordered. "Ted Abernathy, Mr. Commissioner. One of my pitchers. Good relief man. Yes sir, Mr. Commissioner. Fine boys. Yes sir."

The Cubs almost won that game, but after they botched two double plays, a homer beat them. They did not approach two for three. They lost all their games, and before the last one on Sunday Durocher did not hold court near home plate. Instead, he stood at second base where he could relay outfield throws to the batting practice pitcher and be safe from anyone who might ask how he thought things were going. Sunday was the day that Sinatra, Dean Martin and Joey Bishop were supposed to have flown in from Las Vegas to watch Durocher manage. But reporters found three anonymous children occupying Sinatra's seats. "I see," said Sinatra in Las Vegas, "my man Leo, he's not doing so good." That was not much comfort to a manager hell-bent on victory and losing games at the age of 59 going on 61.

Opening day in Chicago was not much better. Already the Cubs were one and five, and now they had to play against the Giants again. On the way to Wrigley Field, Durocher turned into Lake Shore Drive on a changing light, and a car plowed into the back of his Buick Riviera, disabling it. He was not hurt, but he had to ride the rest of the way in a squad car. That bothered him and so did a forthright series of articles in the Chicago *Daily News* called "Durocher: The Legend and the Man." It was a wet day and chilly, and the stands were not full, but on the field Durocher found himself surrounded by interviewers. For a little while he was cordial, saying orthodox things. "I don't see how this club didn't finish higher with all the talent it's got. We're gonna cause a little trouble. Make a little noise."

After a while he was talking into a microphone held by Rudy Bukich, quarterback of the Chicago Bears, and when that was through it was time to attack again. "Ya gettin' this all down?" he barked at a newspaperman. "Yeah, yeah. The writers come around and they're real nice, like that guy from the *Daily News*. He was sitting by the pool, and I couldn't have been nicer, and all the while ya know what he had up his sleeve? A—hatchet. Well, yah, you can all get your hatchets out, boys, and work on me all you want, 'cause I got news for you boys, it's been done before. When they hatchet me they ain't getting no—maiden."

The style is first to try intimidation. After that, perhaps amiability. "Now there is no sense," Durocher says, "if you are going for a pennant, of being mean to a bad club. If I'm on the contender and we're playing the last place team, it's how do ya do. Glad to see ya. Welcome to town. Take 'em out. Buy 'em a drink. Beat 'em a run or two. That's fine. Don't show 'em up. They're sleeping dogs, kid, and you know what they say about them." The style is always loud, but flexible.

He is an absolute pragmatist in all things. "With a girl, you've got to make your move fast," Durocher once instructed a younger man. "Say you pick her up at seven o'clock. Well, then make your first strong move at 7:05. No go? Tough, but hell it's early yet. There's still time to call another broad. But say that move you make at 7:05 works. She says okay. Well, then, hello my dear. You'd be surprised. Some damned famous broads say okay quick."

Within baseball Durocher's pragmatism is not everywhere admired. Wes Westrum, who once caught for Durocher, has gone out of his way this season to point out that he is not playing injured men "like Durocher made me play when my hands were hurt." Westrum feels that playing with bad hands was his ruination as a hitter. His lifetime batting average in the majors was .199, and Westrum reguards Durocher with appropriate warmth.

Billy Herman, a superb second baseman with the Cubs, later under Durocher at Brooklyn, manages the Boston Red Sox. During spring training Herman let slip a fantasy when a reporter asked about Durocher in Chicago. "I don't think he'll last a month," Herman said. "They play the Dodgers the second series of the season. There will be a rhubarb started in one of the games. There has to be. Leo will run out onto the field to get into it, and the big guy with number twenty-four on his shirt will pinch his head off." The big guy with number twenty-four on his shirt is Walter Alston.

Herman Franks, the manager of the Giants, dissents from all criticism. "I can't tell ya about him," says Franks. "You make something up. You make up anything you want and say I said it, long as it's good, okay? Look, when they made that guy, they threw away the mold."

Durocher came out of West Springfield, Mass., schooled in poolrooms and streets, with a blurred background. There have been reports in the past that he is part Jewish. Durocher says no, that is not so. The name is French. His antecedents are French Canadian. He seldom talks about his father. Once he told a biographer that he had spent his life looking for father images.

He was an expedient ballplayer rather than gifted. He had good hands, quickness, drive and profound self-knowledge. He played shortstop, a good position for a weak hitter since defensive shortstops are at a premium. His throwing arm was not outstanding, but he taught himself to scoop and throw with remarkable speed. He is credited by baseball men with being the best of all shortstops at getting rid of the ball in a hurry.

He never could hit. His lifetime major league average

of .247 was acquired in decades when batting averages were higher than they are now. Someone who played with him on the sandlots of West Springfield says that he could not hit even then. "I don't know what it was," Durocher once said. "The guy would pitch, and my butt would fly out. Good-bye." The reference is to a slight, significant, involuntary movement that carried his weight away from the speeding pitch. Excellent self-defense; poor batting form.

He appeared, incredibly, on what may have been the greatest of all hitting teams, the Yankees of Babe Ruth and Lou Gehrig. Up for a cup of coffee in 1925, Durocher made the Yankees in 1928 and played in 102 games. Some of the older men called him "Fifth Avenue" because of his penchant for garish clothing, and he seems to have been nothing more than a boisterous spear carrier for two years. But there he was, the expedient ballplayer with a great Yankee team, until he told off his employer and had to play for Cincinnati, an exile that lasted four years.

He was always moving, wearing out a welcome, and at 28 he was dealt to St. Louis where he played shortstop for the Gashouse Gang, loudly and well. He came to Brooklyn in 1938, when the Cardinals tired of his noise after a season in which he batted .203. Larry MacPhail, a skilled and raucous promoter, had come into Brooklyn, and word was that MacPhail was looking for a new manager for 1939.

There were two prominent candidates for the job. One was Durocher, by now famous for his ferocious drive to win. The other was Babe Ruth, whom MacPhail had hired as a coach. Late in that lost season in Brooklyn long ago, a young baseball writer reported that Ruth, coaching at first, had flashed the hit-and-run sign to a batter.

Now that was a joke, Durocher said in the clubhouse at Ebbets Field. How could the big baboon have flashed a hit-and-run sign when he didn't even know what the sign was? Probably what Durocher said was true. Signs and inside baseball were alien to Ruth. But he had been publicly humiliated, and Ruth decided to avenge himself on Durocher with his fists. He made the threat while seated on a three-legged stool before a narrow locker.

Quickly Durocher shoved Babe Ruth into the locker and cuffed him about the face. "I knew," Durocher said later, "that if the big guy got to me first, I'd be a goner. I also knew fights get broken up fast. By shoving him in there, I figured I'd get my shots in, and before he could come back at me, the fight would be over."

Just before the season ended, Durocher was playing bridge on a train when Cookie Lavagetto made an inept play. "Dammit, aincha got any brains?" Durocher said.

Ruth had been reading a comic strip. Now he looked up. "Yeah, Bananas," Ruth said to Lavagetto. "Don't ya know that the only guy on this club with any brains is the big man?" And Babe Ruth solemnly pointed to the big man, Leo Durocher.

Durocher became manager in 1939, and the Dodgers jumped from seventh place to third. They won the pennant in 1941 and have been contenders more often than not ever since.

In mid-1948 he became the manager of the Giants, then a team of strong, slow sluggers. "I'm gonna build my kind of team," Durocher promised. A swift, gifted opportunistic Durocher Giant team won the pennant in 1951. Since then the Giants, too, have been contenders more often than not.

Durocher's Giant welcome wore out in 1955, the season after his club had won the World Series. With familiarity, he became inclined to make sarcastic remarks about the Giant management, telling a story here, and another there among his friends. One friend, Danny Kaye, later entertained scores of people at a banquet with an imitation of a Giant executive. It was a crude performance, but it made Durocher laugh out loud. When the laughter reached the highest offices of the Giants, it became one more of the complex of reasons that led the Giants to fire him.

After that Leo announced that he would never manage again unless he was given "a piece of the club." Sour years followed. He worked at NBC, but that job dried up. He missed the chance at Cleveland. His marriage to Laraine Day ended, transporting him from a comfortable home to bachelor quarters. He was hard put to maintain his lavish standard and so, with much talk of swallowing pride and a great dumbshow of humility, he took a job in 1961 as coach under a farmer.

There were painful days for coach Durocher and manager Walter Alston. "We're in Cincinnati," Durocher says, recalling one day of frustration, "and they got a man on and Don Drysdale is pitching to Gordie Coleman, which is a low-ball pitcher pitching to a low-ball hitter, and the fellows on the bench, some of the players, said, 'What would you do, Leo?'

"I said, I'd put him on because Marty Keough, the hitter after Coleman, is a high-ball hitter. Well, Alston don't put him on, and the first ball pitched to Coleman, boom, a home run, and now we're down 3 to 0. But I'm not second-guessing Alston. I made this statement before Drysdale ever pitched the ball.

"All right. The eighth inning. We score a run. We tie it in the ninth 3 to 3. In the tenth we score three, and now it's 6 to 3. Looks great. They're up. First man singles and the next man doubles. The tying run at the plate and nobody out.

"Alston finally tells me to bring relief pitcher Ed Roebuck in. The next man hits a fly ball, scoring a run, making it 6 to 4, and the man on second went to third. Next man hit another fly. It's 6 to 5. Two outs. Nobody on. Next man doubled. Coleman the batter.

"*Now* they ask me. I said, 'Why didn't you ask me earlier, that other time? You're asking me now.' And I said, 'Put him on.'

"They said, 'How can you put the winning run on?'

"I says, '*If you're scared go home.*'

"So Alston got teed off, but finally they did what I said,

put him on, and the first ball pitched to Keough, the next hitter, right back to the pitcher. Game's over. We're in the clubhouse."

Afterward Durocher and Alston were undressing in front of adjoining lockers, when a newsman asked Alston, "How come you put the winning run on?"

"Well, I thought about that," Alston said slowly. "It was a kinda tough decision but I thought it was the right thing to do."

Durocher moved his gear and dressed a good distance from Alston after that. He will not talk about him any longer.

Durocher did not have to take the job with the Cubs, although he had gone deeply into debt building a mansion while he was a Dodger coach. The house, which cost perhaps $200,000, is located in Trousdale Estates, a Beverly Hills development that advertises sites for $54,000 and up. But his radio program was lucrative. He landed some television jobs. According to a former agent, Durocher out of baseball in 1965 earned more than $75,000.

The real reason he took the Chicago job, Durocher says, is that he didn't see how the Cubs could "finish eighth with all those good ballplayers." Would you believe it? (Would you believe tenth?)

Last winter he went on the road in Illinois, through Peoria, Joliet and the rest, with some players and a spiel. "Now look at my club," he'd say. "Mr. Ellsworth, the left-hander. Who's a better one? Koufax? Right. Who else is better? Nobody. There's nobody. Mr. Williams in my outfield. One of the five best players in the game. Let me tell you, we got speed, leg men and some power and . . ."

He doubled the Cubs' advance sale. It is kindless to point out that Ellsworth lost his first four starts and that Williams was batting .215 on May 15th. "Leo had those guys convinced back in January," says Joe Black, a former Dodger, who caught some of the road show. "They really thought they were good. Trouble is they didn't open the season till April. The spell wore off."

He has a three-year contract in Chicago and he says it will be July at the earliest before he has the Cubs really playing his game. If trades work out well (and his usually do), and young talent develops fast, he might have a presentable team sometime next year. Not contending, but presentable; good enough, say, to lure Dean and Joey to the ball park once in a while.

Meanwhile he has to wait and see his players stumble and watch his former pupils drive better teams toward the pennant. For all the bravado, this is still the down-beat phase, the sort of thing that Frank Sinatra would condense or cut from a movie.

Not long ago Durocher took a drink and talked about old times with Herman Franks, who had caught for him 26 years ago and batted .183. "Couple of outs," Leo said. "Me and Herman the Whale." He talked some more. "If I can't win this myself . . ." And now he seemed about to say that the pennant might as well go to his friend, Herman the Whale.

One does not speak that way in baseball. By ritual and by fiat, all managers are supposed to hate all others equally. Nobody favors anybody else in public. "Come on, Leo," Frank said firmly, cutting him short. Then gently, "Come on, ol' buddy. Let's go."

Durocher turned and walked away on the arm of his pupil. "Damn," he said, "we shoulda beat you today."

How Durocher
Blew the Pennant

by WILLIAM BARRY FURLONG

Leo Durocher, manager of the Chicago Cubs, destroyed
two of his center fielders, and when the pennant crunch
came, he had none. He called one of his players "quitter."
He tried to out-scramble his players to the money pot. He
cultivated a broad and earnest enmity. "He's the most
unprincipled man in sports," says Jack Brickhouse, the in-
domitably cheerful man who telecasts Cub games. And
what it all cost the Cubs was a chance to win their first
pennant in 24 years.

It was, to be sure, Leo Durocher who brought the Cubs
to the point where a pennant was even a possibility. "This
is not an eighth-place ball club," he snapped when he took
over the Cubs in 1966. He promptly managed them into
tenth place. After that, he cajoled and goaded, he growled
and he praised, and by 1969 he had the Cubs in first place
in the Eastern Division of the National League. The way
Leo Durocher was going in Chicago, he was one-up on
God and only a step-and-a-half behind Mayor Daley.

There were those who detected developing disaster,
however. "This club will never win the pennant as long
as Leo is manager," said one of the Cub regulars last May,
when the team was far out in front. "He just doesn't
know how to handle players." A teammate—a supporter
of Durocher's—nodded. "He keeps the tension too high,"
he said.

They were right. When the pressure descended, the
tense and tired Cubs collapsed like a stale soufflé. In one
of the great turnabouts of baseball, they blew an 8½-game

lead and slid to second place, eight games behind, as the New York Mets roared past them to win the division title, the pennant and the World Series.

During this terrible span, from September 4 to 23, they went from five games ahead to six behind and had the worst record in the major leagues. When the rubble was cleared, it became apparent that these were some of the reasons:

Leo lost touch with his players.

In a wrath-filled, closed-door meeting during the big crunch in September, he flayed Ferguson Jenkins as a "quitter." Jenkins was his hardest working pitcher and the only one who won 20 games in each of the last three years. "He really laid me out," Jenkins admits.

What happened was that Jenkins had watched Durocher do some wild things with his pitchers. For example, he'd let Dick Selma go a week or more without a start. Then suddenly he would start him three times in a week —twice in two days. It didn't work, and when Jenkins was asked to pitch out of turn, he demurred. Which is when Durocher laid him out.

In another heated clubhouse session after the Cubs blew a critical game to the Mets in July, he publicly destroyed his rookie center fielder, Don Young. "That kid in center field gave it away," Durocher howled. "Two little fly balls—he just stood there watching one and he gave up on the other." Durocher made no move to relieve the bitterness or pull the team together when Ron Santo, the Cub third baseman, similarly blasted Young. Santo later apologized. Leo remained silent. He simply yanked Young from the lineup—and had no center fielder to replace him.

At another public session—this time in a speech in downtown Chicago—he wasted Adolfo Phillips, the Cubs' only experienced center fielder. "Nobody wants Phillips," Durocher said. "You can't give him away." The day this appeared, in huge headlines, Phillips, a moody Panamanian, struck out twice, popped up once, and dropped a fly ball for a three-base error. In no time, he was batting .115 and had hit the ball out of the infield only once in 16 tries.

Leo was once closely attuned to the Phillips psyche. He had showered him with all his special affection. He even called him "Dummy!" during clubhouse gin rummy games. He seemed to know how to get the most out of the man. There was a time in 1967 when Phillips took the Cubs into first place in the National League—for a brief, exhilarating moment—by pacing them in homers, hitting and runs-batted-in. But by last year, Durocher could talk to him only through the newspapers. And Phillips responded purely through enmity. He didn't begin to hit until he discovered that his aversion to his manager was shared by many. At that point—publicly congratulating newsman Jerome Holtzman of the Chicago *Sun-Times* for his corrosive conquest of Leo in a shouting match over what the reporter insisted was a lie Durocher told about a pitching selection—Phillips went on a six-game hitting streak in which he batted .411. Leo took one look—and benched him. Then he traded him, leaving a gaping hole in center field, a hole he still hasn't filled.

Leo was not much admired, even within his own ball club, for the way he handled his pitchers last year. One of them, Ken Holtzman, he had much earlier begun to call out to in the clubhouse: "Hey, Jew!" or "C'mon, kike!" There was nothing malicious in this. It was Durocher's way of bringing a rookie into the inner faith of the clubhouse, part of the glowing warmth of baseball. And no different from Durocher calling Ron Santo "wop," or college-grad Don Kessinger "dumb hillbilly."

But in the case of Holtzman, though, Durocher really started to lose touch with his player when these labels were paired with a rumor sweeping the clubhouse that Ken lacked guts, that he didn't hang in there when the pressure was on.

Holtzman suspected he knew the reason. Whenever he was in a tight game, and Leo stomped out to ask him if he was tired, he'd answer with the truth. Of course he was tired. You can't pitch six or seven strenuous innings of major-league ball without getting tired. But he wasn't tired to death. He did not need to be relieved. He found out that this is not the way the game is played. Managers are used to being lied to. If a pitcher admits he's tired, then he's too tired to pitch anymore. The result was that in his first few years with the Cubs, Holtzman found himself being yanked fast and early.

The solution was simple. Holtzman learned to lie. He stopped admitting he was tired. Last year, he completed six of his first ten starts and had a 10-1 record by early June.

When Leo learned of this ploy, he threatened to fine anybody $500 who lied to him about being tired. At that point, the only thing that counted was that Durocher was no longer in contact with his young pitcher. A world had come between them. In the September crunch, Holtzman won one game, lost five.

Durocher destroyed not only his players but a little of himself—or at least the boldly manipulated legend that he lived by.

Durocher has an almost visceral need to big-man it, to demonstrate that he's apart from and above the rest of mankind. "It's the $300-suit syndrome—he thinks he puts on class when he puts on clothes," says one observer. With some people, this is effective. Ron Santo, the third baseman, is mesmerized by Leo's *persona;* he calls him a "fantastic man." Others are less enthralled, especially those whom Durocher steps on in order to step up. He calls Jack Brickhouse, "Mental Midget." He calls George Langford, a promising young sportswriter for the Chicago *Tribune,* "stupid." He forces his quirks and whims on anybody who'll bend to them. When Vince Lloyd, a radio announcer for the *Tribune*-owned WGN in Chicago, lit up a pipe in his presence, Durocher—who detests tobacco smoke—ripped it out of his mouth and threw it into a toilet bowl.

But the legend of his being a special man began coming apart at his wedding last June. It was to be a Great

Social Event, what with the expected arrival of Durocher's pals in the Frank Sinatra-Dean Martin axis. Indeed,
some of the radio-TV people in Chicago were offended
when Durocher didn't invite them. Some of the players
were when he did; Ken Holtzman turned down the invitation, and pitching coach Joe Becker confided that he'd
like to do the same, "But my wife bought a new dress.
. . ." (The rest of the players attended and chipped in to
buy—through a discount house in Atlanta—a silver en-
semble as a gift. The name of Durocher's bride was mis-
spelled in the engraving.)

The ceremony was a success, but the celebrity bit was
a flop. Frank didn't show. Neither did Dean. Or Joe E.
Or Sammy. Toots got in only for the tail end of the reception.

Among those who did show up, in addition to the scattering of baseball people were real estate hustlers, retired
politicians, contractors, and a few of the gang who deal
in a minor way in the shadow areas—high-interest loans
or stocks that the Securities and Exchange Commission
indicated might be rigged in price. These guests did
something for Durocher that he would never have done
for himself: put him exactly in his place.

Even more critical was his trip to Camp Ojibwa in
Wisconsin. After it was discovered that he'd lied when
he left the club during a game—complaining that he was
ill—in order to catch a chartered plane to Wisconsin
where he could visit his stepson, there was much speculation that the players felt Durocher had deserted in the
midst of a pennant fight. Hardly. There was a minimum
of six games that Leo missed last year. One time, he left
the club without even telling his coaches he was going.
But at least several players felt that the club tried harder to win when he wasn't there. What *did* impress the
players was the way Durocher's carefully constructed
self-image was tainted. No longer did he seem a man
apart from—or above—them. When he wanted to get
away from the pressure of the pennant race, he did just
what they did: he lied, went on the sneak. The difference

was that he'd never let a player get away with it. It became obvious that Durocher's standards for himself were lower than those for his players. That's a dangerous insight for men asked to believe unquestioningly in a famous manager. Within three weeks, the Cubs were plummeting swiftly into their great collapse.

Durocher did not crack down on outside distractions. Indeed, he wound up becoming something of a distraction himself to the players.

The Cub clubhouse was a hustler's paradise. Hectic card games went on all the time. Some of the players skipped practice in order to stay in them. From June on, there was always an agent in the clubhouse. He got the players TV spots, recording opportunities, speaking dates; he sold Cub bumper stickers, Cub tumblers, Cub T-shirts ("More than 200,000 the first week," he gloated) and Cub place mats. He aroused excitement—and avarice —about the fortunes that were there for the plucking. Cub players demanded money to talk on radio or TV for more than 90 seconds; they asked $18,000 for a 30-minute special on a local television station (and didn't get it); they insisted they be cut in on the income from a book to which they planned to contribute nothing but their gift for breathing. (Astonishingly, the publisher agreed, and when the players learned that, they upped their price.) "The greed in that clubhouse," says a TV man, "was unbelievable."

But the agent also brought them problems. Ernie Banks asked him to help clean the air when one sportswriter arranged to ghostwrite an autobiography. The agent fixed everything by bringing two more publishers and two or three more writers into the deal, telling them he had a movie contract set. He didn't; his movie-studio contact had been fired. And all he wanted for this contribution was 15 to 33 percent of everything. Ultimately, Banks tried to solve the problem by dumping the man who'd worked out the first book contract, which was not to his taste or temperament. Whatever the reason—or distraction—Banks batted only .156 during the crunch, thus helping to ruin the reason for publishing a book at all.

There were those who felt that the agent's clubhouse hustling was intruding on the time the Cubs would have devoted to (a) gin rummy or (b) baseball. But Leo did not banish him, possibly because he stood to gain as much as anybody from the agent's hustling, maybe more. For everything the agent promoted went into a common pool from which the whole team would benefit, instead of just the name players. Durocher, openly avaricious (despite the club's and baseball's desire for publicity, he refuses to be interviewed by magazines unless he is paid important money, which results in no interviews and no publicity), had to see this as the best of all possible worlds. Since his own side deals—big-money speaking dates, a beer commercial on television—were set up before the pool came into existence, he could draw money from it without contributing anything to it. In addition, once the Cubs forged far into the lead—at one point they led the Mets by 9½ games—Leo was demanding of the ad agency handling the beer account that he get more money and other concessions. And although any added cash would have been a fruit of the team's recent success, there was positively no mention of putting it into the pool. All Durocher wanted to do, after all, was extend some old deals.

In any case, Durocher finally restricted the card playing; all games had to be over 60 to 120 minutes before game time. But he did not banish the agent from the clubhouse until the final day of the season. The agent, Jack Childers, thought that showed a lack of gratitude. "Leo and his coaches got $3,000 each . . . and did absolutely nothing for it," he said.

Leo fumbled his grotesque attempts to unite the ball club against outsiders before its internal tensions tore it apart.

He tried to use umpires as a tension target. One day he got umpire Shag Crawford so mad, by dancing around him yelling "Dummy! Dummy!" that Crawford offered to fight him right there. But in the end, his umpire-baiting worked against the Cubs. They were the victims of some outrageously bad calls, and there was no place to turn; the league had become polarized against Durocher and the Cubs. Once, Leo was overruled by the league president, Warren Giles, on a protest involving a play that cost the Cubs a run and conceivably a ball game. (It was a judgment call on how many bases a runner could advance on a ball thrown into the stands.) Less than two weeks later, exactly the same play developed again, but with the team situation reversed, so that the Cubs—on the basis of the previous precedent—would save a run and perhaps a game. "They can't have it both ways," Durocher crowed of the umpires' decision. He was wrong. They could and they did. Not only that, the league office upheld them when Durocher protested. Whether or not Leo ever united the Cubs against the umpires, he certainly united the umpires against the Cubs.

Similarly, during the great collapse, he organized news people into a common band of hostiles, a ploy that did less than nothing for unifying the ball club. Baseball players are like actresses in heat; they need to be loved. By choosing this particular time to antagonize reporters, Durocher mainly made sure his players didn't get loving while losing—which was when they needed it most.

More, he brought an almost intolerable pressure on them. The first step was to withdraw from any discussion with any newsmen. ("No comment! No bleep-bleep comment. I don't care how bleep long you ask—until the snow is up against the bleep door—it'll still be no bleep comment.") The second step was to inspire doubts and anxieties in his players if *they* dared to answer questions. It developed this way:

One day in August, a Chicago sportswriter asked casually if Leo planned to give some of his beat-tired regulars a rest. That they were reeling with fatigue was no secret. But they didn't want to talk about it, for Durocher's $500-fine edict had squeezed them neatly in the middle. If they lied about being tired, it would cost $500; if they admitted it and dropped out of the lineup, they risked the manager screaming "quitter" at them. Durocher exploded at the reporter. "Don't ask me that bleep question!" he yelped. "If you've got a silly bleep question, go ask the players." He stormed out of his office into the players' quarters and bellowed, "I want all my players out here!" As the players straggled—wet and bedraggled—out of the showers, Leo gestured imperiously toward the reporter. "Are any of you tired? Anybody want to sit down for a while? This man wants to know. Go ahead—anybody who's tired just speak up!" Of course, nobody opened his mouth. There was, obviously, no future in it.

The fact is that when it counted most, both Don Kessinger at short and Glenn Beckert at second were letting ground balls by them that they'd have gobbled up earlier. And what Santo says about it now is, "Next season I'm sure Leo will rest the regulars from time to time."

After the big confrontation, Durocher refused to deal with reporters, and the pressure set in. The manager had a refuge, his office. He could close his door, he could lock it. But when, inevitably, the reporters came to the players, they had no place to hide. They didn't worry over the kind of answers to give—most were clichés anyway—but over what Durocher would think about those who gave them. He can read, and remember. Anybody who talked to a reporter could go on Durocher's bleep list. The anxiety grew until some of the players were thinking more about how to handle the press than how to handle a ground ball. Finally they appointed a committee of Ron Santo and Phil Regan, Durocher's favorite relief pitcher, to go to the manager and ask him to take some pressure off by resuming normal relations with the press. Leo agreed. He'd just come from an all-night session with several reporters at which a truce of sorts was arranged. It was, of course, too late. The Cubs had collapsed.

Leo and his followers provoked his enemies in baseball even more than they inspired the Cubs.

In a key game in September, Tommie Agee, the lead-off batter for the Mets, was knocked down by a Cub pitch in his first time at bat. He was not intimidated. He got up and hit a two-run homer and a double and scored two runs as the Mets beat the Cubs, 3-2.

In another key game, at the peak of the pennant race, Bob Gibson of St. Louis, who talks about Durocher with a curled lip, passed up a chance to pitch against the Mets and went out of rotation to meet—and beat—the Cubs. One reason: On a previous appearance, Gibson's outfielders had been victimized by Durocher's tough, noisy fans in the bleachers, who released white mice whenever a ball was hit to the outfield. In the confusion, the Cubs got 12 extra-base hits.

The same Cub fans, whom Durocher called the best in America, learned the names of the "Chicago girls" of some of the visiting outfielders and shouted the names aloud as the players circled under Cub fly balls. (One Los Angeles outfielder became so enraged that he hit two home runs in one game and ran around the bases brandishing a fist at Durocher and at his fans.) On another occasion, Durocher hurled a gratuitous insult at Gene Mauch, manager of the Montreal Expos: "Stick with that little genius [Mauch], and you'll stay in last place." Mauch waited until the Cubs were scrambling for survival in September and started Bill Stoneman, an ex-Cub pitcher who had little love for Durocher ("I don't talk to anybody named Leo"). He pitched a six-hitter that ended all the Cubs' hopes.

Cal Koonce, another pitcher unloaded by Durocher ("There goes garbage for garbage," Leo says about trades like this), waited a long time to "send a little love note to Leo." He did it in a key win for the Mets in which he pitched five innings of shutout ball against the Cubs. "It's the longest I've pitched this season," said Koonce, "but the incentive was there. Look around the clubhouse—everybody is enjoying this because they know that big-shot Leo will be unhappy."

When the unbelievable flop became fact, Durocher was quick to spot the reason. The players, he said on his own pregame radio show, "quit" on him. It was a harsh, unjust judgment. Indeed, Leo himself struggled to qualify it. But the damage was done. The players sensed that Leo was shifting the responsibility for the team's failure as far away from himself as was possible. One Cub regular, who'd been taken from the lineup for a much-needed rest once the race was pretty much over, insisted on going back into the lineup. He didn't want to take the rap, he said, for being one of the quitters.

Can Leo change it all this year?

It will be difficult. He's set in his ways. At 63, he will be the oldest manager in the big leagues. He sniffles a lot. He has a cough like electric static. Even when the sun is high, his handkerchief is never far from his hand, and in the spring, he stuffs towels under the door of his office to keep drafts from his feet. More than most, Leo Durocher is aware of the cool chill of advancing years and the burden of his own past friendships with people like George Raft; whenever his team suffers a dramatic failure, or whenever there are rumblings of gambling in sports, there are people ready to investigate Durocher.

He can still swagger and strut, but it is no longer an earned conceit. Perhaps he can take solace in the memory that he began managing in the big leagues over 30 years ago and he *did* win a world championship.

But only one.

Charlie Dressen

COMMENTS

There are three kinds of managers, Charlie Dressen, or somebody, once pointed out: the "I," "we" and "they" types. Charlie Dressen, himself, no doubt about it, was the "I" type. He was an itinerant managerial superstar, managing here, coaching there, managing somewhere else, through the 1930s, 40s, 50s and 60s. He'd pack his toothbrush and his scorecards and his personality as he moved on to dominate another town. Charlie would go anywhere: He was a professional manager and his ego wouldn't—couldn't—be hurt if he was fired. He got fired a lot, maybe because he was an old-time manager at a time when managerial styles—and ballplayers—were changing. John Lardner shows just how well Charlie adapted to the change.

Advisor to Presidents

by JOHN LARDNER

Charlie Dressen has been thrown out of baseball, temporarily, two different times, by two different high commissioners, Judge Landis and Happy Chandler. Serious thinkers believe that these moves were necessary, for the country's good. Dressen's exuberant confidence in Dressen must, they feel, be checked and subdued at regular intervals. If Charlie had not been banished in 1943, and again in 1947, he might have run for President in 1944 and 1948. If he had not been removed from the big leagues once more in 1953, with Mrs. Dressen's help, he might have been ready to seize national or global power in 1954 or 1956.

The theory goes a little too far. Dressen doesn't want to be President. He merely wants to help the President out—or, generally speaking, to be sure that nobody, anywhere, has to go without advice from Dressen, if Dressen is in a position to give it. When Charlie was a coach with the New York Yankees, he noticed that Joe DiMaggio was trying to get his hits the hard way—that is, without Dressen's help. So he gave DiMaggio tips on hitting. Also, as is his custom, he tried to save Joe the trouble of thinking, by working out a private system of letting him know what the next pitch would be, fast ball or curve. Once, when Dressen tipped the wrong pitch—or, what is more likely, when DiMaggio misunderstood the signal—the famous batsman almost got cracked in the ear. He immediately asked Dressen to stop calling pitches for him.

"Desist, before I get killed," said the ungrateful slugger, or words to that effect.

"Okay," said Charlie, more in sorrow than in anger. He did not add, "You'll regret it," but it's a fact that three or four years later, DiMaggio was all through.

At the opening of the 1955 season in Washington, Dressen, now manager of the Senators, heard that D. D. Eisenhower, the righthanded, crowd-pleasing Chief Executive, had bursitis in his pitching arm. "I'll tell you how to fix that," Dressen said to the President. He then described a machine he had just discovered (and maybe, if the truth be known, had invented) for curing sore arms. "I'll make a note of the name for you," Charlie said. From this, it is only a short step to installing a wire to the White House from Dressen's office in Griffith Stadium. Then, when and as necessary, Charlie can steal Bulganin's hit-and-run sign for the Administration, tip off Mao Tse-tung's fast ball, and decide whether Dulles should bat ahead of Wilson. But—and this is the point—if the government doesn't ask him, there's a fair chance that Dressen won't tell them. It has always been good will, not a thirst for power, that has led Charlie to give advice. If Eisenhower doesn't need him, Dressen will have enough to do running a ball club, or ball clubs.

In the spring of 1955, Dressen managed two clubs. The Washington team expected it, having hired him for the purpose. To the Brooklyn team, it came as a surprise, when Dressen, during the training season, announced which Dodgers would be cut from the squad, mapped out a Brooklyn batting order, and stated confidently that the Brooks could not fail to win the pennant. Walter Alston, the manager of record, turned a lively mulberry color when these remarks were quoted to him. On recovering his powers of speech, he sought out Walter O'Malley, the Brooklyn president.

"This Dressen," he said. "Are you sure he's not still managing the club?"

"Absolutely, Walter," said Mr. O'Malley. "I distinctly remember letting the fellow go. He didn't want—or his wife didn't want—a one-year contract."

O'Malley had strong reasons for liking one-year contracts. Once, when the Brooklyn club fired Casey Stengel before his three-year contract was up, it found itself obliged to pay him $15,000 a year not to manage. The memory left a scar. "It must not happen again," said O'Malley firmly. "With a one-year contract, when we fire a manager, he's through." That's what O'Malley thought. Dressen simply reversed the Stengel pattern. Where Casey stopped managing, but went on collecting, Dressen stopped collecting, but went on managing.

His post-graduate advice to Brooklyn—much of which Brooklyn was forced to follow, because it was good advice—annoyed many Dodgers besides Alston.

"Dressen should keep his mouth shut," said Tom La-Sorda, young Dodger lefthander. "He'll have his hands full managing his own *blank blank blank* ball club, without trying to run this one."

"The trouble with him is, he *can't* keep his mouth shut," said Ken Lehman, another young Brooklyn southpaw, a few days before he was cut from the squad, just as Dressen had said he would be cut. "That's why he's managing those humpties in Washington, instead of a real team."

It's true that Dressen is managing, in Washington, a team of what appears to be humpties. But that's not to say that he won't eventually produce a winner. The record suggests that there is more in the talent of this Napoleon-sized advice-distributor than a busy epiglottis, a sunny smile, a tuneful whistle, and a tendency to imitate Emily Post. As a coach or player, he has been in World Series with all three New York clubs. ("I'm unique," says Charlie shyly, if inaccurately, inasmuch as Casey Stengel also played in the Series for the Dodgers and Giants and managed the Yankees in a few recent classics.) As a manager, he won pennants in Oakland in 1950 and 1954, and in Brooklyn in 1952 and 1953.

It's also true that Dressen talks too much, mostly in sentences beginning with "I," "I'm," or "I'll." (It should be remembered that he spent some of his formative days in the Three-I League.) But the men on his side have usually liked and admired Charlie. Pee Wee Reese, who doesn't deny that he has thought of being a manager himself some day, says that he studied Dressen's methods closely, and with profit, when Dressen had the Dodgers. Now and then, with his own players, Charlie will even listen—as he listened one day to Lee Grissom, a large, fast, strong-willed pitcher who worked for him in Cincinnati in the 1930s. Dressen was going over the New York batting order with Grissom, before a Giants-Reds game. He came to the name of Johnny McCarthy, New York first baseman.

"Now, with this guy—" Dressen began.

"You don't need to tell me about him," said Grissom, brushing McCarthy aside. "I pitched to him in the minors. He could never get a foul off me."

At the last moment, McCarthy was replaced at first base and in the batting order by the solid-hitting Sam Leslie. Dressen let nature take its course. Coming up against Grissom, Leslie lined a single to right field. After the inning was over, Charlie took Grissom aside.

"What's the matter, Griss?" he said. "I thought you knew how to pitch to McCarthy?"

Grissom scratched his head. "I don't know what the hell happened," he said. "In all the years I worked against him, he never got his bat on the ball before."

"Maybe it's because he's put on weight," said Dressen.

"You're right," said Grissom, relieved. "He's as fat as a pig."

After Dressen left Brooklyn, a question came up, would he have won the pennant for Brooklyn in 1954 where Alston—or something, or somebody—failed? There were three possible answers to the question: no comment, no or yes. Two of these answers are good ones. Dressen selected the third. "Why, yes," said Charlie. "Even with the injuries that year, the Dodgers had enough stuff on the bench to do it. I knew the fellas better, and I could've gotten more out of them."

Once, in the season of 1952, when the powerful Brooklyns were pouring it on the helpless Cardinals, Dressen made remarks and gestures that flamed the temper of Eddie Stanky, then managing the Cardinals. "I don't mind jockeying at all," said Stanky later, "if it comes from a man of character." It's not easy to say where Dressen falls short in the matter of character, but it may be that Stanky had in mind the fact that Charlie is not over-burdened with education. Some years later, when Dressen made his sudden—and accurate—remark, "The Giants is dead," his words were quoted all over the country. The sentence became a national institution. Dressen was sur-prised at first to hear it repeated so often. Then he real-ized that his grammar had something to do with it. At once, he made the position clear.

"You know," he said eagerly, "I talk English either way—good or bad. If they wanted 'The Giants are dead,' I could've given it to them that way too."

Charlie is nonchalant about education—so long as you take note that he could have had it if he'd wanted it. When he was a youth in Illinois, hitting, fielding, pitching, punting, passing and thinking, he got an offer for an ath-letic scholarship from Millikin University. At the moment, Dressen was making $67 a week playing quarterback for the Decatur Staleys, the forerunners of the Chicago Bears. "Can you imagine what 67 bucks meant to a kid in them days?" he says. He passed education by, and went on using brains in its place.

While pitching semi-pro in Illinois for $7.50 a week, he had also learned enough to be able to tell pitchers how to pitch for the next few years. With Minneapolis and Cincinnati, as a third baseman, he learned to tell fielders how to field and hitters how to hit. Along the line, he learned about horses.

History shows that when Dressen is thrown out of base-ball, or out of a league, it is usually because some great idea or principle is at stake. In 1953, the principle was Walter O'Malley's right to fire managers yearly. In 1943, it was Judge Landis' right to hate horses. Dressen at that time was a Brooklyn coach. Leo Durocher was the Brooklyn manager. This combination—representing the strongest concentration of intellect in the annals of the game—had worked harmoniously for four years. There was some card playing on the club, and some horseplaying, too. As regards racing, Charlie's approach was similar to Napoleon's approach to war: He thought he could handicap all the tracks in the country simultaneously. Most of the time, however, he and Durocher devoted their minds to baseball. Some doubt existed as to which of them was the true brains of the team—it depended on which you talked to, Durocher or Dressen. There is no doubt that Brooklyn practically crawled with genius. But Commissioner Landis did not look at it that way. When Branch Rickey took over the Dodgers in 1943, the Judge grabbed the telephone.

"You must break up that nest of horseplayers and card sharks!" the Judge said.

Rather than fire the whole team, Rickey fired Dressen. Apparently, the gesture satisfied the Judge. It also pleased Rickey, for other reasons. Charlie had been getting $10,500 a year, the highest salary ever paid a coach, up to then. A few months later, when the heat was off, Rickey hired him back for $6,500. It was one of the great man's most sagacious strokes. He had saved the club $4,000, pleased the commissioner, and he still owned the smartest coach in baseball. It took Dressen three years to work his way up again to his old salary. At that point, Larry MacPhail offered him $20,000 a year to coach the Yankees.

"You'll be sorry," Rickey said to Dressen, when he heard this painful news. "I was just going to raise you to $12,500." Charlie brought his keen brain briefly to bear on these figures. He joined the Yanks.

In 1947, he was sacrificed to principle again. War had broken out in the spring of that year between MacPhail on the one hand and Rickey and Durocher on the other. The new commissioner, Happy Chandler, showed an iron hand by tossing Durocher out of the game.

"But, Happy," wailed Mr. Rickey, "where is the equity?"

"The what?" the commissioner said. "We must have equity," said Rickey. "You have punished us. What are you going to do to punish MacPhail?"

"I'll think of something," said Happy, and suspended

Dressen. A month later, however, Charlie was back teaching DiMaggio how to hit.

Dressen's brainwork reached its finest flower when he was leading the Dodgers of the 1950's against Durocher's Giants. The clash of mind against mind was audible for miles. One day, Durocher put in a pinch-hitter with a big Coast League reputation, Artie Wilson, to bat for the pitcher. Dressen had managed Wilson at Oakland. With an irritating smile of wisdom, he called in Carl Furillo, his rightfielder, to play between first and second and stationed three men between second and third. Thus—though Wilson was a lefthanded hitter—Dressen was leaving the whole right field open, and playing a five-man infield. Durocher's haughty face turned gray with strain as he waited to see what would come of this insulting strategy. Wilson grounded out.

"I knew this fella just can't pull to right field," said Dressen.

"#$%&%$#!" said Durocher.

It used to be said of Dressen, when he was coaching the Yankees, that the American League didn't understand him. His "I told him there was something wrong with his swing," and "I told MacPhail," and "I said to Harris," and "I taught him how to throw a screwball," and "I used that same play myself in 1935" were a little too brash for the big, rich, stuffy tastes of the big, rich, stuffy Yankees. Charlie, they said, with his noisy ways and his happy, lowdown egomania, belonged in a lowdown league, like the National. That may have been true of Dressen's stay with the Yanks. They were proud and standoffish. Charlie didn't fit. They looked at him, as MacPhail once admitted, down their noses. They looked at MacPhail in somewhat the same way.

But what was true for the Yankees, in regard to Dressen, may not be true for all the American League. Going back to the American League last year, for the second time in his life, Charlie cast his lot with a pretty lowdown club. Right away, he let the Senators know—as he let President Eisenhower know—that Charlie Dressen knew what was best for them.

Dressen introduced the Dressen Foreign Policy: how to handle Spanish-speaking ballplayers. Under the Dressen Policy, Dressen doesn't learn Spanish, the Latin-American players learn English. "They're bright enough to learn," says Charlie. "They don't have no trouble ordering their meals." In other words, why should the manager, at his age, take the trouble to learn the Spanish word for "I"? The boys from Venezuela and Cuba, he figures, should be able to master five simple signals, with 109 sub-divisions in each. At last report, things have improved since the day last spring when, with a Cuban runner on third base, Dressen gave the squeeze sign. The runner did not know the squeeze sign. Charlie called for another player to interpret. The interpreter failed. By this time, everyone in the park, except the runner, knew that the squeeze was on. So Charlie put the interpreter on third in place of the Cuban, changed from "squeeze" to "hit away," and formed the Dressen Foreign Policy.

"If I can't squeeze when I want to squeeze," he said, "where am I?"

He also introduced the Dressen Women Policy: spread the wives out. Washington players' wives were told to scatter around the stands, instead of sitting together. "When they sit all in one box," said Charlie, "they needle each other about their husbands, and the next thing I know my ball club breaks up. I seen it happen once in 19—"

These are deep waters. There are no profounder questions in the world than the woman question and the foreign question. And Charlie Dressen has them well in hand. And the government knows where to find Charlie.

Squawks Magrew

COMMENTS

Some of the best managers of all never set spike in Yankee Stadium. Some of the most interesting never took a chaw of tobacco and never spit it on a reporter. Some of the most memorable never kicked a real live umpire in the real life shins. Some of the best exist only on paper and in our heads. Squawks Magrew (love that name), James Thurber's creation, is one of them.

You Could Look It Up

by JAMES THURBER

It all begun when we dropped down to C'lumbus, Ohio, from Pittsburgh to play an exhibition game on our way out to St. Louis. It was gettin' on into September, and though we'd been leadin' the league by six, seven games most of the season, we was now in first place by a margin you could'a' got it into the eye of a thimble, bein' only a half a game ahead of St. Louis. Our slump had given the boys the leapin' jumps, and they was like a bunch a old ladies at a lawn fete with a thunderstorm comin' up, runnin' around snarlin' at each other, eatin' bad and sleepin' worse, and battin' for a team average of maybe .186. Half the time nobody'd speak to nobody else, without it was to bawl 'em out.

Squawks Magrew was managin' the boys at the time, and he was darn near crazy. They called him "Squawks" 'cause when things was goin' bad he lost his voice, or perty near lost it, and squealed at you like a little girl you stepped on her doll or somethin'. He yelled at everybody and wouldn't listen to nobody, without maybe it was me. I'd been trainin' the boys for ten year, and he'd take more lip from me than from anybody else. He knowed I was smarter'n him, anyways, like you're goin' to hear.

This was thirty, thirty-one year ago; you could look it up, 'cause it was the same year C'lumbus decided to call itself the Arch City, on account of a lot of iron arches with electric-light bulbs into 'em which stretched acrost High Street. Thomas Albert Edison sent 'em a telegram, and they was speeches and maybe even President Taft opened the celebration by pushin' a button. It was a great week for the Buckeye capital, which was why they got us out there for this exhibition game.

Well, we just lose a double-header to Pittsburgh, 11 to 5 and 7 to 3, so we snarled all the way to C'lumbus, where we put up at the Chittaden Hotel, still snarlin'. Everybody was tetchy, and when Billy Klinger took a sock at Whitey Cott at breakfast, Whitey throwed marmalade all over his face.

"Blind each other, watta I care?" says Magrew. "You can't see nothin' anyways."

C'lumbus win the exhibition game, 3 to 2, whilst Magrew set in the dugout, mutterin' and cursin' like a fourteen-year-old Scotty. He bad-mouthed everybody on the ball club and he bad-mouthed everybody offa the ball club, includin' the Wright brothers, who, he claimed, had yet to build a airship big enough for any of our boys to hit it with a ball bat.

"I wisht I was dead," he says to me. "I wisht I was in heaven with the angels."

I told him to pull hisself together, 'cause he was drivin' the boys crazy, the way he was goin' on sulkin' and bad-mouthin' and whinin'. I was older'n he was and smarter'n he was, and he knowed it. I was ten times smarter'n he was about this Pearl du Monville, first time I ever laid eyes on the little guy, which was one of the saddest days of my life.

Now, most people name of Pearl is girls, but this Pearl du Monville was a man, if you could call a fella a man who was only thirty-four, thirty-five inches high. Pearl du Monville was a midget. He was part French and part Hungarian, and maybe even part Bulgarian or somethin'. I can see him now, a sneer on his little pushed-in pan, swingin' a bamboo cane and smokin' a big cigar. He had a gray suit with a bit black check into it, and he had a gray felt hat with one of them rainbow-colored hatbands onto it, like the young fellas wore in them days. He talked like he was talkin' into a tin can, but he didn't have no foreign accent. He might a been fifteen or he might a been a hundred, you couldn't tell. Pearl du Monville.

After the game with C'lumbus, Magrew headed straight for the Chittaden bar—the train for St. Louis wasn't goin' for three, four hours—and there he set, drinkin' rye and talkin' to this bartender.

"How I pity me, brother," Magrew was tellin' this bartender. "How I pity me." That was alwuz his favorite tune. So he was settin' there, tellin' this bartender how heartbreakin' it was to be manager of a bunch of blindfolded circus clowns, when up pops this Pearl du Monville outa nowhere's.

It gave Magrew the leapin' jumps. He thought at first maybe the D.T.'s had come back on him; he claimed he'd had 'em once, and little guys had popped up all around him, wearin' red, white and blue hats.

"Go on, now!" Magrew yells. "Get away from me!"

But the midget clumb up on a chair across the table from Magrew and says, "I seen that game today, Junior, and you ain't got no ball club. What you got there, Junior," he says, "is a side show."

"Whatta ya mean, 'Junior'?" says Magrew, touchin' the little guy to satisfy hisself he was real.

"Don't pay him no attention, mister," says the bartender. "Pearl calls everybody 'Junior,' 'cause it alwuz turns out he's a year older'n anybody else."

"Yeh?" says Magrew. "How old is he?"

"How old are you, Junior?" says the midget.

"Who, me? I'm fifty-three," says Magrew.

"Well, I'm fifty-four," says the midget.

Magrew grins and asts him what he'll have, and that was the beginnin' of their beautiful friendship, if you don't care what you say.

Pearl du Monville stood up on his chair and waved his cane around and pretended like he was ballyhooin' for a circus. "Right this way, folks!" he yells. "Come on in and see the greatest collection of freaks in the world! See the armless pitchers, see the eyeless batters, see the infielders with five thumbs!" and on and on like that, feedin' Magrew gall and handin' him a laugh at the same time, you might say.

You could hear him and Pearl du Monville hootin' and hollerin' and singin' way up to the fourth floor of the Chittaden, where the boys was packin' up. When it come time to go to the station, you can imagine how disgusted we was when we crowded into the doorway of that bar and seen them two singin' and goin' on.

"Well, well, well," says Magrew, lookin' up and spottin' us. "Look who's here. . . . Clowns, this is Pearl du Monville, a monseer of the old, old school. . . . Don't shake hands with 'em, Pearl, 'cause their fingers is made of chalk and would bust right off in your paws," he says, and he starts guffawin' and Pearl starts titterin' and we stand there givin' 'em the iron eye, it bein' the lowest ebb a ball-club manager'd got hisself down to since the national pastime was started.

Then the midget begun givin' us the ballyhoo. "Come on in!" he says, wavin' his cane. "See the legless base runners, see the outfielders with the butter fingers, see the southpaw with the arm of a little chee-ild!"

Then him and Magrew begun to hoop and holler and nudge each other till you'd of thought this little guy was the funniest guy than even Charlie Chaplin. The fellas filed outa the bar without a word and went on up to the Union Depot, leavin' me to handle Magrew and his new-found crony.

Well, I got 'em out there finely. I had to take the little guy along, 'cause Magrew had a holt onto him like a vise and I couldn't pry him loose.

"He's comin' along as masket," says Magrew, holdin' the midget in the crouch of his arm like a football. And come along he did, hollerin' and protestin' and beatin' Magrew with his little fists.

"Cut it out, will you, Junior?" the little guy kept whinin'. "Come on, leave a man loose, will you, Junior?"

But Junior kept a holt onto him and begun yellin', "See the guys with the glass arm, see the guys with the cast-iron brains, see the fielders with the feet on their wrists!"

So it goes, right through the whole Union Depot, with people starin' and cat-callin', and he don't put the midget down till he gets him through the gates.

"How'm I goin' to go along without no toothbrush?" the midget asts. "What'm I goin' to do without no other suit?" he says.

"Doc here," says Magrew, meanin' me—"doc here will look after you like you was his own son, won't you, doc?"

I give him the iron eye, and he finely got on the train and prob'ly went to sleep with his clothes on.

This left me alone with the midget. "Lookit," I says to him. "Why don't you go on home now? Come mornin', Magrew'll forget all about you. He'll prob'ly think you was somethin' he seen in a nightmare maybe. And he ain't goin' to laugh so easy in the mornin', neither," I says. "So why don't you go on home?"

"Nix," he says to me. "Skiddoo," he says, "twenty-three for you," and he tosses his cane up into the vestibule of the coach and clam'ers on up after it like a cat. So that's the way Pearl du Monville come to go to St. Louis with the ball club.

I seen 'em first at breakfast the next day, settin' opposite each other; the midget playin' "Turkey in the Straw" on a harmonium and Magrew starin' at his eggs and bacon like they was an uncooked bird with its feathers still on.

"Remember where you found this?" I says, jerkin' my thumb at the midget. "Or maybe you think they come with breakfast on these trains," I says, bein' a good hand at turnin' a sharp remark in them days.

The midget puts down the harmonium and turns on me. "Sneeze," he says, "your brains is dusty." Then he snaps a couple drops of water at me from a tumbler. "Drown," he says, tryin' to make his voice deep.

Now, both them cracks is Civil War cracks, but you'd of thought they was brand new and the funniest than any crack Magrew'd ever heard in his whole life. He started hoopin' and hollerin', so I walked on away and set down

with Bugs Courtney and Hank Metters, payin' no attention to this weak-minded Damon and Phidias acrost the
aisle.

Well, sir, the first game with St. Louis was rained out,
and there we was facin' a double-header next day. Like
maybe I told you, we lose the last three double-headers
we play, makin' maybe twenty-five errors in the six games,
which is all right for the intimates of a school for the
blind, but is disgraceful for the world's champions. It was
too wet to go to the zoo, and Magrew wouldn't let us go
to the movies, 'cause they flickered so bad in them days.
So we just set around, stewin' and frettin'.

One of the newspaper boys come over to take a pitture
of Billy Klinger and Whitey Cott shakin' hands—this reporter'd heard about the fight—and whilst they was standin'
there, toe to toe, shakin' hands, Billy give a back lunge
and a jerk, and throwed Whitey over his shoulder into
a corner of the room, like a sack a salt. Whitey come
back at him with a chair, and Bethlehem broke loose in
that there room. The camera was tromped to pieces like
a berry basket. When we finely got 'em pulled apart, I
heard a laugh, and there was Magrew and the midget
standin' in the door and givin' us the iron eye.

"Wrasslers," says Magrew, cold-like, "that's what I got
for a ball club, Mr. Du Monville, wrasslers—and not very
good wrasslers at that, you ast me."

"A man can't be good at everythin'," says Pearl, "but
he oughta be good at somethin'."

This sets Magrew guffawin' again, and away they go, the
midget taggin' along by his side like a hound dog and
handin' him a fast line of so-called comic cracks.

When we went out to face that battlin' St. Louis club
in a double-header the next afternoon, the boys was
jumpy as tin toys with keys in their back. We lose the first
game, 7 to 2, and are trailin', 4 to 0, when the second
game ain't but ten minutes old. Magrew set there like a
stone statue, speakin' to nobody. Then, in their half a the
fourth, somebody singled to center and knocked in two
more runs for St. Louis.

That made Magrew squawk. "I wisht one thing," he says, "I wisht I was manager of an old ladies' sewin' circus 'stead of a ball club."

"You are, Junior, you are," says a familyer and disagreeable voice.

It was that Pearl du Monville again, poppin' up outa nowheres, swingin' his bamboo cane and smokin' a cigar that's three sizes too big for his face. By this time we'd finely got the other side out, and Hank Metters slithered a bat acrost the ground, and the midget had to jump to keep both his ankles from bein' broke.

I thought Magrew'd bust a blood vessel. "You hurt Pearl and I'll break your neck!" he yelled.

Hank muttered somethin' and went on up to the plate and struck out.

We managed to get a couple runs acrost in our half a the sixth, but they come back with three more in their half a the seventh, and this was too much for Magrew.

"Come on, Pearl," he says. "We're gettin' outa here."

"Where you think you're goin'?" I ast him.

"To the lawyer's again," he says cryptly.

"I didn't know you'd been to the lawyer's once, yet," I says.

"Which that goes to show how much you don't know," he says.

With that, they was gone, and I didn't see 'em the rest of the day, nor know what they was up to, which was a God's blessin'. We lose the nightcap, 9 to 3, and that puts us into second place plenty, and as low in our mind as a ball club can get.

The next day was a horrible day, like anybody that lived through it can tell you. Practice was just over and the St. Louis club was takin' the field, when I hears this strange sound from the stands. It sounds like the nervous whickerin' a horse gives when he smells somethin' funny on the wind. It was the fans ketchin' sight of Pearl du Monville, like you have prob'ly guessed. The midget had popped up onto the field all dressed up in a minacher club uniform, sox, cap, little letters sewed onto his chest, and

all. He was swingin' a kid's bat and the only thing kept
him from lookin' like a real ballplayer seen through the
wrong end of a microscope was this cigar he was smokin'.

Bugs Courtney reached over and jerked it outa his
mouth and throwed it away. "You're wearin' that suit on
the playin' field," he says to him, severe as a judge. "You
go insultin' it and I'll take you out to the zoo and feed
you to the bears."

Pearl just blowed some smoke at him which he still has
in his mouth.

Whilst Whitey was foulin' off four or five prior to
strikin' out, I went on over to Magrew. "If I was as comic
as you," I says, "I'd laugh myself to death," I says. "Is
that any way to treat the uniform, makin' a mockery out
of it?"

"It might surprise you to know I ain't makin' no
mockery outa the uniform," says Magrew. "Pearl du Monville here has been made a bone-of-fida member of this
so-called ball club. I fixed it up with the front office by
long-distance phone."

"Yeah?" I says. "I can just hear Mr. Dillworth or Bart
Jenkins agreein' to hire a midget for the ball club. I can
just hear 'em." Mr. Dillworth was the owner of the club
and Bart Jenkins was the secretary, and they never stood
for no monkey business. "May I be so bold as to inquire,"
I says, "just what you told 'em?"

"I told 'em," he says, "I wanted to sign up a guy they
ain't no pitcher in the league can strike him out."

"Uh-huh," I says, "and did you tell 'em what size of a
man he is?"

"Never mind about that," he says. "I got papers on me,
made out legal and proper, constitutin' one Pearl du
Monville, a bone-of-fida member of this former ball club.
Maybe that'll shame them big babies into gettin' in there
and swingin', knowin' I can replace any one of 'em with
a midget, if I have a mind to. A St. Louis lawyer I seen
twice tells me it's all legal and proper."

"A St. Louis lawyer would," I says, "seein' nothin'
could make him happier than havin' you makin' a mock-

ery outa this one-time baseball outfit," I says.

Well, sir, it'll all be there in the papers of thirty, thirty-one year ago, and you could look it up. The game went along without no scorin' for seven innings, and since they ain't nothin' much to watch but guys poppin' up or strikin' out, the fans pay most of their attention on the goin's-on of Pearl du Monville. He's out there in front a the dugout, turnin' handsprings, balancin' his hat on his chin, walkin' a imaginary line, and so on. The fans clapped and laughed at him, and he ate it up.

So it went up to the last a the eighth, nothin' to nothin', not more'n seven, eight hits all told, and no errors on neither side. Our pitcher gets the first two men out easy in the eighth. Then up comes a fella name of Porter or Billings, or some such name, and he lammed one up against the tobacco sign for three bases. The next guy up slapped the first ball out into left for a base hit, and in come the fella from third for the only run of the ball game so far. The crowd yelled, the look a death come onto Magrew's face again, and even the midget quit his tomfoolin'. Their next man fouled out back a third, and we come up for our last bats like a bunch a school girls steppin' into a pool of cold water. I was lower in my mind than I'd been since the day in Nineteen-four when Chesbro throwed the wild pitch in the ninth inning with a man on third and lost the pennant for the Highlanders. I knowed something just as bad was goin' to happen, which shows I'm a clairvoyun, or was then.

When Gordy Mills hit out to second, I just closed my eyes. I opened 'em up again to see Dutch Muller standin' on second, dustin' off his pants, him havin' got his first hit in maybe twenty times to the plate. Next up was Harry Loesing, battin' for our pitcher, and he got a base on balls, walkin' on a fourth one you could a combed your hair with.

Then up come Whitey Cott, our lead-off man. He crouches down in what was prob'ly the most fearsome stanch in organized ball, but all he can do is pop out to short. That brung up Billy Klinger, with two down and

a man on first and second. Billy took a cut at one you
could a knocked a plug hat offa this here Carnera with it,
but then he gets sense enough to wait 'em out, and finely
he walks, too, fillin' the bases.

Yes, sir, there you are; the tyin' run on third and the
winnin' run on second, first a the ninth, two men down,
and Hank Metters comin' to the bat. Hank was built like a
Pope-Hartford and he couldn't run no faster'n President
Taft, but he had five home runs to his credit for the season and that wasn't bad in them days. Hank was still hittin'
better'n anybody else on the ball club, and it was mighty
heartenin', seein' him stridin' up towards the plate. But he
never got there.

"Wait a minute!" yells Magrew, jumpin' to his feet. "I'm
sendin' in a pinch hitter!" he yells.

You could a heard a bomb drop. When a ball-club
manager says he's sendin' in a pinch hitter for the best
batter on the club, you know and I know and everybody
knows he's lost his holt.

"They're goin' to be sendin' the funny wagon for you,
if you don't watch out," I says, grabbin' a holt of his arm.

But he pulled away and run out towards the plate,
yellin', "Du Monville battin' for Metters!"

All the fellas begun squawlin' at once, except Hank, and
he just stood there starin' at Magrew like he'd gone crazy
and was claimin' to be Ty Cobb's grandma or somethin'.
Their pitcher stood out there with his hands on his hips
and a disagreeable look on his face, and the plate umpire
told Magrew to go on and get a batter up. Magrew told
him again Du Monville was battin' for Metters, and the
St. Louis manager finely got the idea. It brung him outa
his dugout howlin' and bawlin' like he'd lost a female dog
and her seven pups.

Magrew pushed the midget towards the plate and he
says to him, he says, "Just stand up there and hold that
bat on your shoulder. They ain't a man in the world can
throw three strikes in there 'fore he throws four balls!"
he says.

"I get it, Junior!" says the midget. "He'll walk me and

force in the tyin' run!" And he starts on up to the plate
as cocky as if he was Willie Keeler.

I don't need to tell you Bethlehem broke loose on that
there ball field. The fans got onto their hind legs, yellin'
and whistlin', and everybody on the field begun wavin'
their arms and hollerin' and shovin'. The plate umpire
stalked over to Magrew like a traffic cop, waggin' his
jaw and pointin' his finger, and the St. Louis manager kept
yellin' like his house was on fire. When Pearl got up to the
plate and stood there, the pitcher slammed his glove down
onto the ground and started stompin' on it, and they ain't
nobody can blame him. He's just walked two normal-sized
human bein's, and now here's a guy up to the plate they
ain't more'n twenty inches between his knees and shoulders.

The plate umpire called in the field umpire, and they
talked a while, like a couple doctors seein' the bucolic
plague or somethin' for the first time. Then the plate umpire come over to Magrew with his arms folded acrost
his chest, and he told him to go on and get a batter up,
or he'd forfeit the game to St. Louis. He pulled out his
watch, but somebody batted it outa his hand in the scuf-
flin', and I thought there'd be a free-for-all, with everybody yellin' and shovin' except Pearl du Monville, who
stood up at the plate with his little bat on his shoulder,
not movin' a muscle.

Then Magrew played his ace. I seen him pull some papers outa his pocket and show 'em to the plate umpire.
The umpire begun lookin' at 'em like they was bills for
somthin' he not only never bought it, he never even
heard of it. The other umpire studied 'em like they was a
death warren, and all this time the St. Louis manager
and the fans and the players is yellin' and hollerin'.

Well, sir, they fought about him bein' a midget, and
they fought about him usin' a kid's bat, and they fought
about where'd he been all season. They was eight or nine
rule books brung out and everybody was thumbin'
through 'em tryin' to find out what it says about midgets,
but it don't say nothin' about midgets, 'cause this was

somethin' never'd come up in the history of the game before, and nobody'd ever dreamed about it, even when
they has nightmares. Maybe you can't send no midgets in
to bat nowadays, 'cause the old game's changed a lot,
mostly for the worst, but you could then, it turned out.

The plate umpire finely decided the contrack papers
was all legal and proper, like Magrew said, so he waved
the St. Louis players back to their places and he pointed
his finger at their manager and told him to quit hollerin'
and get on back in the dugout. The manager says the
game is percedin' under protest, and the umpire bawls,
"Play ball!" over 'n' above the yellin' and booin', him
havin' a voice like a hog-caller.

The St. Louis pitcher picked up his glove and beat at it
with his fist six or eight times, and then got set on the
mound and studied the situation. The fans realized he was
really goin' to pitch to the midget, and they went crazy,
hoopin' and hollerin' louder'n ever, and throwin' pop bottles and hats and cushions down onto the field. It took
five, ten minutes to get the fans quieted down again,
whilst our fellas that was on base set down on the bags
and waited. And Pearl du Monville kept standin' up there
with the bat on his shoulder, like he'd been told to.

So the pitcher starts studyin' the setup again, and you
got to admit it was the strangest setup in a ball game
since the players cut off their beards and begun wearin'
gloves. I wisht I could call the pitcher's name—it wasn't
old Barney Pelty nor Nig Jack Powell nor Harry Howell.
He was a big right-hander, but I can't call his name. You
could look it up. Even in a crotchin' position, the ketcher
towers over the midget like the Washington Monument.

The plate umpire tries standin' on his tiptoes, then he
tries crotchin' down, and he finely gets hisself into a
stanch nobody'd ever seen on a ball field before, kinda
squattin' down on his hanches.

Well, the pitcher is sore as a old buggy horse in fly
time. He slams in the first pitch, hard and wild, and maybe two foot higher'n the midget's head.

"Ball one!" hollers the umpire over 'n' above the racket,

'cause everybody is yellin' worsten ever.

The ketcher goes on out towards the mound and talks to the pitcher and hands him the ball. This time the big right-hander tried a undershoot, and it comes in a little closer, maybe no higher'n a foot, foot and a half above Pearl's head. It would a been a strike with a human bein' in there, but the umpire's got to call it, and he does.

"Ball two!" he bellers.

The ketcher walks on out to the mound again, and the whole infield comes over and gives advice to the pitcher about what they'd do in a case like this, with two balls and no strikes on a batter that oughta be in a bottle of alcohol instead of up there at the plate in a big-league game between the teams that is fightin' for first place.

For the third pitch, the pitcher stands there flat-footed and tosses up the ball like he's playin' ketch with a little girl.

Pearl stands there motionless as a hitchin' post, and the ball comes in big and slow and high—high for Pearl, that is, it bein' about on a level with his eyes, or a little higher'n a grown man's knees.

They ain't nothin' else for the umpire to do, so he calls, "Ball three!"

Everybody is onto their feet, hoopin' and hollerin', as the pitcher sets to throw ball four. The St. Louis manager is makin' signs and faces like he was a contorturer, and the infield is givin' the pitcher some more advice about what to do this time. Our boys who was on base stick right onto the bag, runnin' no risk of bein' nipped for the last out.

Well, the pitcher decides to give him a toss again, see-in' he come closer with that than with a fast ball. They ain't nobody ever seen a slower ball throwed. It come in big as a balloon and slower'n any ball ever throwed before in the major leagues. It come right in over the plate in front of Pearl's chest, lookin' prob'ly big as a full moon to Pearl. They ain't never been a minute like the minute that followed since the United States was founded by the Pilgrim grandfathers.

Pearl du Monville took a cut at that ball, and he hit it! Magrew give a groan like a poleaxed steer as the ball rolls out in front a the plate into fair territory.

"Fair ball!" yells the umpire, and the midget starts runnin' for first, still carryin' that little bat, and makin' maybe ninety foot an hour. Bethlehem breaks loose on that ball field and in them stands. They ain't never been nothin' like it since creation was begun.

The ball's rollin' slow, on down towards third, goin' maybe eight, ten foot. The infield comes in fast and our boys break from their bases like hares in a brush fire. Everybody is standin' up, yellin' and hollerin', and Magrew is tearin' his hair outa his head, and the midget is scamperin' for first with all the speed of one of them little dashhounds carryin' a satchel in his mouth.

The ketcher gets to the ball first, but he boots it on out past the pitcher's box, the pitcher fallin' on his face tryin' to stop it, the shortstop sprawlin' after it full length and zaggin' it on over towards the second baseman, whilst Muller is scorin' with the tyin' run and Loesing is roundin' third with the winnin' run. Ty Cobb could a made a three-bagger outa that bunt, with everybody fallin' over theirself tryin' to pick the ball up. But Pearl is still maybe fifteen, twenty feet from the bag, toddlin' like a baby and yeepin' like a trapped rabbit, when the second baseman finely gets a holt of that ball and slams it over to first. The first baseman ketches it and stomps on the bag, the base umpire waves Pearl out, and there goes your old ball game, the craziest ball game ever played in the history of the organized world.

Their players start runnin' in, and then I see Magrew. He starts after Pearl, runnin' faster'n any man ever run before. Pearl sees him comin' and runs behind the base umpire's legs and gets a holt onto 'em. Magrew comes up, pantin' and roarin', and him and the midget plays ring-around-a-rosy with the umpire, who keeps shovin' at Magrew with one hand and tryin' to slap the midget loose from his legs with the other.

Finely Magrew ketches the midget, who is still yeepin'

like a stuck sheep. He gets holt of that little guy by both his ankles and starts whirlin' him round and round his head like Magrew was a hammer thrower and Pearl was the hammer. Nobody can stop him without gettin' their head knocked off, so everybody just stands there and yells. Then Magrew lets the midget fly. He flies on out toward 'second, high and fast, like a human home run, headed for the soap sign in center field.

Their shortstop tries to get to him, but he can't make it, and I knowed the little fella was goin' to bust to pieces like a dollar watch on a asphalt street when he hit the ground. But it so happens their center fielder is just crossin' second, and he starts runnin' back, tryin' to get under the midget, who had took to 'spiralin' like a football 'stead of turnin' head over foot, which give him more speed and more distance.

I know you never seen a midget ketched, and you prob'ly never ever seen one throwed. To ketch a midget that's been throwed by a heavy-muscled man and is flyin' through the air, you got to run under him and with him and pull your hands and arms back and down when you ketch him, to break the compact of his body, or you'll bust him in two like a matchstick. I seen Bill Lange and Willie Keeler and Tris Speaker make some wonderful ketches in my day, but I never seen nothin' like that center fielder. He goes back and back and 'still further back and he pulls that midget down outa the air like he was liftin' a sleepin' baby from a cradle. There wasn't a bruise onto him, only his face was the color of cat's meat and he ain't got no air in his chest. In his excitement, the base umpire, who was runnin' back with the center fielder when he ketched Pearl, yells, "Out!" and that give hysteries to the Bethlehem which was ragin' like Niagry on that ball field.

Everybody was hoopin' and hollerin' and yellin' and runnin', and the fans swarmin' onto the field, and the cops trying to keep order, and some guys laughin' and some of the women fans cryin', and six or eight of us holdin' onto Magrew to keep him from gettin' at that midget and fin-

ishin' him off. Some of the fans picks up the St. Louis
pitcher and the center fielder and starts carryin' 'em
around on their shoulders, and they was the craziest
goin's-on knowed to the history of organized ball on this
side of the 'Lantic Ocean.

I seen Pearl du Monville strugglin' in the arms of a
lady fan with a ample bosom, who was laughin' and cryin'
at the same time, and him beatin' at her with his little
fists and bawlin' and yellin'. He clawed his way loose
finely and disappeared in the forest of legs which made
that ball field look like it was Coney Island on a hot summer's day.

That was the last I ever seen of Pearl du Monville. I
never seen hide nor hair of him from that day to this, and
neither did nobody else. He just vanished into the thin
of the air, as the fella says. He was ketched for the final
out of the ball game and that was the end of him, just
like it was the end of the ball game, you might say, and
also the end of our losing streak, like I'm goin' to tell
you.

That night we piled onto a train for Chicago, but we
wasn' snarlin' and snappin' any more. No, sir, the ice was
finely broke and a new spirit come into that ball club.
The old zip come back with the disappearance of Pearl
du Monville out back a second base. We got to laughin'
and talkin' and kiddin' together, and 'fore long Magrew
was laughin' with us. He got a human look onto his pan
again, and he quit whinin' and complainin' and wishtin' he
was in heaven with the angels.

Well, sir, we wiped up that Chicago series, winnin' all
four games, and makin' seventeen hits in one of 'em. Funny thing was, St. Louis was so shook up by that last game
with us, they never did hit their stride again. Their center
fielder took to misjudgin' everything that come his way,
and the rest a the fellas followed suit, the way a club'll
do when one guy blows up.

'Fore we left Chicago, I and some of the fellas went
out and bought a pair of them little baby shoes, which
we had 'em golded over and give 'em to Magrew for a

souvenir, and he took it all in good spirit. Whitey Cott and Billy Klinger made up and was fast friends again, and we hit our home lot like a ton of dynamite and they was nothin' could stop us from then on.

I don't recollect things as clear as I did thirty, forty years ago. I can't read no fine print no more, and the only person I got to check with on the golden days of the national pastime, as the fella says, is my friend, old Milt Kline, over in Springfield, and his mind ain't as strong as it once was.

He gets Rube Waddell mixed up with Rube Marquard, for one thing and anybody does that oughta be put away where he won't bother nobody. So I can't tell you the exact margin we win the pennant by. Maybe it was two and a half games, or maybe it was three and a half. But it'll all be there in the newspapers and record books of thirty, thirty-one year ago and, like I was sayin', you could look it up.

Joe McCarthy

COMMENTS

Joe McCarthy won a lot of pennants and a lot of world championships, but what he'll probably be remembered for most is the Yankee image. That's what I'll remember him for.

Probably more than anybody else, McCarthy was responsible for that image. He made the Yankees win, but he also homogenized the Yankees. He gave the Yankees the Yankee Way. Dress like a Yankee. Act like a Yankee. Be a Yankee. Think Yankee.

I got to know that Yankee image very well. My first spring training I remember checking into the old Soreno Hotel in St. Petersburg, where the only people there were Yankees and old ladies. The Yankees were the ones with the spikes.

You walked past the old green benches and then into the lobby, and the first thing you noticed was the little old ladies and the little old violin music and the ambulance sirens in the background. I checked in and found a mimeographed form in my mailbox explaining what would be required of me as a Yankee. Jackets and ties in the dining room. Jackets at all times, always, absolutely, anywhere. If you wanted to go out and take a boat ride, or go swimming, you had to wear a jacket. It was great to be young and a Yankee. And just in case you couldn't read, there was Bruce Henry, the traveling secretary, coming up to you to explain the rules and regulations. "Don't forget, tie and jacket." And then he mentioned Ted Williams.

"You," Henry said to me, "have to wear a tie and jacket. You're not Ted Williams."

The Red Sox, Henry said, also had a rule about ties and jackets, which meant that Williams, who hates ties, had to wear one. Except he didn't. One time he was in the lobby of a hotel wearing an open sport shirt—no tie —and a minor club official came over to him and said, "You better put on a shirt and tie."

"What am I hitting?" said Williams.

The Yankees, you were supposed to believe, didn't make those kinds of exceptions. From McCarthy's time on, we were all supposed to look the same, act the same, play the same, be efficient the same. McCarthy gave them this team idea. Interchangeable parts. The whole is more important than its parts. Individuals need not apply. No room for flakes. Up to about ten years ago, even if a guy was a good ballplayer, if he was a flake he wouldn't become a Yankee. There was always a ballplayer just as good who wasn't flakey—a ballplayer who would bring honor to the Yankee tradition.

I remember, in the minor leagues, lots of times our managers would tell us that Pepitone would *never* go up because he never acted like a Yankee. I mean, if Joe Pepitone could be a Yankee, *anything* was possible.

The Yankees themselves, the players, not only upheld the tradition, but some of them were its self-appointed guardians. You'd show up at the airport or to meet the bus and there'd be Moose Skowron, looking at the way you were dressed, looking you up and down, checking you out, making sure you weren't going to embarrass the Yankees. Even today, I bet Moose Skowron dresses 1950s. Very Yankee.

He was constantly calling you a rook and telling you things like "Rookies should be seen and not heard," and "You're lucky to be a Yankee" and other inspirational verses. He was always looking at me and Phil Linz and Joe Pepitone, even if we hadn't done anything. Well, maybe we had just been talking or doing something silly, but Moose didn't think Yankees ought to do that. That wasn't the Yankee Image.

I hated that image. In fact, I hated the Yankees when I was a kid. I was a Giant fan. I couldn't like the Yankees. They were too cold, too efficient for an apprentice flake like me.

So why did I sign with the Yankees?

I considered all the options very carefully. My dad considered all the options very carefully. Then we both considered all the options together. And then we both realized that the Yankees were the only people who would give me any money.

Actually, the way the Yankees signed me should have told me something about the Yankee image of cold-blooded efficiency. It should've told me it was dying.

This is how efficiently the Yankees worked to sign me. In high school and in college, I was never a star. Even then, I batted ninth. Anyway, this one summer in Chicago I was playing on an amateur team and I was about the third-string pitcher. But I was having a pretty good summer when we went to this national tournament, and the rotation worked out so that I ended up pitching against the top team in the tournament.

I beat this team, on a two-hitter, and it was the only game they lost as they went on to win the tournament. Well, there were a lot of scouts there that day and they all saw me and they were saying, "Wow, who is this kid who just shut out that great team from Cincinnati?" No one had ever heard of me before.

So, while the other guys in college were spending their weekends drinking beer, here I was, 18 years old and flying off to Philadelphia and Detroit. The only bad thing was that once all these teams got to see me, it turned out that none of them were interested in signing me.

It got to be about Thanksgiving and I said to my dad, "What happened? Where are all the scouts? Where is everyone? Where is all that money?"

My dad said we'd try one more thing. So he wrote up

a form letter. Dear (blank) major-league team: My son Jim is prepared to sign a major-league contract. If you do not have your bid in by (blank) date, we will not be able to consider you and you will lose out, etc., etc.

A total lie.

And the Yankees fell for it. Out of all the major-league teams, they were the only ones who thought they were in the middle of a bidding contest and had better get in a good offer quick. And they did. They were the only ones.

And right after I signed, as the scout walked out the door, my dad and me threw our arms around each other and hugged, and said, "Boy, did we pull a fast one on them!"

On the other hand, I did make the big leagues. I did win 20 games for the Yankees. I did make the All-Star team. I'm the last pitcher to win a World Series game for the Yankees. (In fact I'm the last *two* Yankee pitchers to win a World Series game.)

Maybe the Yankees were more efficient than I thought. I think my dad sold me short. A really smart dad would've gotten me a lot more money. That's what I keep telling him.

But even though the Yankees lucked out with me, by the time I got to the major leagues, the image was changing. By the time I left the Yankees, it was gone. The act-like-a-Yankee, dress-like-a-Yankee thing became less and less important as the Yankees got bad and the type of ballplayer available to them changed.

Once Dan Topping decided to stop spending money to sign kids, and once the draft came in, you couldn't just take a flake and get rid of him. The flake and the malcontent might be all you had. That's why the Yankees brought up Linz, Pepitone and Bouton.

They told us Pepitone would never get up there, and there he was, up there. Joe Pepitone was living proof that it didn't matter anymore what you looked like or if you were a little crazy. If you could hit the ball, you'd go up.

Actually, the change happened quickly. When I first came up to the Yankees, if a club had one or two flakes, that was a lot. Now flakes are almost in the majority. Tomorrow the world.

Of course, the Yankees would still like to be old, cold Yankees. They just don't have the choice anymore. And yet, even when the image was going, the guys on other teams still had that look in their eyes when they played us. They looked at us with awe. Even when the Yankees weren't really the Yankees anymore, they won a lot of games because of the name on their uniforms. Other teams would get on the field with us and you knew that they knew they were expecting something to happen to them. And sooner or later, something did.

Like we'd be playing the White Sox, and it was 0-0 in the seventh. Then we'd hit a ground ball to short and the guy would kick it and all of a sudden you'd see the look in their eyes that said *this is it*. And as soon as they got into that frame of mind, we had them.

Or we'd come into Cleveland, open the newspaper to the sports page, and there was a cartoon of a very large Mickey Mantle and a whole trail of Yankees and there were Indians lying in the street, bloodied, dead. The Yankees were coming to town, and we had already won three games. McCarthy would've been proud.

Nobody's Neutral

by ED FITZGERALD

Jerking his head toward the radio, the man at the end of the bar heard the announcer give the introduction for the sports newscast. He took a long drink of his beer and offered some friendly advice to the bartender.

"May as well shut that thing off," he said. "No ball game this afternoon. They're playin' them all tonight."

The barkeep, busy with the usual 5:30 crowd, shrugged. "Okay," he said disinterestedly.

He turned to shut off the radio, when the urgent voice stopped him in his tracks. "Lightning struck the baseball world in the same place for the second time today," it said excitedly, "when Joe McCarthy resigned his job as manager of the staggering Boston Red Sox."

For a few seconds, the rush of words from the loudspeaker was lost in the general chorus of astonishment from the drinkers lining the bar. Then a tense, attentive silence fell over the room again as the staccato voice went on. "It is the second time the famous Marse Joe, winningest manager in modern baseball history, with nine major league pennants and seven world championships to his credit, has quit a great post under similar conditions. In 1946, McCarthy left the New York Yankees on a road trip and flew home to his farm outside Buffalo for a rest. He was said to have been tired, sick, in no condition to stay on the job. The next day, he resigned." The voice paused for a second. "Well, it's the same old story. McCarthy left the Red Sox in Chicago yesterday, and today, from his home, he announced his retirement. In Boston, the Red Sox front office named Steve O'Neill, coach under McCarthy, to take over the direction of the club that was such a heavy favorite to win the American League pennant but has stumbled so badly to date. . . ."

The voice trailed off and the bar man had to bustle to set up fresh drinks. The pitch of conversation became a roar. Why? What happened? Was he really sick? Did he quit or was he fired?

Some of the questions may never be answered; others will have to wait a long time. But this much is sure. On June 23, 1950, ended the career of a man whose imprint will never be completely erased from major league baseball, a giant among managers, a fighter who in the end had proved that he could lick every problem in baseball except that posed by his own nerves and his brooding introspective Irish mind.

The following is Marse Joe, before the blowup.

Vast numbers of people regard Mac as the smartest field manager in the whole multimillion dollar baseball business. What makes him such a controversial figure is that almost as many others subscribe to Jimmy Dykes' scathing characterization of him as a push-button manager who made his reputation with custom-tailored clubs that couldn't have lost with Shirley Temple in the dugout. Everybody agrees he is a mighty hard man to know and to understand, but except for that, the voters line up passionately either for or against him. One thing is sure. Nobody is neutral about Joe McCarthy. In the words once applied by the Right Honourable Winston Churchhill to a certain large country in the Near East, he is a mystery wrapped up in an enigma.

He looks formidable enough in the shade of the Red Sox dugout. Without actively doing anything to browbeat you, McCarthy manages very nicely to keep you at your distance. Especially when he puts on his working clothes and settles his ample frame in his dugout throne. With the visor of his cap pulled down over his eyes, his mouth tight-lipped, his eyes businesslike and cool, and the grim line of that over-sized jaw like an anatomical busy signal, Joe is not the kind of person with whom you bandy small talk about the funny thing that happened to you on your way to the ball park.

Talking over the telephone that morning, he had lived up to every inch of his title as baseball's champion interview-dodger. He didn't come right out and say no, but he certainly didn't say yes. "Call me tomorrow morning and I'll see," was as far as he would go, and if those words have a chilly ring in type, you ought to hear Mc-Carthy pronounce them. Each word, properly flavored and impaled on a stick, could have been sold as a Popsicle.

At the ball park, though, things picked up. To begin with, Joe shook hands just like other people do—quickly, but firmly. He discussed a mutual acquaintance politely and voluntarily set a time for a meeting the next morning.

"I won't make you talk too much," I told him, diplomatically.

McCarthy turned to Frank Graham and winked. "Not much chance of that is there?"

Graham laughed and said, "No. Not much." He sounded as if he knew what he was talking about.

But the next morning, when I knocked at McCarthy's suite in the Hotel Commodore, the New York stopping-place of the Red Sox, Joe opened the door quickly and greeted me as if I were an old friend dropping in for a visit. I was hardly inside the room before he had offered me a cigar. If this was the McCarthy who ate reporters for breakfast, he must have already eaten his fill.

In street clothes, McCarthy looks much younger, more vigorous and less grim than he does in uniform. He has a pleasant smile that softens his whole face when he lets it go, and when his still-thick brown hair isn't covered by a baseball cap, Joe's deep brown eyes are much warmer. He wore a dark gray business suit, a striped shirt, gaily figured red tie, and garterless socks. Sinking back in an easy chair while I sat across from him on a couch, he didn't seem at all forbidding.

He talked easily and intelligently about a great many subjects. He begged off a few, but always without rancor, and each time he waited patiently for a new question. Every once in a while, when he was trying to make an important point, he got up and walked around the room, puffing furiously on his stogie, blowing thick curls of blue smoke ahead of his measured words. What he had to say was always short, stripped of unnecessary wordage, and to the point. Contrary to his warning of the day before, there was quite a lot of it, and it covered most of the highlights of his career and the wellsprings of his philosophy. A few of his general statements are almost enough for a character sketch. Listen to him talk:

"Politics should never enter into baseball."

"You can't freeze the ball in this game. You have to play till the last man is out."

"Of course, we all know you can't get blood out of a stone. A good ball club always makes a good manager."

"You have to improve your club if it means letting your own brother go."

"Just don't make me sound like a pop-off. . . . Don't have me doing too much of that 'I' stuff. . . ."

That's the way McCarthy has always operated. Not too much of that "I" stuff. He has always liked to sit quietly in the dugout and concentrate on his job. You hardly ever see him chug out on the field to challenge the umpires and you rarely see him thrown out of a ball game. In fact, Joe has had so little experience in such matters that on two separate occasions he has completely misunderstood the intentions of an umpire with whom he was discussing a decision he didn't like.

There was the time the Yankees played a double-header with the Athletics on June 2, 1934. In the second inning, umpire Lou Kolls called a fourth ball on Jimmy Foxx of the As. McCarthy thought old Double-X had taken a cut at the pitch and he jogged out of the dugout to offer his thoughts on the matter.

Joe asked Kolls to confer with the base umpires and get their opinion. Kolls refused, declaring that his own judgement was quite sufficient, thank you. McCarthy glared at him. "Fathead!" he said, coldly.

Kolls was outraged. He pointed to the dugout and yelled angrily, "Get out!"

"I went back to the bench," said McCarthy, "and kept on running the club, shifting the pitchers and giving the signs. Then, in the seventh inning Ben Chapman came back from the plate and told me I was supposed to be out of the ball park.

" 'Who says so?' I asked him.

" 'Kolls,' Ben said. 'He says it's going to cost you money every inning you stay here.'

"Well," Joe finished, "it looked as though I had the most expensive seat in the ball park, but I wasn't going to leave it until Kolls told me to himself, so I stayed until the end. The next day, I got word that Will Harridge had fined me $50 and suspended me for three days."

Just this year, early in the season, he engaged umpire Bill McKinley in a heated conversation at home plate at Griffith Stadium. McKinley objected to McCarthy's attitude and concluded the tête-à-tête with a loud invitation to the Red Sox manager to "Get out of here!" Quite possibly, Joe remembered what had happened 16 years before. At any rate, he turned on his heel, walked into the dugout, opened the door, and marched straight through to the visitors' dressing room. It wasn't until after the game that he found out he hadn't been banished at all. McKinley merely had desired him to retreat to the dugout.

Such misunderstandings would never plague a more experienced umpire-baiter. It would, for example, be hard to imagine Leo Durocher taking himself off to the showers on the mere suspicion that the umpire would be happier without his presence. But McCarthy is not an umpire-baiter and never has been. He prefers to sit in majestic silence on the bench. Joe being a man who figures all the percentages right down to the last decimal point, the chances are good that he thinks the umpires know when they have booted one and can be relied upon to square things at the earliest opportunity. You certainly can't condemn his technique as unsuccessful.

That is, not unless you are one of those people who like to forget everything that went before and merely assess McCarthy on the basis of what he has done with the Boston Red Sox. Of course, even that is far from the worst managerial record in history. Second twice in a row by one game, but, true, it isn't the same as first, and in the old days Joe made a habit of being first. So if you always thought he was a bum who was shot full of luck, you are probably overjoyed that he has been unable to boot home a winner at Boston. What's more, you are probably convinced that his two seconds constitute proof positive that McCarthy is a lousy manager who is lost when the buttons he pushes don't automatically turn up the right answers.

It would be wholly wrong to say that such a conclusion on your part would be of no concern to McCarthy. Joe has for years been portrayed as the Great Stone Face of baseball, the Sphinx of the Dugout. But that is only a surface judgement. Actually, Joe has enough Irish in his blood to be profoundly troubled by the thought that any of his fellow men think poorly of him. He is richly sentimental, passionately proud. He has painfully taught himself to hide his feelings from the outside world, but that doesn't mean that the feelings don't exist.

An incident that demonstrates how inaccurate it would be to class McCarthy as an automaton occurred at the winter major league meetings at Chicago in 1937. The supposedly cold, unemotional, businessman manager of the Yankees almost had a fist fight with the hot-headed boss of the Giants, Bill Terry.

For two years in a row, Terry, boiling over the way the surging Yankees had taken the play away from the Giants in New York, hadn't bothered to congratulate McCarthy on winning the world championship. But Joe, smiling amiably, approached Terry in the lobby of the Congress Hotel and said, "I have an idea for you, Bill."

The thin-skinned Terry, misconstruing the McCarthy grin, barked back sulkily, "Keep your tips to yourself. I'm doing all right." He bit down hard on his half-smoked cigar.

Joe was determined to be friendly. "You shouldn't smoke, Bill," he said, cheerfully. "It makes a man too contented."

Memphis Bill spun around and lit into McCarthy like a taxi driver spitting fire at somebody who had just cut him off. Just as Joe's right hand jumped out of his pocket, a group of onlookers stepped between the two highest-paid managers in the game.

Later, McCarthy tried to smooth it over. "It was just a little popping off," he said. "No punches were thrown."

Terry was still sore. "Too many beers for that guy," he sputtered.

The point is, McCarthy is anything but the human cash register, the soulless overseer that so many detractors like to make him out to be. His skin can be pierced just as easily as the next man's. But, being in the line of work he's in, he can't afford to scream with anguish and call for a choice of weapons every time he's pinked. He figures it's all in a day's work.

Fortunately, Joe has a good Irish sense of humor. He can cleanse his anger by laughing it off, he can forget a tough day at the ball park by spinning long, funny stories about the hundreds of droll characters he has encountered during his lifetime in baseball. His Irishness is apparent also in his tendency to go down the line of strong hunches and to commune with "the little people" so dear to Gaelic mythology on matters like the choice of a starting pitcher for the next day's game. Naturally, the leprechauns of Joe's acquaintance aren't always right, but he doesn't hold that against them.

One thing that should be mentioned in connection with the steady stream of criticism fired at the Red Sox manager is that so vehement a booing section is acquired only by worthwhile targets. You've got to be important to draw so much ammunition. Look at the company he has in this respect—men like Ty Cobb, Bob Feller, Ted Williams. Only the truly great get the really big blasts.

Unfortunately, a lot of people are always ready to believe the worst about any successful man. So McCarthy, like Cobb before him, like Feller and Williams today, gets a carload of bum raps every season. Take, for example, the yarn that circulated last spring to the effect that Ted Williams had bluntly defied McCarthy's authority in front of the whole ball club in the dressing room at the Sarasota training camp. According to this fable, Teddy was approached by a photographer who wanted him to pose for some pictures. Before the great hitter could say yes or no, a lesser club official stepped in and told the photographer he couldn't do it. At which point, Ted is supposed to have blown up and yelled that nobody, not McCarthy or anybody else, was going to tell him when he could have his picture taken and when he couldn't.

Naturally, this morsel of gossip was relayed around the baseball circuit in no time at all, and it didn't exactly boost anybody's opinion of manager McCarthy. Then Dan Parker, the forthright sports editor of the New York *Daily Mirror,* tracked down the photographer in question and got his side of the story.

"It was nothing like that," said the picture-taker. "I was getting the runaround from some minor club officials when I tried to go in the clubhouse to see Ted. He happened to overhear one of them arguing with me, so he shouted to me to come in and take as many pictures as I wanted. McCarthy wasn't involved in the incident at all and Ted never mentioned his name."

Gossip is an unreliable yardstick of a man's character but it has been used more than once to measure Joe McCarthy.

On the other hand, winning a sackful of league pennants and world championships hasn't endowed Mister McCarthy with a halo of infallibility. He makes mistakes. He isn't always being put upon when the boys unlimber their big guns and draw a bead on him. This year, for instance, it is possible to conclude that Joe got exactly what was coming to him when he was belted without mercy by the press corps for whatever part he may have played in the foolish action of the Red Sox in barring reporters from their clubhouse for 30 minutes after each game. (Later softened to 15 minutes.)

It was Joe's contention, when I spoke to him about this silly fuss, that the nation's columnists fired on him too hastily. He implied that he had nothing to do with the pronunciamento. The news stories, of course, merely said that the Red Sox players had instituted the ban and that the announcement had been made by Dominic Di-Maggio, the players' representative.

Nevertheless, at this stage of the game, it should come as no surprise to McCarthy that the manager is held responsible for the actions of his players and that one of the manager's duties is to stop his players from making damn fools of themselves.

Apparently, Happy Chandler remembered this fundamental rule, even if McCarthy didn't. Asked for an opinion on the fuss between the Red Sox and the reporters, the commissioner seemed to think that there was no reason for him to have an opinion. "The manager," said Chandler, "has complete authority over the clubhouse."

"But this was the players," suggested Bill Cunningham, the famous columnist of the Boston *Herald*.

"The manager has charge of the players," said Chandler.

But if Joe was wrong that time, he is still way out in front. He has been right far more often than not. He has followed the right turns instinctively—perhaps with the help of his beloved "little people"—ever since he was a small boy in Philadelphia. Not in every little detail, maybe, but in the big things, in the things that counted, Joe has always known where he was going.

Joe, who is a vigorous 63 now, was born in Philadelphia on April 21, 1887. Right from the time he was big enough to go out and play with the other boys, he was crazy about baseball. He would stand for hours outside the gate of the old Athletics ball park waiting for Connie Mack to come out after the game. Then, hands in his pockets and head down bashfully, he would follow the great man as he walked to the streetcar. He never bothered Mack, never pestered him for his autograph. All he wanted was just to look at him.

After finishing grade school, Joe had to go to work. His father, who was a contractor, had been killed on a job when Joe was only three years old. The money young McCarthy could earn was badly needed at home, so he went into a textile mill. The standard wage in the plant was $5.50 a week, but it didn't take Joe long to become a "head tender" at $6.50. He picked up an occasional extra dollar by playing semi-pro baseball on weekends.

Joe didn't go to high school, but strangely, he did put in two full years at college. Niagara University at Buffalo, New York, impressed by his ballplaying on the Philadelphia sandlots, offered Joe a scholarship and he went there in 1905 and for part of 1906 before quitting the academic world for good.

It was an offer to join the Wilmington club of the Tri-State League that lured the ambitious young Irishman away from college. He played a few games for Wilmington in 1907 and then finished the season with Franklin of the Inter-State League. In 71 games, McCarthy hit a respectable .314 at Franklin. It was good enough to move him up to Toledo of the American Association in 1908.

By now, there was no doubt in Joe's mind what he wanted to do for a living. It was baseball for him, and it has been baseball for him ever since. Not that it was an easy path he followed. On the contrary, it was brutally hard. The plain truth is that Joe was no great shakes as a ballplayer. He drew down paychecks for 15 years as a player simply because he had a ferocious determination to make good that lit up every one of his slender talents like a Christmas tree.

It was the burning dream of McCarthy's young life to play his way into the major leagues. He never made it. After that .314 mark at Franklin, he got above .300

only once more in his years as a player. Joe thought he was going to make the big time in 1916, when he jumped to the Federal League, but the outlaw organization folded before it could give him even a faint taste of major league ball.

When it became crystal clear that his dream was going to die a-borning, Joe soberly took stock of himself. "I wasn't much of a hitter," he says, "and I didn't have good speed either." He had some great assets, though. He loved baseball with all his heart and soul, and he had the honesty to look a fact in the face. He wasn't going to make it as a player, that was plain. Well, why not as a manager?

McCarthy already had served a brief hitch as a manager, at Wilkes-Barre in 1913. Now he turned all his thoughts and energies to the task of learning everything there was to learn about the trade. All the furious effort and unflagging enthusiasm that he had put into his bid for a big league player's berth, Joe threw into his new campaign. They needed managers up there as badly as they need ballplayers, didn't they?

It would be good plotting to have the poor, honest busher with the bright flame of ambition move right up to the majors once he made up his mind in which direction his future lay. But nothing like that happened. McCarthy was destined to pass almost two full decades in the sticks before he got his break. For him, it was the cheap hotels, rickety grandstands, flimsy buses, and low pay of the minors. But he was soaking up an encyclopedia of baseball knowledge.

Joe finally quit the playing field late in the season of 1921, his third year as the Louisville manager. The incident that pushed him off the end of the plank constitutes one of his favorite stories, particularly because it involves one of his pet characters, the fabulous Jay Kirke. A powerful hitter, Kirke was one of the world's worst fielders, and McCarthy can spin dozens of sidesplitting yarns about him.

Louisville was playing St. Paul the day it happened.

Bert Ellison of St. Paul was caught in a rundown between first and second, and finally made a desperation dash for second. Kirke, the Louisville first baseman, lunged madly after him, clutching the ball in his hand. McCarthy, playing second, screamed for him to throw it. Finally it became clear even to Kirke that he wasn't going to win the foot race, so without warning he flung the ball sharply at McCarthy. It hit Joe smack in the middle of the chest and bounced off into the outfield, setting off a stream of McCarthy fireworks.

"You big Kraut-head!" Joe raged. "That's the dumbest play I ever saw in my life! Why didn't you give me the ball sooner?"

Kirke looked at the manager disdainfully. "Listen," he growled back. "What the hell right you got telling a .380 hitter how to play ball?"

"The trouble was," says Joe now, "he was right. I was only hitting about .252 at the time. You couldn't blame Jay for figuring I had no right to be telling him off."

Ever since then, Joe has taken a dim view of player-managers, although he and Lou Boudreau of the Cleveland Indians are good friends and respect each other highly. "You can't blame a player for not listening to you," McCarthy says, "when you bawl him out for swinging at bad ones and you're doing the same thing yourself. A manager shouldn't play unless he's better than anybody else on the team."

Joe had no way of knowing it, although he never stopped hoping and praying for it, but he was getting close to the big jump. The lessons he had learned and the friends he had made during the long, hungry years in the minors were about to pay off.

At the end of the 1925 season, William Wrigley, Jr., whose Chicago Cubs had finished dead last in the National League, began looking around for a new manager. The Cubs were in bad shape. They had been run, in '25, by a bewildering succession of Bill Killefer, Rabbit Maranville, and George Gibson. It was time for a new deal and Wrigley was looking for the right man.

John B. Foster, an old-time baseball writer who had served a stretch as secretary of the Giants and then had returned to sportswriting, suggested to his pal Wrigley that Joe McCarthy would be a good choice. Wrigley was impressed by Foster's arguments in favor of the Louisville manager, but he couldn't help worrying about the wisdom of handing over his ball club to a man who had never had a day's experience in the big leagues. He went around and asked some of his other friends what they thought. Every one of them agreed with Foster. "Get McCarthy," they said, vigorously. "He's your man."

Wrigley got McCarthy. It wasn't hard. Fresh from leading his Colonels to the American Association pennant, Joe was ripe for the move. He was confident that he knew what it was all about, impatient for a chance to prove it. The fact that he was inheriting a last-place club didn't discourage him a bit. The only direction you could move from there was up. He tore into the job like a scrub football player getting a chance to win his letter in the big game.

It wasn't all ice cream and cake, this promotion to the big top. Joe quickly discovered that his ballplayers, most of them veterans, resented him as a "busher." So did the fans. Everywhere Joe went as he swung around the league with the Cubs, he heard the taunting shouts.

"Hey, Busher! Didja learn how to sleep in a lower yet?"

"Ya big busher! I hear you were hot stuff in Wilkes-Barre!"

Whatever McCarthy thought, and it's a cinch he was boiling inside, his poker face gave no hint that he was disturbed. Actually, he was far more worried about the attitude of his players. The fans would be on his side when he won. But he couldn't win unless he got the players on his side first.

The big man of the ball club was the great right-handed pitcher and two-handed drinker, Grover Cleveland Alexander. Fate decreed that it was Alexander who

would have to serve as the medium through which Mc-
Carthy would show the team who was boss.

The trouble built up swiftly. Old Pete was never much
of a hand for punishing himself in training, and that
didn't set well with the new manager. Several times that
spring, Joe called on Alexander to pitch and Old Pete
couldn't make it. McCarthy knew that everybody was
watching the silent struggle between them and he knew
that he had to step on the great veteran or give up. It
was a tough decision to make but he carried it straight to
Wrigley and won his point. On June 22, 1926, Alexander
was sold to St. Louis on waivers.

You could feel the difference right away. Selling Old
Pete was a big step for a club that had finished last the
year before. It was plain to every man on the squad that
McCarthy meant business. There was a tightening up all
the way down the line.

Once his control was established, Joe proved that he
could be as reasonable as the next man. He certainly
took it easy on Hack Wilson, the rookie slugger up from
Toledo. Hack was a young man who would go anywhere,
do anything for a laugh. He loved good company, good
talk, good liquor. He hated to go to bed early at night.
All of which was most disconcerting to McCarthy, but
not so much that Joe lost his head about it.

During spring training, Joe got up early one Sunday
morning and headed for church. Walking down the street,
he was shocked to see his prize outfield recruit bumbling
along in a car jammed to the scuppers with extremely
convivial souls. It was clear that there were no temper-
ance workers in the crowd. McCarthy continued reflec-
tively on to mass.

That afternoon, at the ball park, Hack started in center field along with most of the other regulars. It was a
hot day, the kind of scorcher when even the heavy flannel baseball uniform can't soak up all the sweat that runs
down a ballplayer's body as he runs and throws and takes
his cuts at the ball. Before the exhibition was half over,

McCarthy had released all his regulars for the day—except Hack Wilson. He left Hack in there, sweating his unhappy head off.

Finally, in the seventh inning, Wilson laid into the ball for a tremendous home run. Tired to the point of exhaustion, he jogged slowly around the bases, head down, feet dragging in the dust. When he clattered into the dugout and slumped down on the bench, McCarthy inspected him carefully. "Better go in now, Hack," he said sweetly. "You're liable to be too tired to go out automobile ridin' tonight."

Then there was the time, during the season, when Hack's after dark schedule got to the point where it threatened to interfere seriously with his daytime chores. McCarthy decided that strong measures were called for. So, before game-time one day, he conducted a scientific experiment for the benefit of the assembled squad. In one hand, he held up a glass of water; in the other, a worm. Joe dropped the worm into the water and it wriggled wildly. Reaching in, he fished it out and dropped it into a second glass. "This one," he announced solemnly, "is full of whiskey."

Everybody watched curiously as he dropped the worm into the joy juice. Once again, it wriggled for a moment. Then it sank to the bottom. If it wasn't dead, it was certainly unconscious.

Joe looked straight at Hack. "What did you learn from that?" he barked.

Wilson never batted an eye. "I guess," said the happy-go-lucky slugger, "it means if I keep on drinkin' likker, I ain't gonna have no worms."

But Wilson played ball for McCarthy, and so did the other Cubs. He didn't exactly set the world on fire with them that first year, but he did shove them into the first division in a fourth-place finish that put a big smile on Wrigley's face and made general manager Bill Veeck convinced that they had the right man in the grim-jawed Irishman from Double-A.

In 1927, McCarthy held his own. He finished fourth

again. In '28, he moved up a notch to third. The Chicago fans were getting worked up now. They had pennant fever; they thought they could smell a championship. And they were right. This was Chicago's year.

The purchase of Rogers Hornsby from the Boston Braves for a reported $200,000 in cash and five players fanned baseball interest in Chicago to white heat. McCarthy was really on the spot now. He was expected to win. His fans thought he had the players to do it.

Joe had his troubles that year—it was far from a walkaway—but he got Wrigley the pennant he wanted so badly. With Charlie Root chalking up 19 victories, Pat Malone and Guy Bush pitching effectively all summer, and Hack Wilson batting in 159 fat runs, the Cubs outfought the league and roared home in front. Hornsby, the expensive addition, batted .380. Everything was beautiful. It was on to the world championship.

That's when McCarthy's luck ran out. The champions of the American League were the Philadelphia Athletics, and they were tough. They were, in fact, so tough that they slaughtered the Cubs in five games. That was bad enough, but the finishing touch was supplied by the way the As took the fourth game right out of the Cubs' mouths. It was murder.

Trailing in the Series, two games to one, McCarthy's boys got off to a flying start in that fourth game. They pounded Jack Quinn, Rube Walberg, and Ed Rommel unmercifully. By the time the Athletics came to bat in the last of the seventh, they were losing 8-0. It looked like a rout.

Al Simmons, foot in the bucket and all, led off the inning by belting the ball out of the park. "Too bad," said the experts in the press box. "There goes Charlie Root's shutout."

Nine hits and one hit batter later, there went more than that. Nine more runners crossed the plate and made it 10-8 for Philadelphia, and that's the way it ended.

The fifth game of the Series was anticlimactic. The Cubs were a beaten team and everybody knew it. They had nothing left. They walked out on the field as though they were shell-shocked, and that's just about the way it was. They lost, 3-2, and it was all over.

All over, that is, but the second-guessing. That went on for days, for weeks, even months. All through the winter, through spring training, even through the 1930 season, the arguments raged. The Cub fans couldn't and wouldn't believe that the As were that much better. They blamed McCarthy for everything.

McCarthy knew it was time for him to look around for something else to do. He knew that he couldn't be happy in Chicago any longer. So he was interested when Warren Brown, then the sports editor of the Chicago *Herald-Examiner,* asked him one day in the dugout, "Would you like to manage the Yankees?"

Poker-faced Joe looked at Brown skeptically. "Who wouldn't?" he asked, eloquently.

But Brown wasn't talking through his hat. He knew that Bob Shawkey, the stopgap manager the Yankees had appointed to succeed the late Miller Huggins, wasn't going to be able to keep the job. He knew that Ed Barrow, the general manager, and Colonel Jacob Ruppert, owner of the Yankees, respected McCarthy. And he knew that both McCarthy and Wrigley would be happier if Buffalo Joe left the Cubs.

After Jake Ruppert checked personally with Wrigley and made sure the Cub owner wouldn't object to McCarthy's departure, the deal was inevitable. Ed Barrow and Ruppert discussed terms with Joe, and in late September, the Cubs announced that McCarthy had resigned as manager and would be succeeded by second baseman Rogers Hornsby. Joe's appointment as boss of the Yankees wasn't made public until after the three principal parties—Ruppert, Barrow, and McCarthy—had met in a Philadelphia hotel room during the 1930 World Series between the Athletics and the Cardinals.

Joe was no nervous when he stood before a newsreel microphone at the Yankee's offices in New York at the ceremonies introducing him to the big town's sportswriters and fans that he made a gigantic blunder. Asked to say something to his new employer, he blurted: "Colonel Huston, I . . ." A roar of laughter cut him short and Joe turned a flaming red. Colonel Huston, Ruppert's original partner in the Yankee venture, hadn't been connected with the club for years.

Ruppert laughed along with everybody else. "Maybe," he said in his meaningful way, "McCarthy will be around here long enough so he will get to know me better."

McCarthy was to be around for 16 years, long enough to get to know Jake Ruppert very well indeed, long enough to win eight pennants and seven world championships for him and his heirs, long enough to engrave his name permanently on the roster of the game's greatest managers.

He knew he was taking on a tough assignment. Ruppert made that plain. "McCarthy," Jake told him sternly, "I finished third last year. I realize that you are confronted with problems that it will take you a little while to solve, so I'll be satisfied if you finish second this year. But," and the ruddy-faced beer baron leaned forward to emphasize his point, "I warn you, McCarthy, I don't like to finish second!"

Not all of the Yankees welcomed the new manager. A good many of the older stars thought McCarthy was getting a job that rightfully belonged to Babe Ruth. The Babe had never indicated that he wanted it, but—well, he was the big man of the club, wasn't he?

McCarthy won them over by grabbing the reins in both hands. An incident during spring training gave the Yanks their first indication of the kind of man they were working for. The club went into Milwaukee for an exhibition game, and the players, observing McCarthy's serious approach to the game, resolved to give him a big victory. "Maybe," they figured, "that'll make him happy." Piling into the startled Brewers right from the beginning, they ran up a lopsided 19-1 score.

As the Yankees climbed aboard their buses after the game, Jimmy Reese, a kid second baseman up from the

Pacific Coast League, approached McCarthy. "Well, Joe," he said breezily, "how'd you like that? Pretty good, huh?"

McCarthy glared at him. "Against a bunch of bums like that," he rasped, "you should've made 30 runs!"

Thus did the man from the minors set the pattern for leadership of what was to become the greatest club in the game. He was a perfectionist, a hard-driving wagon master, a fighter. He was proud to be in the majors, proud to wear the uniform of the Yankees, and he communicated that feeling to his ballplayers. If some of them failed to catch on, you could count on seeing them change to another uniform before long. McCarthy's years in the bushes had taught him to be patient with the mechanical mistakes of young players, but he was downright intolerant of flaws of the spirit. Clubhouse lawyers, prima donnas, rowdies, malcontents, drinkers—he cleaned them out as fast as he spotted them.

"You're in the big leagues now," Joe would remind a young ballplayer who was getting out of line. And the way he said it, it usually was enough. The dumbest rookie was able to grasp the fact that it meant a lot to McCarthy to be in Yankee Stadium and that he didn't want anybody around him who didn't feel the same.

From Jake Ruppert, Barrow and McCarthy through Babe Ruth and Gehrig, down to the lowest-ranking man on the squad, the Yankees all felt the same way. They didn't like to finish second.

But that's exactly where they did finish that first year under McCarthy. The As were still too good in '31. Nobody was able to stop them until Pepper Martin and the rest of the Cardinals ran away with them in the World Series. The Yankees, with Ruth and Gehrig each hitting 46 home runs, and Ben Chapman electrifying the crowds by stealing 61 bases, made a fight of it but couldn't quite get there.

"I'll make it next year," Joe swore to himself—and he did. His confident, smartly trained crew roared through the schedule to add up 117 victories and knock the Athletics off the perch they had occupied for three years.

The old Colonel grinned at McCarthy as though he were his favorite son.

The Yankees, and Joe McCarthy, were sitting on top of the world. They stayed there for a long time.

There was a convincing air of confidence about the Yankees, an atmosphere that clung to the club at home or on the road, that never varied in victory or defeat, that surrounded the executives as well as the players, that enveloped the team with a blanket of invincibility. Whether they won the pennant or not, the Yankees were still the Yankees. Hustling, aggressive, proud, precise— they played like champions and most of the time they were champions.

Joe McCarthy was the architect of this remarkable club spirit. He was also its guardian. When the invisible structure grew shaky, or appeared to be in danger at any given point of stress, Joe swung into action with deceptive calmness. Sitting back there in the dugout the way he did, not running around much, keeping hs mouth shut unless he had something useful to say, he didn't seem to be doing a great deal. But nothing got by him. Joe knew everything that was going on, and if he didn't like what he saw, he took positive steps to correct it. Except for one problem, which had to be resolved differently.

The Yankees followed that first McCarthy pennant by running second three years in a row. It was a difficult, troubled period for the manager, and not just because he wasn't winning pennants. The first great crisis of Joe's relationship with the Yankees was coming to a boil, festering daily. Babe Ruth's string was running out and the Babe wanted McCarthy's job.

McCarthy tried to minimize the situation, but it was clear to everybody that Ruth, always cool to him, was now actively trying to undermine Joe. The Babe had slipped to a .301 batting average in '33, and had skidded badly to a puny .288 in '34. At 39, he was too old, too fat, and too tired to play regularly. He appeared in only two-thirds of the Yankee games and was only a shadow of the old time Bambino.

The normally garrulous Ruth never had much to say to McCarthy. They were polite, but they kept out of each other's way as much as possible. As the '34 season wore on, Joe allowed the great slugger to put himself in or take himself out of the lineup as he chose. Above all, the shrewd manager desired to avoid an open breach. He was acutely aware of the unique position the Babe held in the hearts of the fans and he had no intention of challenging it.

In the end, it was Ruth who provoked the inevitable blowoff. He confronted Ruppert with a blunt demand that the Colonel remove McCarthy and install him as manager of the Yankees. Ruppert refused, countering with an offer to give the Babe the direction of the Newark farm club. "Prove to me that you can manage a ball club," Ruppert told him, "and you will be in line for the job on the Yankees whenever I decide to make a change."

Ruth's pride was stung. He was the biggest of all the big leaguers, wasn't he? Why should he go down to the minors? Let McCarthy go down. He was a minor leaguer, anyway. "No," he told Ruppert, angrily. "No. I won't do it."

"Then I'm sorry," Ruppert said, spreading his hands expressively.

McCarthy had won. He was in; Ruth was out. On February 26, 1935, soon after he had returned from an Oriental barnstorming tour, the greatest home run hitter in baseball history, the most colossal drawing card the game had ever known, was released by the Yankees, waived out of the American League, and signed to a contract by the Boston Braves. Busher Joe, the man who hadn't been good enough to play a single game under the big top, had held his job in the face of a frontal assault launched by the superstar whose name was the symbol of major league magnificence.

Now the last restraining cord had been cut. As they never had been before, as they never could have been while Ruth remained on the roster, the Yankees were McCarthy's team. He turned his back on the past and went to work. He had to get Colonel Ruppert another pennant.

It wasn't to be in 1935. "I warn you, McCarthy," Ruppert had said. "I don't like to finish second." And now Joe had finished second for three years in a row.

There was a new note of determination about the Yankee camp at St. Petersburg that spring of 1936. There was also—and this is one of the points always hammered by the anti-McCarthy bloc—a new ballplayer in camp. He was a tall, taciturn Italian boy from San Francisco, the hottest minor league player in the country in 1935, and his name was Joseph Paul DiMaggio.

Despite the pressure that was on him as he trained the club for that '36 season, Joe held to his rule of just one practice session a day. His player regulations were light. He enforced no blue laws, had no bed check. He regarded his men as professionals and his discipline was implicit rather than explicit. By now, all the players knew that if they didn't act like professionals, both on and off the field, they wouldn't be Yankees long. Not many of them cared to run the risk.

One did, and McCarthy cut him off like he would a wart. Ben Chapman, the flashy outfielder, was a hothead. He let his temper get the better of him once too often, and before he had time to reflect on his sins, he had been traded to Washington even up for Jake Powell. That was the tip-off. It didn't look like an even trade, or anything like it. Chapman may have been a hard man to control, but he was a gifted ballplayer. Powell was nothing more than a good journeyman outfielder. Apparently, McCarthy wouldn't stop at anything once you got on his blacklist.

Whether it was McCarthy or the ballplayers, or both, that Yankee team ripped through the league like a forest fire sweeping over a drought-ridden stand of timber. When the final standing was tabulated, they were 19½ games in front of the second place Detroit Tigers. Once again, they were the toast of baseball, and once again McCarthy allowed himself the luxury of an occasional smile.

He didn't spend much time gloating, though. He had a big World Series coming up, a Subway Series, with the Giants, and he didn't ease up until the fence-rattling, window-breaking power of his long-ball hitters had smashed the Giants in four out of six games to raise another World Championship banner to the top of the flagpole at Yankee Stadium.

Those were the great years for McCarthy. His was the mightiest, the richest, the most successful team in all baseball. "Marse Joe," the sportswriters called him. "Mister McCarthy," the young rookies reporting to the Yankees in a steady stream from George Weiss's farm system called him. "Lucky!" his critics called him.

But the dissenting voices were drowned out by the unchallengeable splendor of the Yankees' performance. Four straight years they scourged the American League, four straight years they overpowered the opposition in the World Series. They even appropriated the mid-summer All-Star game as their own special show, and in it gave the bruised National Leaguers a few more lumps for good measure.

Their pictures were in all the papers, their names were on everyone's lips. Great crowds turned out to see them wherever they played, from spring training right through the World Series in the fall. They were the aristocrats of baseball, and it was Joe McCarthy's job to keep them fighting for the honor of staying up there and at the same time prevent them from meditating too much on the pleasures and privileges of success.

"My greatest worry is keeping the boys on the jump," Joe told reporters during 1938 spring training. "I know they have to be in there playing ball every game, and after winning two pennants in a row, the tendency is to ease off. I'm here to stop any easing off."

But he didn't have to worry in '38. At least, not once Joe DiMaggio broke his protracted holdout and signed for the $25,000 the Yankees were willing to pay him for his third season in the league. As the big fellow regained his batting eye, the club picked up speed and it was the same old story all over again. It was the same in the Series, too. Again a clean sweep. Once again, the Yankees sang "The Sidewalks of New York" in their dressing room, shook hands with Judge Landis, and posed for victory pictures. They were happy, but not delirious. They were getting used to it.

And all around the major leagues, in front offices, in newspaper columns, in the bull sessions of the fans, the cry went up: "Break up the Yankees."

Colonel Ruppert was unmoved. "The other clubs," he said bluntly, "would do better to stop worrying about breaking up the Yankees and start worrying about catching up to the Yankees!"

For Christmas, 1938, McCarthy's players gave him a handsome silver plaque which bore the pictures of 23 Yankee ballplayers and officials, with the signature of each reproduced in silver. "The boys let me see a blueprint of it last summer," Joe grinned. "They hadn't won the pennant yet, but they described themselves as 1938 world champions. Then they went out and made good."

The Yankees kept it up in 1939, but in many ways it was a sad year for them—and for McCarthy. Jake Ruppert died in January and Lou Gehrig benched himself on May 2 after having played first base for the club in 2130 consecutive games beginning in June of 1925. Both events were loaded with grief for the Buffalo Irishman. He had never been exactly intimate with Ruppert, but the Yankee owner had been his patron and his strength. He had stood squarely behind him at all times. He had kept faith with Joe even when it meant letting Babe Ruth go. McCarthy knew he would miss him—but even he didn't know how much.

Gehrig had always been a McCarthy favorite. Quiet, self-contained, modest, hard-working, the Iron Horse was Joe's kind of ballplayer. He typified the Yankee ideal in McCarthy's mind. Joe hated to see him come to the end of the line and he was shocked when the news broke that Lou was suffering from a malignant form of chronic infantile paralysis.

But the Yankees moved on in their accustomed fashion. They spread-eagled the field and wound up 17½ games ahead of the Red Sox. Then they took on Bill McKechnie's Cincinnati Reds, and the Reds made noises like a gang of fighters. But it was four straight for the Yankees again.

Frank Graham wrote about hearing a dazed Cincinnati fan groaning in a bar that last night. "Break up the Yankees?" he was saying. "Hell, I'll be satisfied if they just break up that Charlie Keller!"

The Yankees were never quite that good again. They blew the pennant to Detroit in 1940, then came back to take it all in 1941, whipping the Brooklyn Dodgers in the World Series. In '42, they won the pennant but were taken in the Series by a fighting bunch of St. Louis Cardinals. In '43, they got even with the Cards, and once again they were the champions of the world.

It was a magnificent record that stretched out behind them. Seven American League pennants in eight years, six world championships in those eight years. Baseball had never known a wrecking crew like this one. And Mc-Carthy's personal record: Eight pennants and seven world championships in 13 years. Wasn't he obviously the greatest of all managers?

"Like hell he is!" the opposition shrieked. "Anybody could win with the players he's got! Look at the way he blew the '42 series!"

That always made McCarthy sore. He didn't know himself what had happened to the Yankees that fall. Maybe it was simply that the Cards were hungrier, the Yankees filled to the ears with praise and rich living. Whatever it was, the Redbirds from St. Louis gave the almighty Yankees a taste of how the other half lives. Stan Musial, Terry Moore, Country Boy Slaughter, Marty Marion, Whitey Kurowski—they slashed their base-hits and careened around the bases until the cocky New Yorkers were beaten to their knees.

Joe McCarthy got the first big dose of second-guessing he had been forced to swallow since his Cubs lost to the Athletics in 1929. He didn't like it, either. "What's the matter?" he growled. "Has everybody forgotten the other years? What do we have to do, win them all?"

It would have been easier for him if he hadn't been so openly resentful. You have to walk on eggs when you're way up on top; it doesn't take much to make the mob turn on you. But Joe was bitter. "Well," he said, talking about the criticism of his strategy, "at least I got my name in the papers this time."

It got much worse in the spring of '44. Jimmy Dykes, the fast-talking manager of the Chicago White Sox, summed it all up for the fans who didn't like Marse Joe. He gave them a neat little package to throw at McCarthy's head—and the package had a rock in it.

"Joe McCarthy," said Dykes, discussing the season prospects with reporters, "will really have to go to work this season. He won't be able to sit back the way he did in other years and simply push buttons. . . ."

The crack exploded around the league and Joe heard it everywhere he went. If there was ever a man in baseball who was free of rabbit ears, it was McCarthy. But this needling got under his skin.

"Hiya, Joe!" they yelled at him. "Got yer push buttons?"

"Hey, Joe, what's the matter? You lose your buttons?"

"Push button Joe! Ya bum, ya!"

It's an old story in sports, this jeering and cat-calling heaped on a loser. It's always hard to take, expecially when you've been a winner for a long time, as McCarthy had been. But the thing that made Joe burn was the fact that the push-button dig was aimed more at his past successes than at his present troubles. It hurt to see the record of which he was so proud attacked so unreasonably.

Always appreciative of a good drink, Joe drank no-ticeably more. He and his wife, the former Elizabeth McCave, whom he had married back in 1921 in his Louisville days, had no children, and Mrs. McCarthy kept house for Joe in New York during the season. But Babe, as Joe called her, didn't travel with the team very often and on the road trips he had too much time on his hands.

Joe might have sought escape even more assiduously if he had known that he had won his last championship with the Yankees. He finished third in 1944 and had to go back home for a couple of weeks early in the season to rest up from a severe attack of polyneuritis, resulting from influenza. But if he thought he had troubles then, it was only because he didn't know what was coming. On January 26, 1945, the Yankee baseball empire was sold by the Ruppert estate to Larry MacPhail, Del Webb, and Dan Topping.

McCarthy's number was up the moment that Larry MacPhail sat down in the president's chair. Oh, sure, there were dozens of statements about how much Larry thought of Joe, and about how Joe intended to manage the Yankees as long as his health would permit. But the handwriting was on the wall and a lot of people read it clearly—including Joe McCarthy.

It looked as though Joe was ready to quit when he left the club for three weeks beginning July 22, 1945. The vacation was billed as being caused by a recurrence of a chronic gallbladder condition, but most of the sports-writers covering the team thought there was more to the situation than met the naked eye. But Joe came back to work on August 8, relieving Art Fletcher of the burden.

It was learned later that Joe had offered his resigna-tion to MacPhail the night before he took off for his rest cure. MacPhail refused to accept it.

The season ran its course, the Yankees finished fourth, and McCarthy said he would be back again in '46. He was, but he didn't stay long.

On the Yankees' first western trip, McCarthy reported

sick for the last game of a series in Cleveland. His gall-bladder was acting up again. He went with the team to Detroit but had to stay in his hotel room during both games there.

It was on that flight to Detroit that McCarthy made his famous speech to Joe Page, then a largely unsuccessful pitcher suspected by McCarthy of being a playboy. Squatting down in the aisle next to Page's seat on the plane, Joe ripped into the embarrassed left-hander with all the sarcasm and violence at his command. It is possible that that outburst cost him two pennants when he moved to Boston, for Page has never forgotten the incident, never forgiven McCarthy for the public humiliation to which he subjected him. The Gay Reliever would rather beat McCarthy once than any other club three times.

On May 23, 1946, still unable to go to the park, Joe got on a 9:50 A.M. plane from Detroit for Buffalo. The feeling on the team which he had left behind was that he would never come back. The boys were right. He never did.

The next day, MacPhail met the club as it arrived in Boston. He had with him a telegram containing McCarthy's resignation. "My doctor advises me that my health would be seriously jeopardized if I continued," it stated. "This is the sole reason for my decision which, as you know, is entirely voluntary on my part. I have enjoyed our pleasant relations. . . ."

Larry had a hard time making the baseball writers buy all that. They thought, and many of them still think, that McCarthy was fired, or that at best it was a mutual proposition brought on by a severe case of incompatibility. Whatever the reason, Joe McCarthy was no longer the Yankee manager. First Ruth, then Ruppert, then Gehrig, then Barrow, and now McCarthy. Where, a poetic sportswriter wondered, were the Yankees of yesteryear?

So old Marse Joe, sick of body and sicker of heart, shuffled off to the Buffalo farm he had bought in '43. He read the box scores in *The Sporting News* and listened to some games on the radio, but other than that he was through with baseball. At least, that's what he said.

He sounded a little different in September, when an Associated Press writer interviewed him at the farm. Joe looked a lot better. His face was tanned, his body looked active and hard, his eyes were clear. "There's no use denying I'd like to be back," he said. "There are a couple of good jobs reported open. I have my health back. So far, I've had no offers. We'll see what goes at the World Series."

The Democrats of Erie County, New York, asked Joe if he'd like to run for County Sheriff, but McCarthy just smiled. "No, thanks," he said. "I have no political ambitions."

Branch Rickey made the first attempt to lure Joe back to the majors. After Happy Chandler suspended Leo Durocher at the beginning of the 1947 season, Rickey tried to interest McCarthy in the job. Joe might have grabbed it, but it was only for a year. Rickey reserved the right to bring back Durocher when the pepperpot's sentence had expired.

On April 21, 1947, as Joe observed his 60th birthday, Mrs. McCarthy told reporters, "Joe is through with baseball forever. He likes this life out here. It's made a new man out of him. It's given him back his health. He won't go back as a baseball manager. He has new hobbies now. He's interested in flowers . . . and birds."

Less than five months later, Joe was back in the thick of things. On September 29, 1947, after a year and a half on the farm, he signed a two-year contract to succeed Joe Cronin as manager of the Boston Red Sox. Cronin, who was moving up to general manager, was obviously delighted at his catch. "Joe's going to have more power," he said, "than probably any manager since Mc-Graw. He will have complete charge of the team and will have the power to make any deals he wants."

McCarthy's appointment was announced on the eve of the World Series between the Yankees and the Dodgers, and Joe's room at the Hotel Commodore looked more like the hotel lobby as people filed in and out to congratulate him on his return to the game. Telegrams piled up on the furniture.

"Naturally, I'm pleased," said Joe. "When you've been in baseball as long as I have, it gets in your blood."

It has to be in his blood for him to stay in it after what has happened to him in Boston. The sportswriters of the town, who greeted him with open arms when he took the job, have been beating him over the head ever since. Not all of them, but most of them. They predict his resignation every week. They criticize his handling of his players, his relations with the press, his every positive or negative act.

Joe prefers to ignore such things. He believes it is beneath his dignity to answer personal attacks.

"I always figure," he told me, "the truth comes out in the end. If I make a fuss, I just give the writer more publicity, and that's probably just what he wants." Thinking it over, Joe added, "When somebody writes something bad about me, and I know it's not true, well, I just figure I don't want anything more to do with that fellow, that's all."

At the root of it all, of course, is his record in Beantown. Marse Joe has finished second twice in a row. His margin of defeat on each occasion was one game. The Cleveland Indians beat him in an extraordinary special playoff in 1948 after the two teams had finished in a dead heat, and the Yankees beat him in a climactic final series at Yankee Stadium at the end of the '49 season. Joe went into the last two days of the battle with a one-game lead over the Bombers. His old club beat the Red Sox twice in a row to win by a game.

What caused those two one-game defeats? Joe pulled his cigar out of his mouth and leaned forward in his chair. He blew a big fat cloud of smoke across the room. "You tell *me!*" he said.

Which is a reminder of Joe's favorite interview technique. When the writers start crowding him for information about player problems, lineup changes, or other club headaches, Joe is fond of cutting them short with "Let me worry about that. I'll do the managing around here."

The newspaper boys all thought Joe would have a tremendous collision with Ted Williams, the problem-child slugger of the Red Sox, when he first took over in Boston. But he didn't. He told them in advance that he wouldn't. "Listen," said the practical McCarthy, "any manager who can't get along with a .400 hitter ought to have his head examined."

When they remembered the way Marse Joe used to insist that his Yankees dress "like major leaguers" all the time, including a shirt and tie, even during spring training, the Boston scribes were certain there would be trouble between McCarthy and Williams. The individualistic Teddy Boy never wears a tie. So what happened? On the first day of spring training, McCarthy showed up in the hotel lobby wearing an open-collar sport shirt. A smart Irishman, is Buffalo Joe.

"I don't know anything much about his personal life," he says regarding Williams, "but I've had the boy for two years now, and I couldn't ask for anything more."

Joe gets along well with all his players, even though you could hardly describe their relationship as intimate. He doesn't make them call him Mister McCarthy. They all call him Joe. But, an old-fashioned manager, he believes in keeping his men at arm's length, and there is nobody who knows how to do that any better than Joseph Vincent McCarthy.

After all these years in the game, Joe has friends all around the league, but when the club is at home, he spends most of his spare time with his wife. They have a suite in a downtown Boston hotel and Joe likes to walk the 15 minutes to Fenway Park when the weather is good. On the road, he is more sociable. Babe isn't with him and he spends more time with his coaches, with Tom Dowd, the traveling secretary, and with old acquaintances along the route.

Joe doesn't read much for pleasure, but he still checks every line of the baseball box scores and retains every shred of information in his bear-trap memory.

He goes to the movies once in a while, mostly on the road. "When you're managing a ball club," he says, "you don't have much time for that stuff. When you're not actually working, you're thinking about it." He used to play golf in the spring and fall, but he gave it up a couple of years ago. Too tiring. He likes prizefights. When he was a young blood around Philadelphia, he managed a couple of fighters. (They weren't very good.)

He doesn't play cards. Maybe he developed a hatred for the pastime when he was first up with the Yankees. He used to get aggravated watching the fierce intensity with which the ballplayers tackled their nonstop games on train trips and in the clubhouse on rainy days. "If you guys would concentrate half as hard on baseball as you do on those damn cards," he complained, "we'd never lose."

His farm, in Amherst, New York, a few miles outside Buffalo, is a sprawling 61 acres, but Joe doesn't work it for profit. A tenant farmer takes care of the place and does some truck farming, cutting McCarthy in on the profits, if any.

There's no getting away from it, Joe's whole life—except for his enormous affection for his wife—is baseball. That's why he puts up with it all—the train trips, the airplane flights, the hotel meals, the abuse from the fans, the criticism in the papers. He's a baseball man and he can't get along without the game.

If you're lucky, you may catch him sometime when he's feeling mellow and, between puffs on that omnipresent cigar, he'll tell you a little of what he keeps inside him. "When you know in your heart you've helped some of these young fellows make good, when you know you played a part in their success, that's when you know you're accomplishing something, you're not wasting your time. When I think of fellows like Crosetti and Dickey, and I see what they've made of themselves, and they come to me and tell me I helped them do it, why, I feel I've done something important."

That's when Joe realizes that it doesn't make any difference whether the crowds cheer him or boo him, whether the papers pet him or pound him. Joe has never been neutral himself, so he doesn't expect other people to be.

All of Joe McCarthy is wrapped up in the simple answer he gave me when I asked him if he thought he could win this year. Joe seemed surprised that I should ask him that. He took the cigar out of his mouth and examined it carefully. The brown eyes were wide open and the square jaw was sticking out like the bumper on a Mack truck.

"Why else would I be here?" he said. "What would anybody play for except the championship?"

Dick   Williams

How Dick Williams Became the World Champion Manager

by JIM BOUTON

I really was born too soon. When I was in the major leagues, the managers would look at me and think my hair was too long, my sweat shirt wasn't the right color, my opinions were too opinionated. Because of all that, I was a known flake. Worse than that, I had also been seen in the company of known flakes. (Are you now, or have you ever been . . . ? I am, I was.)

Now it's the managers who look like flakes. Well, at least one manager. Dick Williams.

I can just see it now. I'm pitching for the Oakland Athletics and I walk into the clubhouse on the first day of spring training. And there, in the middle of the clubhouse, wearing a funny colored sweat shirt, wearing hair that curls way below his collar, wearing a mustache, for God's sake, is my manager. My *manager*. It is not Ralph Houk.

I would feel warm all over if Dick Williams was my manager. I would feel nice. I would feel confident. I would be able to spend the entire spring knowing that if I didn't make the club it would be because I wasn't a good pitcher. It wouldn't be because of my hair, my sweat shirt or my opinions. If I could pitch, I think Dick Williams wouldn't have minded if I liked to run without my cap on, or if I supported the Players Association, or if I liked to listen to The Beatles in the clubhouse.

Which is not to say that Dick Williams would run without his hat on, or support the Players Association, or like The Beatles. Maybe he prefers the Rolling Stones. I don't know Dick Williams. I never played for him.

Even though he comes on hip and flexible and ultramodern around baseball, maybe Dick Williams doesn't believe in any of it. Perhaps he hates mustaches and thinks that only commies and hairdressers have long hair. Maybe when he's away from the ball park he beats his wife. It doesn't matter.

In 1967 Williams was the manager of the Boston Red Sox. He didn't have long hair and a mustache then. He had a crew cut. He also had a very bad temper and a very inflexible attitude. He was a tyrant with the Red Sox, a manager who wanted his players to do everything his way. He couldn't have been so bad there, because in 1967 the Red Sox came within one game of the world championship. Still, two years later, he was fired because, they said, he was too tough.

And then, a couple of years later, he turned up at Oakland and he wasn't so tough anymore. He let people do things their own way, just as long as it helped win baseball games. "Times change," Williams said. "I had to change with them."

Williams made a conscious effort to change. Or at least a conscious effort to suppress the old crew-cut personality. I think he realized what's the point of having rules if they don't make guys play better. He realized that the A's weren't going for good conduct medals or the best punctuality record in the major leagues. They were trying to win more baseball games than anyone else. And in 1972, they did. Maybe there's a connection.

From what I know of the new Dick Williams and the bunch of guys on the 1972 Oakland team, they didn't have many rules. Oh, maybe they weren't allowed to punch each other in public. No punching a teammate, I suppose, in a nightclub. Fighting only allowed in the clubhouse. No screaming at each other when the wives are around. And don't embarrass the manager to more than two wire services during any one homestand.

Williams understood that screaming and fighting and complaining about the other guys on the team and about the manager, too, wasn't so terrible. Being permissive, letting the guys get angry at each other, didn't stop you from winning games. Most managers have grown up on the old axiom that dissension is bad. So they tell their players, "Fellas, you've got to be together to win. We can't win this thing unless we're together. And blah. And blah. And blah." Well, once you start placing limits on yourself, of course, you reduce your chances of winning. Because then the players start saying, hell, we have dissension, that means we can't win. It gives them a ready-made excuse. That's all ballplayers need. The season is over.

Williams didn't give the 1972 A's a ready-made excuse. It may have made them world champions.

Which doesn't mean the A's won the championship just because they had long hair, or their manager had long hair, or their manager was permissive and let them do things their own way. That was maybe 10 or 15% of the reason. The other 85% was because they had a lot of good baseball players. Williams could have tried his long hair, his mustache and his lack of rules with the Cleveland Indians, for instance, and he would have gotten a lot of long-haired .220 hitters. In fact, there would have been a lot of people blaming his permissive ways for why the Indians didn't do so good.

The best manager in the world wouldn't worry much about hair. He would make sure that he had Richie Allen hitting third, Reggie Jackson hitting fourth, Tom Seaver pitching and so on. He'd make sure they knew what town the game was in and that he had nine guys dressed in their uniforms when the game was ready to start. And then he would disappear.

Still, Williams with his new ways did prove something. He showed that you don't have to have short hair and believe in God to win. He might have done for baseball what Joe Namath did for football when he won the Super Bowl. He showed that you can like the ladies, like the bottle and still throw a great pass. He showed that there is more than one way to win.

Now that doesn't mean baseball is going to learn anything from Williams's success. I mean, I don't think Ralph Houk is going to grow a mustache. Well, maybe he'll wear a pink sweat shirt. But the point is, baseball managers aren't going to change that easily. For the most part, they're still the same traditional kind, the type that will say, when Williams's A's don't finish first some year, "Well, that's what you get for letting those damn players do anything they damn please."

So they're not going to change. The people who may change are the owners, of all people. See, it's their money. If they found out you needed flakes to win, they'd hire Andy Warhol. Like Dick Williams said during the World Series, "I'll take all the criticism there is if we win the World Series. Criticism doesn't bother me. Only losing does."

And speaking of owners, there's Charles O. Finley. Williams probably deserves more credit for adapting to Finley than for adapting to his players. Finley isn't the easiest man in the world for managers to get along with. He fires them at the drop of a white hat. Or a gold hat. Or a green hat. With all those hats around, Williams knew he didn't have a lot of time to mold the Athletics to his liking. So he molded himself to their liking.

Actually, I suppose the best way to handle an owner like Finley is to post the standings on your office door and every time the owner comes down to complain, just run to the door and point. Just make sure you're in first place.

Williams made sure in 1972. But now Williams has to watch out. This year's flexibility can become next year's dogma. I can hear him telling some future team, "Let me tell you how we won it in '72. And that's how we're going to do it this year."

Maybe the ballplayer of the future won't want flexibility. He'll want direction, discipline. He'll want to be treated like a child of the family.

Sure.

George Stallings

The Miracle Man

by TOM MEANY

George Tweedy Stallings was a man of infinite impatience. One of baseball's greatest legends, Stallings may also have been baseball's first bona fide split personality. Away from the ball park, he was a dignified, fastidious man, meticulous in dress, Chesterfieldian in his manners. Nobody ever would take him for a baseball manager. Swarthy, moon-faced, bright-eyed, he would have been a cinch for today's men-of-distinction ads.

On the bench during a ball game, Stallings was another person. No man, not even John McGraw or Leo Durocher, ever reached the heights of invective stormed by George. He could fly into a schizophrenic rage at the drop of a pop fly. Sputtering with a fury which invited apoplexy, Stallings told off ballplayers as they haven't been told off since.

And, curiously enough, nobody minded the tongue lashings of Stallings. "It was an art with him," Hank Gowdy remarked with awesome reverence over three decades later.

In 1915, a year after his baseball miracle with the Boston Braves, Stallings walked home from the ball game with owner Jim Gaffney. All the Braves rode home, for they all had purchased cars out of their series shares, all but Johnny Evers, who had won a Chalmers car as the National League's most valuable player for 1914. Stallings knew the make of every car owned by his players, and in that 1915 season he prefaced his derogatory remarks to his men by inserting the name of the automobile. Thus Rabbit Maranville became an "Aperson

Jack-rabbit bonehead," others were "Packard dunces," "Stanley Steamer clowns" and "White simpletons."

Only once did Stallings forget the name of a car owned by one of his players. Seeking to call attention to the mental shortcomings of Gowdy, who missed a sign one day, the Braves' manager turned to the rest of the bench.

"Look at him up there," he sputtered derisively, "the— the—" And there was a pause as Stallings tried in vain to recall the name of the car driven by Gowdy. He was stumped, but not for long.

"Look at him," yelled Stallings, "the bicycle-riding so-and-so."

It was Stallings' habit to sit on the same spot on the bench day after day, his knees and his feet close together. As he grew agitated—and he did so every day, win, lose or draw—he would slide his feet, still close together, back and forth over the floor of the dugout. And sometimes he would slide his body, too. He wore the seat of a pair of trousers clean through during the second game of the 1914 World Series.

Not only was Stallings superstitious but he encouraged his ballplayers in superstition. He couldn't abide scraps of paper anywhere within range of his vision, an idiosyncrasy rival ballplayers exploited to the hilt when they learned of it.

Years after Stallings had left the Braves, when he managed and owned the Rochester Club in the International League, his legend persisted. Even today, two stories of the Stallings repartee are still part of baseball folklore.

One deals of his trials with two collegians, twin brothers who were infielders. Sometimes they're identified as the Shannon twins from Seton Hall, often they're not from Seton Hall at all, neither twins nor brothers and not even infielders. Through all versions of the story, however, they remain collegians.

The story goes that one day the twins were on second and third, with one out. The Rochester batter hit to the shortstop, who threw home to cut off the run. The twin on third was caught in a run-down and eventually tagged out. And the twin on second chose that particular moment to try and make third where he, too, was exterminated and the inning was over.

The enormity of what he had just witnessed left Stallings speechless. But only briefly. The inning over, the twins returned to their defensive positions in the field. George darted off the bench and beckoned the two tyros to him.

Paternally draping an arm on the shoulder of each, Stallings inquired, "You boys are both college graduates, aren't you?"

"Yes, Mr. Stallings," they chorused in assent.

"Well, then," said Stallings briskly and, changing his voice to imitate the staccato bark of a cheerleader, he roared: "Rah, rah, rah! Rah! Rah! Rah! Rah! Rah! Rah!"

Perhaps the most hallowed of all the Stallings legends concerns itself with the time when he retired to his plantation at Haddock, Georgia, The Meadows, broken in health and through with baseball. He was suffering from a serious cardiac disturbance.

"Mr. Stallings," said the specialist at the completion of the examination, "you have an unusually bad heart. Is there any way you can account for it?"

"Bases on balls, you so-and-so, bases on balls," cursed Stallings softly, turning his face to the wall.

Stallings managed before it became the baseball style to address managers as "Skipper," but his position with his players may be judged from the fact that they usually called him "Chief." Some of the more intimate called him "George," but none ever took any liberties with him. Baseball, to Stallings, was too serious to permit of any levity.

There were, of course, "meetings" before Stallings' day, as those baseball skull sessions are called, but the Chief intensified these daily conclaves at which strategy was mapped. He was as careful in detail of play as he was in detail of dress, a precise, methodical planner.

Stallings is generally given the credit for being the

first to use different outfield combinations for left- and right-handed pitchers. The "percentage" of having a left-hander bat against a right-handed pitcher and vice versa was recognized long before 1914, particularly in the selection of pinch hitters and relief pitchers, but Stallings was the first to play the percentage wholesale. He almost was forced into it, because the Braves did not have a strong outfield that season, but Stallings made the best of it, by having Herbie Moran, Larry Gilbert and Joe Connolly as one set of outfielders, against right-handed pitching, and Leslie Mann, Ted Catcher and George Whitted against southpaws.

There were others who broke into these combinations, of course—Stallings used nearly a dozen different outfielders during the year—and Connolly, the only member of the team to hit .300 for the season, frequently was used against both right- and left-handed pitchers. It was, nevertheless, the first full outfield switch in history and Stallings stuck to it during the World Series.

One thing Stallings must get credit for introducing into baseball is the "tooth" sign. The Chief would call a certain play by baring his teeth. Dark-complexioned and with teeth of pearly white, Stallings could give his sign from the shadows of the dugout and have it picked up by his coaches or players every time. When the Chief bared his fangs his men knew it was time to run—but literally, since the Braves used it as a steal sign.

COMMENTS

Managers today don't tell off their ballplayers like they used to, not like George Stallings did. During my first year in pro ball, after giving up a couple of home runs on high pitches, my minor-league manager, gentle Jimmy Gleeson, came out to tell me off and remove me from the game.

Putting his hand on my shoulder and reaching for the ball, he said kindly, "James, if you're going to continue pitching the ball above the waist, you're going to be pitching for me again next year."

Jimmy Gleeson could really rip a guy.

Joe Schultz

The Manager
Who Wasn't

by JIM BOUTON

Joe Schultz managed the new expansion Seattle Pilots in their one and only year of existence. Aside from the fact that Schultz was suspicious of knuckle balls and people who threw them, I enjoyed pitching for him more than any other manager I ever played for.

The great thing about Joe Schultz was that he had things in perspective. Either that or he didn't give a damn. I'm sure it was perspective.

Joe understood very early that the assortment of cast-offs that made up the Seattle Pilots was not going to win many games. Rather than whip a dead horse, he at least tried to make the summer bearable for all of us.

We'd lose nine out of seven on mental errors, physical errors, and just plain old lack of ability, and Joe Schultz would call a team meeting to chew us out. He'd holler for a while and then he'd look around the room at all those forlorn faces belonging to nobody and you could see him start to feel sorry for us. He wanted to motivate us, but he didn't want to break our spirit. So at the end of his lecture—or maybe you'd call it harangue—he'd pause, then finish with, "Aww, shitfuck, we're not that bad. What the hell, we're as good as anybody. Fuckshit, we're better than anybody." We went from worse than anybody to better than anybody in the time it took to transpose a shitfuck. (In *Ball Four* I quoted Joe Schultz saying shitfuck 211 times. Schultz now coaches for Detroit and the Tiger players call him "Ol' Shitfuck." I take full credit.)

Then Joe Schultz would end his lecture with, "Let's go

get 'em and then pound some Budweiser." Occasionally,
we would. Go get 'em, I mean. We *always* pounded Budweiser.

Usually, we got beat no matter what Joe (you have to
use his full name wherever possible—it's such a great name
for a manager) Schultz said. Sometimes we got beat so
bad Joe Schultz would try to take our minds off the
game. We'd be losing to Minnesota 9-1 in the eighth inning of the first game of a doubleheader. We already
knew we were going to lose the second game, too. We
just didn't know what the score was going to be. Joe
would be pacing back and forth in the dugout, and then
in a serious voice he'd say, "Men, between games of this
doubleheader, we have a choice of ham, roast beef or
tuna salad."

Of course this broke up the whole bench, and as a result we'd be so relaxed that we'd lose the second game
only 5-3 instead of 8-0.

Another time we'd be losing to Baltimore 9-3 in the
seventh inning. (We were always losing to Baltimore in
the seventh inning. Also in the eighth inning and the
ninth inning.) Fred Talbot, a pitcher (giving him the benefit of the doubt), once said we had no business schedul-
ing those guys. It wasn't that we didn't try. We tried every
conceivable way to win. We tried jumping off to an early
lead. We tried falling behind and catching up later. We
tried winning by forfeit. We tried winning by rain delay.
We tried winning by day, by night, by astroturf, by real
ground. Nothing worked. Anyway, we're losing 9-3 to
Baltimore in the seventh, and suddenly Joe Schultz hollers down to the end of the bench, "Gelnar, get down
here."

John Gelnar is keeping a chart on each pitch thrown,
and everybody thinks Joe wants to find out if Baltimore
is getting too many fast balls to hit, or what. So with
everyone watching, Joe Schultz points across the field and
says, "Gelnar. Gelnar, look over there by that section-23
sign. Check the rack on that broad."

Instead of crying all summer, we laughed a lot. Joe

Schultz turned what could have been a miserable summer into a memorable one.

On the other hand, Joe Schultz wasn't a real manager. He was a perfect coach type who was given a shot at managing because he had spent time in a winning St. Louis organization. Baseball people think a winning organization means that everybody in it knows something about winning. Something might've filtered down. Or maybe they hired Joe Schultz because he had such a great manager's name.

And how could Joe Schultz turn them down? Maybe he didn't want to be a manager because he knew he shouldn't be, but how can the secretary who's been at the company for 20 years turn down the vice-presidency, whether he wants it or not? If you're a baseball coach, you want to become a baseball manager. There are some things you just don't say no to.

Since Joe Schultz wasn't really a manager, it was frustrating to players trying to have a good season. And there were some. Most managers are very thorough and spend hours thinking about little ways to improve the ball club. Not Joe Schultz.

I spent all summer long trying to convince Joe Schultz that me and my knuckle ball should be starting instead of sitting in the bullpen. But the knuckle ball was always jumping around, and Joe thought it was risky to give me a start. I didn't think that should matter since it was risky for us to even take the field, regardless of who was pitching. I'd go to Joe and start to tell him that my statistics showed that I'd only walked two guys in my last nine innings of relief. Before I could finish, Joe Schultz would wave his hand and say, "Aww, I don't want to hear any statistics. I can see what's going on with my own eyes." Joe Schultz was as interested in statistics as he was in Gelnar's pitching chart.

Joe's idea of attention to detail was to make sure that we all had our socks cut the same and wore the same color sweat shirts. And Joe's idea of strategy was to come out to the mound, pick up the resin bag, slam it down, and say, "What the shit. Give 'em some low smoke and we'll catch an early plane the hell out of here." We never knew if Joe Schultz thought that pitch would get the guy out or get hit out. Either way, it was an early plane.

It's doubtful Joe Schultz would have been a winner even with a team that could play baseball. He'd have been outsmarted by guys like Gene Mauch or Billy Martin or Earl Weaver or some clever manager who kept all the charts and used all the edges that would make a difference over a long season. But it is possible that if Joe Schultz had better players he would have been more scientific. Maybe he figured that with us marginal players the little things didn't matter. The only thing that mattered was coming out of that summer of '69 with our sanity.

That was the summer I tried to hang on in the big leagues with an elusive knuckle ball that could make you crazy. After all, look what it did to me. It was also the summer that I took notes to write *Ball Four* and needed quotable people.

Some people only get passing mention in books. And others, like Joe Schultz, because of their star quality, sell books all by themselves. That's why he's in this book, too. It took great restraint not to put his picture on the cover.

Under the circumstances I couldn't have had a better manager that summer than Joe Schultz.

National League Managers 1876–1972

Atlanta Braves

Year	Manager	Finish	Year	Manager	Finish	Year	Manager	Finish
	BOSTON[1]		1910	Fred Lake	8		Del Bissonette	6
			1911	Fred Tenney	8	1946	Billy Southworth	4
1876	Harry Wright	4	1912	John Kling	8	1947	" "	3
1877	" "	1	1913	George Stallings	5	1948	" "	1
1878	" "	1	1914	" "	1[s]	1949	" "	4
1879	" "	2	1915	" "	2	1950	" "	4
1880	" "	6	1916	" "	3	1951	" "	
1881	" "	6	1917	" "	6		Tommy Holmes	4
1882	John F. Morrill	3	1918	" "	7	1952	" "	
1883	Jack Burdock[2]		1919	" "	6		Charlie Grimm	7
	John F. Morrill	1	1920	" "	7			
1884	" "	2	1921	Fred Mitchell	4		MILWAUKEE	
1885	" "	5	1922	" "	8			
1886	" "	5	1923	" "	7	1953	Charlie Grimm	2
1887	" "	5	1924	Dave Bancroft	8	1954	" "	3
1888	" "	4	1925	" "	5	1955	" "	2
1889	Jim Hart	2	1926	" "	7	1956	" "	
1890	Frank Selee	5	1927	" "	7		Fred Haney	2
1891	" "	1	1928	Jack Slattery		1957	" "	1[s]
1892	" "	1		Rogers Hornsby	7	1958	" "	1
1893	" "	1	1929	Judge Fuchs[4]	8	1959	" "	2
1894	" "	3	1930	Bill McKechnie	6	1960	Chuck Dressen	2
1895	" "	5	1931	" "	7	1961	" "	
1896	" "	4	1932	" "	5		Birdie Tebbetts	4
1897	" "	1	1933	" "	4	1962	" "	5
1898	" "	1	1934	" "	4	1963	Bobby Bragan	6
1899	" "	2	1935	" "	8	1964	" "	5
1900	" "	4	1936	" "	6	1965	" "	5
1901	" "	5	1937	" "	5			
1902	Al Buckenberger	3	1938	Casey Stengel	5		ATLANTA	
1903	" "	6	1939	" "	7			
1904	" "	7	1940	" "	7	1966	Bobby Bragan	
1905	Fred Tenney	7	1941	" "	7		Billy Hitchcock	5
1906	" "	8	1942	" "	7	1967	" "	
1907	" "	7	1943	" "	6		Ken Silvestri	7
1908	Joe Kelley	6	1944	Bob Coleman	6	1968	Luman Harris	5
1909	Frank Bowerman		1945	" "		1969	" "	1
	Harry Smith	8						

Atlanta Braves (continued)

Year	Manager	Finish	Year	Manager	Finish
1970	Luman Harris	5	1972	Luman Harris	
1971	" "	3		Eddie Mathews	4

[1] Franchise originated in Boston in 1876; transferred to Milwaukee in 1953; transferred to Atlanta in 1966.
[2] Not listed by 1972 National League Green Book.
[3] World Champions.
[4] 1972 National League Green Book lists Rabbit Maranville as having managed the latter part of 1929.

Chicago Cubs

Year	Manager	Finish	Year	Manager	Finish	Year	Manager	Finish
1876	Al Spalding	1	1906	Frank Chance	1		Charlie Grimm	1
1877	" "	5	1907	" "	1[1]	1933	" "	3
1878	Bob Ferguson	4	1908	" "	1[1]	1934	" "	3
1879	Cap Anson	4	1909	" "	2	1935	" "	1
1880	" "	1	1910	" "	1	1936	" "	2
1881	" "	1	1911	" "	2	1937	" "	2
1882	" "	1	1912	" "	3	1938	" "	1
1883	" "	2	1913	Johnny Evers	3		Gabby Hartnett	1
1884	" "	4	1914	Hank O'Day	4	1939	" "	4
1885	" "	1	1915	Roger Bresnahan	4	1940	" "	5
1886	" "	1	1916	Joe Tinker	5	1941	Jimmy Wilson	6
1887	" "	3	1917	Fred Mitchell	5	1942	" "	6
1888	" "	2	1918	" "	1	1943	" "	5
1889	" "	3	1919	" "	3	1944	" "	
1890	" "	2	1920	" "	5		Roy Johnson[2]	
1891	" "	2	1921	Johnny Evers			Charlie Grimm	4
1892	" "	7		Bill Killefer	7	1945	" "	1
1893	" "	9	1922	" "	5	1946	" "	3
1894	" "	8	1923	" "	4	1947	" "	6
1895	" "	4	1924	" "	5	1948	" "	8
1896	" "	5	1925	" "		1949	" "	
1897	" "	9		Rabbit Maranville			Frankie Frisch	8
1898	Tom Burns	4		George Gibson	8	1950	" "	7
1899	" "	8	1926	Joe McCarthy	4	1951	" "	
1900	Tom Loftus	5	1927	" "	4		Phil Cavarretta	8
1901	" "	6	1928	" "	3	1952	" "	5
1902	Frank Selee	5	1929	" "	1	1953	" "	7
1903	" "	3	1930	" "		1954	Stan Hack	7
1904	" "	2		Rogers Hornsby	2	1955	" "	6
1905	" "		1931	" "	3	1956	" "	8
	Frank Chance	3	1932	" "		1957	Bob Scheffing	7

282

Chicago Cubs (continued)

Year	Manager	Finish	Year	Manager	Finish	Year	Manager	Finish
1958	Bob Scheffing	5	1962	El Tappe		1967	Leo Durocher	3
1959	" "	5		Lou Klein		1968	" "	3
1960	Charlie Grimm			Charlie Metro	9	1969	" "	2
	Lou Boudreau	7	1963	Bob Kennedy	7	1970	" "	2
1961[3]	Vedie Himsl		1964	" "	8	1971	" "	3
	Harry Craft		1965	" "		1972	" "	
	El Tappe			Lou Klein	8		Whitey Lockman	2
	Lou Klein	7	1966	Leo Durocher	10			

[1]World Champions.
[2]Not listed by 1972 *National League Green Book.*
[3]For 1961-65, the 1972 *National League Green Book* lists no one as manager of Chicago, who rotated coaches as managers in those years.

Cincinnati Reds

Year	Manager	Finish	Year	Manager	Finish	Year	Manager	Finish
1876	Charlie Gould	8	1906	Ned Hanlon	6	1930	Dan Howley	7
1877	Lipman Pike		1907	" "	6	1931	" "	8
	Bob Addy[1]	6	1908	John Ganzel	5	1932	" "	8
1878	Cal McVey	2	1909	Clark Griffith	4	1933	Donie Bush	8
1879	" "		1910	" "	5	1934	Bob O'Farrell	
	Deacon White	5	1911	" "	6		Burt Shotton[2]	
1880	John Clapp	8	1912	Hank O'Day	4		Chuck Dressen	8
1881-			1913	Joe Tinker	7	1935	" "	6
1889	Not in League		1914	Buck Herzog	8	1936	" "	5
1890	Tom Loftus	4	1915	" "	7	1937	" "	
1891	" "	7	1916	" "			Bobby Wallace	8
1892	Charlie Comiskey	5		Ivey Wingo[2]		1938	Bill McKechnie	4
1893	" "	6		Christy Mathewson	7	1939	" "	1
1894	" "	10	1917	" "	4	1940	" "	1[3]
1895	Buck Ewing	8	1918	" "		1941	" "	3
1896	" "	3		Heinie Groh	3	1942	" "	4
1897	" "	4	1919	Pat Moran	1[3]	1943	" "	2
1898	" "	3	1920	" "	3	1944	" "	3
1899	" "	6	1921	" "	6	1945	" "	7
1900	Bob Allen	7	1922	" "	2	1946	" "	6
1901	Bid McPhee	8	1923	" "	2	1947	Johnny Neun	5
1902	" "		1924	Jack Hendricks	4	1948	" "	
	Frank Bancroft		1925	" "	3		Bucky Walters	7
	Joe Kelley	4	1926	" "	2	1949	" "	
1903	" "	4	1927	" "	5		Luke Sewell[2]	7
1904	" "	3	1928	" "	5	1950	" "	6
1905	" "	5	1929	" "	7	1951	" "	6

Cincinnati Reds (continued)

Year	Manager	Finish	Year	Manager	Finish	Year	Manager	Finish
1952	Luke Sewell		1958	Birdie Tebbetts		1965	Dick Sisler	4
	Earle Brucker[2]			Jimmy Dykes	4	1966	Don Heffner	
	Rogers Hornsby	6	1959	Mayo Smith			Dave Bristol	7
1953	" "			Fred Hutchinson	5	1967	" "	4
	Buster Mills[2]	6	1960	" "	6	1968	" "	4
1954	Birdie Tebbetts	5	1961	" "	1	1969	" "	3
1955	" "	5	1962	" "	3	1970	Sparky Anderson	1[4]
1956	" "	3	1963	" "	5	1971	" "	4
1957	" "	4	1964	" "	2	1972	" "	1[4]

[1]1972 National League Green Book lists Charlie Gould and Lipman Pike as the managers in 1877.
[2]Not listed by 1972 National League Green Book.
[3]World Champions.
[4]National League Champions.

Houston Astros

Year	Manager	Finish	Year	Manager	Finish	Year	Manager	Finish
1962	Harry Craft	8	1966	Grady Hatton	8	1970	Harry Walker	4
1963	" "	9	1967	" "	9	1971	" "	4
1964	" "		1968	" "		1972	" "	
	Luman Harris	9		Harry Walker	10		Leo Durocher	2
1965	" "	9	1969	" "	5			

Los Angeles Dodgers

Year	Manager	Finish	Year	Manager	Finish	Year	Manager	Finish
	BROOKLYN[1]		1899	Ned Hanlon	1	1911	Bill Dahlen	7
			1900	" "	1	1912	" "	7
1890	Bill McGunnigle	1	1901	" "	3	1913	" "	6
1891	Monte Ward	6	1902	" "	2	1914	Wilbert Robinson	5
1892	" "	3	1903	" "	5	1915	" "	3
1893	Dave Foutz	6	1904	" "	6	1916	" "	1
1894	" "	5	1905	" "	8	1917	" "	7
1895	" "	5	1906	Patsy Donovan	5	1918	" "	5
1896	" "	9	1907	" "	5	1919	" "	5
1897	Billy Barnie	6	1908	" "	7	1920	" "	1
1898	" "		1909	Harry Lumley	6	1921	" "	5
	Mike Griffin		1910	Bill Dahlen	6	1922	" "	6
	Charlie Ebbets	10						

Los Angeles Dodgers (continued)

Year	Manager	Finish	Year	Manager	Finish	Year	Manager	Finish
1923	Wilbert Robinson	6	1941	Leo Durocher	1	1957	Walter Alston	3
1924	" "	2	1942	" "	2			
1925	" "	6	1943	" "	3		LOS ANGELES	
1926	" "	6	1944	" "	7	1958	Walter Alston	7
1927	" "	6	1945	" "	3	1959	" "	1[3]
1928	" "	6	1946	" "	2	1960	" "	4
1929	" "	6	1947	Clyde Sukeforth[2]		1961	" "	2
1930	" "	4		Burt Shotton	1	1962	" "	2
1931	" "	4	1948	Leo Durocher		1963	" "	1[3]
1932	Max Carey	3		Burt Shotton	3	1964	" "	6
1933	" "	6	1949	" "	1	1965	" "	1[3]
1934	Casey Stengel	6	1950	" "	2	1966	" "	1
1935	" "	5	1951	Chuck Dressen	2	1967	" "	8
1936	" "	7	1952	" "	1	1968	" "	7
1937	Burleigh Grimes	6	1953	" "	1	1969	" "	4
1938	" "	7	1954	Walter Alston	2	1970	" "	2
1939	Leo Durocher	3	1955	" "	1[3]	1971	" "	2
1940	" "	2	1956	" "	1	1972	" "	3

[1]Franchise originated in Brooklyn in 1890; transferred to Los Angeles in 1958.
[2]Durocher was suspended by Commissioner A. B. Chandler on April 9, 1947, for 1947 season.
Sukeforth was not listed by *1972 National League Green Book* as a manager for Brooklyn in 1947.
[3]World Champions.

Montreal Expos

Year	Manager	Finish
1969	Gene Mauch	6
1970	" "	6
1971	" "	5
1972	" "	5

New York Mets

Year	Manager	Finish	Year	Manager	Finish	Year	Manager	Finish
1962	Casey Stengel	10	1964	Casey Stengel	10		Wes Westrum	10
1963	" "	10	1965	" "		1966	" "	9

New York Mets (continued)

Year	Manager	Finish	Year	Manager	Finish	Year	Manager	Finish
1967	Wes Westrum		1969	Gil Hodges	1¹	1971	Gil Hodges	3
	Salty Parker	10	1970	" "	3	1972	Yogi Berra	3
1968	Gil Hodges	9						

¹World Champions.

Philadelphia Phillies

Year	Manager	Finish	Year	Manager	Finish	Year	Manager	Finish
	PHILADELPHIA		1905	Hugh Duffy	4	1940	Doc Prothro	8
1876	Al Wright	7	1906	" "	4	1941	" "	8
1877-			1907	Bill Murray	3	1942	Hans Lobert	8
1879	Not in League		1908	" "	4	1943	Bucky Harris	
			1909	" "	5		Fred Fitzsimmons	7
	WORCESTER¹		1910	Red Dooin	4	1944	" "	8
			1911	" "	4	1945	" "	
1880	Frank Bancroft	5	1912	" "	5		Ben Chapman	8
1881	Freeman Brown	8	1913	" "	2	1946	" "	5
1882	" "		1914	" "	6	1947	" "	7
	Tommy Bond		1915	Pat Moran	1	1948	" "	
	Jack Chapman	8	1916	" "	2		Dusty Cooke³	
			1917	" "	2		Eddie Sawyer	6
	PHILADELPHIA		1918	" "	6	1949	" "	3
1883	Bob Ferguson²		1919	Jack Coombs		1950	" "	1
	Blondie Purcell	8		Gavvy Cravath	8	1951	" "	5
1884	Harry Wright	6	1920	" "	8	1952	" "	
1885	" "	3	1921	Wild Bill Donovan			Steve O'Neill	4
1886	" "	4		Kaiser Wilhelm	8	1953	" "	3
1887	" "	2	1922	" "	7	1954	" "	
1888	" "	3	1923	Art Fletcher	8		Terry Moore	4
1889	" "	4	1924	" "	7	1955	Mayo Smith	4
1890	" "	3	1925	" "	6	1956	" "	5
1891	" "	4	1926	" "	8	1957	" "	5
1892	" "	4	1927	Stuffy McInnis	8	1958	" "	
1893	" "	4	1928	Burt Shotton	8		Eddie Sawyer	8
1894	Arthur Irwin	4	1929	" "	5	1959	" "	8
1895	" "	3	1930	" "	8	1960	" "	
1896	Billy Nash	8	1931	" "	6		Andy Cohen³	
1897	George Stallings	10	1932	" "	4		Gene Mauch	8
1898	" "		1933	" "	7	1961	" "	8
	Bill Shettsline	6	1934	Jimmie Wilson	7	1962	" "	7
1899	" "	3	1935	" "	7	1963	" "	4
1900	" "	3	1936	" "	8	1964	" "	2
1901	" "	2	1937	" "	7	1965	" "	6
1902	" "	7	1938	" "		1966	" "	4
1903	Chief Zimmer	7		Hans Lobert	8	1967	" "	5
1904	Hugh Duffy	8	1939	Doc Prothro	8	1968	" "	

286

Philadelphia Phillies (continued)

Year	Manager	Finish	Year	Manager	Finish	Year	Manager	Finish
	George Myatt[3]			George Myatt	5	1972	Frank Lucchesi	
	Bob Skinner	7	1970	Frank Lucchesi	5		Paul Owens	6
1969	" "		1971	" "	6			

[1]Franchise was in Worcester in 1880-1882.
[2]1972 *National League Green Book* lists Horace Phillips as manager for 1883.
[3]Not listed by 1972 *National League Green Book*.

Pittsburgh Pirates

Year	Manager	Finish	Year	Manager	Finish	Year	Manager	Finish
1887	Horace Phillips	6	1913	Fred Clarke	4	1940	Frank Frisch	4
1888	" "	6	1914	" "	7	1941	" "	4
1889	" "		1915	" "	5	1942	" "	5
	Fred Dunlap		1916	Jim Callahan	6	1943	" "	4
	Ned Hanlon	5	1917	" "		1944	" "	2
1890	Guy Hecker	8		Honus Wagner		1945	" "	4
1891	Ned Hanlon			Hugo Bezdek	8	1946	" "	
	Bill McGunnigle	8	1918	" "	4		Spud Davis[3]	7
1892	Tom Burns		1919	" "	4	1947	Billy Herman	
	Al Buckenberger	6	1920	George Gibson	4		Bill Burwell[3]	7
1893	" "	2	1921	" "	2	1948	Bill Meyer	4
1894	" "		1922	" "		1949	" "	6
	Connie Mack	7		Bill McKechnie	3	1950	" "	8
1895	" "	7	1923	" "	3	1951	" "	7
1896	" "	6	1924	" "	3	1952	" "	8
1897	Patsy Donovan	8	1925	" "	1[1]	1953	Fred Haney	8
1898	Bill Watkins	8	1926	" "	3	1954	" "	8
1899	" "		1927	Donie Bush	1	1955	" "	8
	Patsy Donovan	7	1928	" "	4	1956	Bobby Bragan	7
1900	Fred Clarke	2	1929	" "		1957	" "	
1901	" "	1		Jewel Ens	2		Danny Murtaugh	7
1902	" "	1	1930	" "	5	1958	" "	2
1903	" "	1	1931	" "	5	1959	" "	4
1904	" "	4	1932	George Gibson	2	1960	" "	1[1]
1905	" "	2	1933	" "	2	1961	" "	6
1906	" "	3	1934	" "		1962	" "	4
1907	" "	2		Pie Traynor	5	1963	" "	8
1908	" "	2	1935	" "	4	1964	" "	6
1909	" "	1[1]	1936	" "	4	1965	Harry Walker	3
1910	" "	3	1937	" "	3	1966	" "	3
1911	" "	3	1938	" "	2	1967	" "	
1912	" "	2	1939	" "	6		Danny Murtaugh	6

287

Pittsburgh Pirates (continued)

Year	Manager	Finish	Year	Manager	Finish	Year	Manager	Finish
1968	Larry Shepard	6	1970	Danny Murtaugh	1	1972	Bill Virdon	1
1969	" "	3	1971	" "	1[1]			

[1]World Champions.
[2]Not listed by *1972 National League Green Book.*

San Diego Padres

Year	Manager	Finish
1969	Preston Gomez	6
1970	" "	6
1971	" "	6
1972	" "	6
	Don Zimmer	6

San Francisco Giants

Year	Manager	Finish	Year	Manager	Finish	Year	Manager	Finish
	NEW YORK[1]		1889	Jim Mutrie	1	1903	John McGraw	2
1876	Bill Cammeyer	6	1890	" "	6	1904	" "	1
1877-			1891	" "	3	1905	" "	1[3]
1878	Not in League		1892	Pat Powers	8	1906	" "	2
			1893	Monte Ward	5	1907	" "	4
			1894	" "	2	1908	" "	2
	TROY		1895	George Davis		1909	" "	3
1879	Horace Phillips			Jack Doyle		1910	" "	2
	Bob Ferguson	8		Harvey Watkins	9	1911	" "	1
1880	" "	4	1896	Arthur Irwin		1912	" "	1
1881	" "	5		Bill Joyce	7	1913	" "	1
1882	" "	7	1897	" "	3	1914	" "	2
			1898	" "		1915	" "	8
	NEW YORK			Cap Anson	7	1916	" "	4
1883	John Clapp	6	1899	John Day		1917	" "	1
1884	James L. Price			Fred Hoey	10	1918	" "	2
	Monte Ward[2]	4	1900	Buck Ewing		1919	" "	2
1885	Jim Mutrie	2		George Davis	8	1920	" "	2
1886	" "	3	1901	" "	7	1921	" "	1[3]
1887	" "	4	1902	Horace Fogel		1922	" "	1[3]
1888	" "	1		Heinie Smith		1923	" "	1
				John McGraw	8			

288

San Francisco Giants (continued)

Year	Manager	Finish	Year	Manager	Finish	Year	Manager	Finish
1924	John McGraw	1	1941	Bill Terry	5		SAN FRANCISCO	
1925	" "	2	1942	Mel Ott	3			
1926	" "	5	1943	" "	8	1958	Bill Rigney	3
1927	" "	3	1944	" "	5	1959	" "	3
1928	" "	2	1945	" "	5	1960	" "	
1929	" "	3	1946	" "	8		Tom Sheehan	5
1930	" "	3	1947	" "	4	1961	Alvin Dark	3
1931	" "	2	1948	" "		1962	" "	1
1932	" "			Leo Durocher	5	1963	" "	3
	Bill Terry	6	1949	" "	5	1964	" "	4
1933	" "	1[3]	1950	" "	3	1965	Herman Franks	2
1934	" "	2	1951	" "	1	1966	" "	2
1935	" "	3	1952	" "	2	1967	" "	2
1936	" "	1	1953	" "	5	1968	" "	2
1937	" "	1	1954	" "	1[3]	1969	Clyde King	2
1938	" "	3	1955	" "	3	1970	" "	
1939	" "	5	1956	Bill Rigney	6		Charlie Fox	3
1940	" "	6	1957	" "	6	1971	" "	1
						1972	" "	5

[1] There was a National League franchise in New York in 1876. The present San Francisco franchise originated in Troy in 1879; transferred to New York in 1883; transferred to San Francisco in 1958.
[2] Not listed by 1972 National League Green Book.
[3] World Champions.

St. Louis Cardinals

Year	Manager	Finish	Year	Manager	Finish	Year	Manager	Finish
1876	Harmon Dehlman[1]	2		Lewis Phelan		1899	Patsy Tebeau	5
1877	J. R. Lucas			Chris		1900	" "	
	George McManus	4		Von Der Ahe	11		Louie Heilbroner	5
1878-			1896	Harry Diddledock		1901	Patsy Donovan	4
1884	Not in League			Arlie Latham		1902	" "	6
1885	H. V. Lucas[2]	8		Chris		1903	" "	8
1886	Gus Schmelz	6		Von Der Ahe[4]		1904	Kid Nichols	5
1877-				Roger Connor		1905	" "	
1891	Not in League			Tom Dowd	11		Jimmy Burke	
1892	Chris		1897	" "			Stanley Robison	6
	Von Der Ahe	11		Hugh Nicol		1906	John McCloskey	7
1893	W. H. Watkins	10		Billy Hallman		1907	" "	8
1894	George Miller[3]	9		Chris		1908	" "	8
1895	Al Buckenberger			Von Der Ahe	12	1909	Roger Bresnahan	7
	Joe Quinn		1898	Tim Hurst	12	1910	" "	7

289

St. Louis Cardinals (continued)

Year	Manager	Finish	Year	Manager	Finish	Year	Manager	Finish
1911	Roger Bresnahan	5	1932	Gabby Street	6	1952	Eddie Stanky	3
1912	" "	6	1933	" "		1953	" "	3
1913	Miller Huggins	8		Frankie Frisch	5	1954	" "	6
1914	" "	3	1934	" "	1⁵	1955	" "	
1915	" "	6	1935	" "	2		Harry Walker	7
1916	" "	7	1936	" "	2	1956	Fred Hutchinson	4
1917	" "	3	1937	" "	4	1957	" "	2
1918	Jack Hendricks	8	1938	" "		1958	" "	
1919	Branch Rickey	7		Mike Gonzalez	7		Stan Hack	5
1920	" "	5	1939	Ray Blades	2	1959	Solly Hemus	7
1921	" "	3	1940	" "		1960	" "	3
1922	" "	3		Mike Gonzalez		1961	" "	
1923	" "	5		Billy Southworth			Johnny Keane	5
1924	" "	6	1941	" "	2	1962	" "	6
1925	" "		1942	" "	1⁵	1963	" "	2
	Rogers Hornsby	4	1943	" "	1	1964	" "	1⁵
1926	" "	1⁵	1944	" "	1⁵	1965	Red Schoendienst	7
1927	Bob O'Farrell	2	1945	" "	2	1966	" "	6
1928	Bill McKechnie	1	1946	Eddie Dyer	1⁵	1967	" "	1⁵
1929	Billy Southworth		1947	" "	2	1968	" "	1
	Gabby Street⁴		1948	" "	2	1969	" "	4
	Bill McKechnie	4	1949	" "	2	1970	" "	4
1930	Gabby Street	1	1950	" "	5	1971	" "	2
1931	" "	1⁵	1951	Marty Marion	3	1972	" "	4

[1] *1972 National League Green Book* lists S. M. Graffen as manager for 1876.

[2] *1972 National League Green Book* lists Fred Dunlap and Benjamin Fine as managers with Lucas for 1885.

[3] *1972 National League Green Book* lists H. B. Martin as manager with Miller for 1894.

[4] Not listed by *1972 National League Green Book.*

[5] World Champions.

Baltimore Orioles

Year	Manager	Finish	Year	Manager	Finish	Year	Manager	Finish
	MILWAUKEE[1]		1923	Lee Fohl		1948	Zack Taylor	6
1901	Hugh Duffy	8		Jimmy Austin	5	1949	" "	7
			1924	George Sisler	4	1950	" "	7
	ST. LOUIS		1925	" "	3	1951	" "	8
1902	Jimmy McAleer	2	1926	" "	7	1952	Rogers Hornsby	
1903	" "	6	1927	Dan Howley	7		Marty Marion	7
1904	" "	6	1928	" "	3	1953	" "	8
1905	" "	8	1929	" "	4			
1906	" "	5	1930	Bill Killefer	6		BALTIMORE	
1907	" "	6	1931	" "	5			
1908	" "	4	1932	" "	6	1954	Jimmy Dykes	7
1909	" "	7	1933	" "		1955	Paul Richards	7
1910	Jack O'Connor	8		Allen Sothoron[2]		1956	" "	6
1911	Bobby Wallace	8		Rogers Hornsby	8	1957	" "	5
1912	" "		1934	" "	6	1958	" "	6
	George Stovall	7	1935	" "	7	1959	" "	6
1913	" "		1936	" "	7	1960	" "	2
	Jimmy Austin[2]		1937	" "		1961	" "	
	Branch Rickey	8		Jim Bottomley	8		Luman Harris	3
1914	" "	5	1938	Gabby Street	7	1962	Billy Hitchcock	7
1915	" "	6	1939	Fred Haney	8	1963	" "	4
1916	Fielder Jones	5	1940	" "	6	1964	Hank Bauer	3
1917	" "	7	1941	" "		1965	" "	3
1918	" "			Luke Sewell	6	1966	" "	1[3]
	Jimmy Austin[2]		1942	" "	3	1967	" "	6
	Jimmy Burke	5	1943	" "	6	1968	" "	
1919	" "	5	1944	" "	1		Earl Weaver	2
1920	" "	4	1945	" "	3	1969	" "	1[4]
1921	Lee Fohl	3	1946	" "		1970	" "	1[3]
1922	" "	2		Zack Taylor	7	1971	" "	1[4]
			1947	Muddy Ruel	8	1972	" "	3

[1]Franchise originated in Milwaukee in 1901; transferred to St. Louis in 1902; transferred to Baltimore in 1954.
[2]Not listed by American League Redbook 1972.
[3]World Champions.
[4]American League Champions.

Boston Red Sox

Year	Manager	Finish	Year	Manager	Finish	Year	Manager	Finish
1901	Jimmy Collins	2	1924	Lee Fohl	7	1951	Steve O'Neill	3
1902	" "	3	1925	" "	8	1952	Lou Boudreau	6
1903	" "	1[1]	1926	" "	8	1953	" "	4
1904	" "	1	1927	Bill Carrigan	8	1954	" "	4
1905	" "	4	1928	" "	8	1955	Pinky Higgins	4
1906	" "		1929	" "	8	1956	" "	4
	Chick Stahl	8	1930	Heinje Wagner	8	1957	" "	3
1907	Cy Young[2]		1931	Shano Collins	6	1958	" "	3
	George Huff		1932	" "		1959	" "	
	Bob Unglaub			Marty McManus	8		Rudy York[2]	
	Deacon McGuire	7	1933	" "	7		Bill Jurges	5
1908	" "		1934	Bucky Harris	4	1960	" "	
	Fred Lake	5	1935	Joe Cronin	4		Pinky Higgins	7
1909	" "	3	1936	" "	6	1961	" "	6
1910	Patsy Donovan	4	1937	" "	5	1962	" "	8
1911	" "	5	1938	" "	2	1963	Johnny Pesky	7
1912	Jake Stahl	1[1]	1939	" "	2	1964	" "	
1913	" "		1940	" "	4		Billy Herman	8
	Bill Carrigan	4	1941	" "	2	1965	" "	9
1914	" "	2	1942	" "	2	1966	" "	
1915	" "	1[1]	1943	" "	7		Pete Runnels	9
1916	" "	1[1]	1944	" "	4	1967	Dick Williams	1
1917	Jack Barry	2	1945	" "	7	1968	" "	3
1918	Ed Barrow	1[1]	1946	" "	1	1969	" "	
1919	" "	6	1947	" "	3		Eddie Popowski	3
1920	" "	5	1948	Joe McCarthy	2	1970	Eddie Kasko	3
1921	Hugh Duffy	5	1949	" "	2	1971	" "	3
1922	" "	8	1950	" "		1972	" "	2
1923	Frank Chance	8		Steve O'Neill	3			

[1]World Champions.
[2]Not listed by American League Redbook 1972.

California Angels

Year	Manager	Finish	Year	Manager	Finish	Year	Manager	Finish
	LOS ANGELES[1]			ANAHEIM		1968	Bill Rigney	8
						1969	" "	
1961	Bill Rigney	8	1965	Bill Rigney	7		Lefty Phillips	3
1962	" "	3	1966	" "	6			
1963	" "	9	1967	" "	5			
1964	" "	5						

California Angels (continued)

Year	Manager	Finish	Year	Manager	Finish	Year	Manager	Finish
1970	Lefty Phillips	3	1971	Lefty Phillips	4	1972	Del Rice	5

[1]Franchise originated in Los Angeles in 1961; transferred to Anaheim, California in 1965.

Chicago White Sox

Year	Manager	Finish	Year	Manager	Finish	Year	Manager	Finish
1901	Clark Griffith	1	1928	Ray Schalk		1952	Paul Richards	3
1902	" "	4		Lena Blackburne	5	1953	" "	3
1903	Jim Callahan	7	1929	" "	7	1954	" "	
1904	" "		1930	Donie Bush	7		Marty Marion[a]	3
	Fielder Jones	3	1931	" "	8	1955	" "	3
1905	" "	2	1932	Lew Fonseca	7	1956	" "	3
1906	" "	1[1]	1933	" "	6	1957	Al Lopez	2
1907	" "	3	1934	" "		1958	" "	2
1908	" "	3		Jimmy Dykes	8	1959	" "	1
1909	Billy Sullivan	4	1935	" "	5	1960	" "	3
1910	Hugh Duffy	6	1936	" "	3	1961	" "	4
1911	" "	4	1937	" "	3	1962	" "	5
1912	Jim Callahan	4	1938	" "	6	1963	" "	2
1913	" "	5	1939	" "	4	1964	" "	2
1914	" "	6	1940	" "	4	1965	" "	2
1915	Pants Rowland	3	1941	" "	3	1966	Eddie Stanky	4
1916	" "	2	1942	" "	6	1967	" "	4
1917	" "	1[1]	1943	" "	4	1968	" "	
1918	" "	6	1944	" "	7		Les Moss[a]	
1919	Kid Gleason	1	1945	" "	6		Al Lopez	9
1920	" "	2	1946	" "		1969	" "	
1921	" "	7		Ted Lyons	5		Don Gutteridge	5
1922	" "	5	1947	" "	6	1970	" "	
1923	" "	7	1948	" "	8		Billy Adair	
1924	Johnny Evers	8	1949	Jack Onslow	6		Chuck Tanner[a]	6
1925	Eddie Collins	5	1950	" "		1971	" "	3
1926	" "	5		Red Corriden	6	1972	" "	2
1927	Ray Schalk	5	1951	Paul Richards	4			

[1]World Champions.
[a]Not listed by *American League Redbook 1972*.

Cleveland Indians

Year	Manager	Finish	Year	Manager	Finish	Year	Manager	Finish
1901	Jimmy McAleer	7	1925	Tris Speaker	6	1951	Al Lopez	2
1902	Bill Armour	5	1926	" "	2	1952	" "	2
1903	" "	3	1927	Jack McCallister	6	1953	" "	2
1904	" "	4	1928	Roger Peckinpaugh	7	1954	" "	1
1905	Nap Lajoie	5	1929	" "	3	1955	" "	2
1906	" "	3	1930	" "	4	1956	" "	2
1907	" "	4	1931	" "	4	1957	Kirby Farrell	6
1908	" "	2	1932	" "	4	1958	Bobby Bragan	
1909	" "		1933	" "			Joe Gordon	4
	Deacon McGuire	6		Walter Johnson	4	1959	" "	2
1910	" "	5	1934	" "	3	1960	" "	
1911	" "		1935	" "			Jo Jo White[2]	
	George Stovall	3		Steve O'Neill	3		Jimmy Dykes	4
1912	Harry Davis		1936	" "	5	1961	" "	
	Joe Birmingham	5	1937	" "	4		Mel Harder[2]	5
1913	" "	3	1938	Ossie Vitt	3	1962	Mel McGaha	6
1914	" "	8	1939	" "	3	1963	Birdie Tebbetts	5
1915	" "		1940	" "	2	1964	" "	6
	Lee Fohl	7	1941	Roger Peckinpaugh	4	1965	" "	5
1916	" "	6	1942	Lou Boudreau	4	1966	" "	
1917	" "	3	1943	" "	3		George Strickland	5
1918	" "	2	1944	" "	5	1967	Joe Adcock	8
1919	" "		1945	" "	5	1968	Alvin Dark	4
	Tris Speaker	2	1946	" "	6	1969	" "	6
1920	" "	1[1]	1947	" "	4	1970	" "	5
1921	" "	2	1948	" "	1[1]	1971	" "	
1922	" "	4	1949	" "	3		Johnny Lipon	6
1923	" "	3	1950	" "	4	1972	Ken Aspromonte	5
1924	" "	6						

[1]World Champions.
[2]Not listed by *American League Redbook 1972.*

Detroit Tigers

Year	Manager	Finish	Year	Manager	Finish	Year	Manager	Finish
1901	George Stallings	3	1908	Hughie Jennings	1	1916	Hughie Jennings	3
1902	Frank Dwyer	7	1909	" "	1	1917	" "	4
1903	Ed Barrow	5	1910	" "	3	1918	" "	7
1904	" "		1911	" "	2	1919	" "	4
	Bobby Lowe	7	1912	" "	6	1920	" "	7
1905	Bill Armour	3	1913	" "	6	1921	Ty Cobb	6
1906	" "	6	1914	" "	4	1922	" "	3
1907	Hughie Jennings	1	1915	" "	2	1923	" "	2

Detroit Tigers (continued)

Year	Manager	Finish	Year	Manager	Finish	Year	Manager	Finish
1924	Ty Cobb	3	1942	Del Baker	5		Jimmy Dykes	4
1925	" "	4	1943	Steve O'Neill	5	1960	" "	
1926	" "	6	1944	" "	2		Billy Hitchcock[1]	
1927	George Moriarty	4	1945	" "	1[2]		Joe Gordon	6
1928	" "	6	1946	" "	2	1961	Bob Scheffing	2
1929	Bucky Harris	6	1947	" "	2	1962	" "	4
1930	" "	5	1948	" "	5	1963	" "	
1931	" "	7	1949	Red Rolfe	4		Chuck Dressen	5
1932	" "	5	1950	" "	2	1964	" "	4
1933	" "	5	1951	" "	5	1965	" "	4
	Del Baker[1]	5	1952	" "		1966	" "	
1934	Mickey Cochrane	1		Fred Hutchinson	8		Bob Swift	
1935	" "	1[2]	1953	" "	6		Frank Skaff	3
1936	" "	2	1954	" "	5	1967	Mayo Smith	2
1937	" "	2	1955	Bucky Harris	5	1968	" "	1[2]
1938	" "		1956	" "	5	1969	" "	2
	Del Baker	4	1957	Jack Tighe	4	1970	" "	4
1939	" "	5	1958	" "		1971	Billy Martin	2
1940	" "	1		Bill Norman	5	1972	" "	1
1941	" "	4	1959	" "				

[1]Not listed by *American League Redbook 1972*.
[2]World Champions.

Kansas City Royals

Year	Manager	Finish	Year	Manager	Finish	Year	Manager	Finish
1969	Joe Gordon	4		Bob Lemon	4	1972	Bob Lemon	4
1970	Charlie Metro		1971	" "	2			

Milwaukee Brewers

Year	Manager	Finish	Year	Manager	Finish	Year	Manager	Finish
	SEATTLE[1]			MILWAUKEE		1971	Dave Bristol	6
						1972	" "	
1969	Joe Schultz	6	1970	Dave Bristol	5		Del Crandall	6

[1]Franchise originated in Seattle in 1969; transferred to Milwaukee in 1970.

Minnesota Twins

Year	Manager	Finish	Year	Manager	Finish	Year	Manager	Finish
	WASHINGTON[1]		1926	Bucky Harris	4	1953	Bucky Harris	5
			1927	" "	3	1954	" "	6
1901	Jimmy Manning	6	1928	" "	4	1955	Chuck Dressen	8
1902	Tom Loftus	6	1929	Walter Johnson	5	1956	" "	7
1903	" "	8	1930	" "	2	1957	" "	
1904	Malachi Kittredge[2]		1931	" "	3		Cookie Lavagetto	8
	Patsy Donovan	8	1932	" "	3	1958	" "	8
1905	Jake Stahl	7	1933	Joe Cronin	1	1959	" "	8
1906	" "	7	1934	" "	7	1960	" "	5
1907	Joe Cantillon	8	1935	Bucky Harris	6			
1908	" "	7	1936	" "	4			
1909	" "	8	1937	" "	6		MINNESOTA	
1910	Jimmy McAleer	7	1938	" "	5	1961	Cookie Lavagetto	
1911	" "	7	1939	" "	6		Sam Mele	7
1912	Clark Griffith	2	1940	" "	7	1962	" "	2
1913	" "	2	1941	" "	6	1963	" "	3
1914	" "	3	1942	" "	7	1964	" "	6
1915	" "	4	1943	Ossie Bluege	2	1965	" "	1
1916	" "	7	1944	" "	8	1966	" "	2
1917	" "	5	1945	" "	2	1967	" "	
1918	" "	3	1946	" "	4		Cal Ermer	2
1919	" "	7	1947	" "	7	1968	" "	7
1920	" "	6	1948	Joe Kuhel	7	1969	Billy Martin	1
1921	George McBride	4	1949	" "	8	1970	Bill Rigney	1
1922	Clyde Milan	6	1950	Bucky Harris	5	1971	" "	5
1923	Donie Bush	4	1951	" "	7	1972	" "	
1924	Bucky Harris	1[3]	1952	" "	5		Frank Quilici	3
1925	" "	1						

[1]Franchise originated in Washington in 1901; transferred to Minnesota in 1961.
[2]Not listed by *American League Redbook 1972*.
[3]World Champions.

New York Yankees

Year	Manager	Finish	Year	Manager	Finish	Year	Manager	Finish
	BALTIMORE[1]		1904	Clark Griffith	2		Hal Chase	2
			1905	" "	6	1911	" "	6
1901	John McGraw	5	1906	" "	2	1912	Harry Wolverton	8
1902	" "		1907	" "	5	1913	Frank Chance	7
	Wilbert Robinson	8	1908	" "		1914	" "	
				Kid Elberfeld	8		Roger Peckinpaugh	6
	NEW YORK		1909	George Stallings	5	1915	Wild Bill Donovan	5
1903	Clark Griffith	4	1910	" "		1916	" " "	4

296

New York Yankees (continued)

Year	Manager	Finish	Year	Manager	Finish	Year	Manager	Finish
1917	Wild Bill Donovan	6	1936	Joe McCarthy	1[2]	1954	Casey Stengel	2
1918	Miller Huggins	4	1937	" "	1[2]	1955	" "	1
1919	" "	3	1938	" "	1[2]	1956	" "	1[2]
1920	" "	3	1939	" "	1[2]	1957	" "	1
1921	" "	1	1940	" "	3	1958	" "	1[2]
1922	" "	1	1941	" "	1[2]	1959	" "	3
1923	" "	1[2]	1942	" "	1	1960	" "	1
1924	" "	2	1943	" "	1[2]	1961	Ralph Houk	1[2]
1925	" "	7	1944	" "	3	1962	" "	1[2]
1926	" "	1	1945	" "	4	1963	" "	1
1927	" "	1[2]	1946	" "		1964	Yogi Berra	1
1928	" "	1[2]		Bill Dickey		1965	Johnny Keane	6
1929	" "			Johnny Neun	3	1966	" "	
	Art Fletcher[3]	2	1947	Bucky Harris	1[2]		Ralph Houk	10
1930	Bob Shawkey	3	1948	" "	3	1967	" "	9
1931	Joe McCarthy	2	1949	Casey Stengel	1[2]	1968	" "	5
1932	" "	1[2]	1950	" "	1[2]	1969	" "	5
1933	" "	2	1951	" "	1[2]	1970	" "	2
1934	" "	2	1952	" "	1[2]	1971	" "	4
1935	" "	2	1953	" "	1[2]	1972	" "	4

[1] Franchise originated in Baltimore in 1901; transferred to New York in 1903.
[2] World Champions.
[3] Not listed by *American League Redbook 1972*.

Oakland Athletics

Year	Manager	Finish	Year	Manager	Finish	Year	Manager	Finish
	PHILADELPHIA[1]		1914	Connie Mack	1	1928	Connie Mack	2
1901	Connie Mack	4	1915	" "	8	1929	" "	1[2]
1902	" "	1	1916	" "	8	1930	" "	1[2]
1903	" "	2	1917	" "	8	1931	" "	1
1904	" "	5	1918	" "	8	1932	" "	2
1905	" "	1	1919	" "	8	1933	" "	3
1906	" "	4	1920	" "	8	1934	" "	5
1907	" "	2	1921	" "	8	1935	" "	8
1908	" "	6	1922	" "	7	1936	" "	8
1909	" "	2	1923	" "	6	1937	" "	7
1910	" "	1[2]	1924	" "	5	1938	" "	8
1911	" "	1[2]	1925	" "	2	1939	" "	7
1912	" "	3	1926	" "	3	1940	" "	8
1913	" "	1[2]	1927	" "	2	1941	" "	8

Oakland Athletics (continued)

Year	Manager	Finish	Year	Manager	Finish	Year	Manager	Finish
1942	Connie Mack	8		KANSAS CITY		1965	Mel McGaha	
1943	" "	8					Haywood Sullivan	10
1944	" "	5	1955	Lou Boudreau	6	1966	Alvin Dark	7
1945	" "	8	1956	" "	8	1967	" "	
1946	" "	8	1957	" "			Luke Appling	10
1947	" "	5		Harry Craft	7			
1948	" "	4	1958	" "	7		OAKLAND	
1949	" "	5	1959	" "	7			
1950	" "	8	1960	Bob Elliott	8	1968	Bob Kennedy	6
1951	Jimmy Dykes	6	1961	Joe Gordon		1969	Hank Bauer	
1952	" "	4		Hank Bauer	9		Jack McNamara	2
1953	" "	7	1962	" "	9	1970	" "	2
1954	Eddie Joost	8	1963	Ed Lopat	8	1971	Dick Williams	1
			1964	" "		1972	" "	1[2]
				Mel McGaha	10			

[1]Franchise originated in Philadelphia in 1901; transferred to Kansas City in 1955; transferred to Oakland in 1968.
[2]World Champions.

Texas Rangers

Year	Manager	Finish	Year	Manager	Finish	Year	Manager	Finish
	WASHINGTON[1]		1965	Gil Hodges	8	1970	Ted Williams	6
			1966	" "	8	1971	" "	5
1961	Mickey Vernon	9	1967	" "	6			
1962	" "	10	1968	Jim Lemon	10		TEXAS	
1963	" "		1969	Ted Williams	4	1972	Ted Williams	6
	Gil Hodges	10						
1964	" "	9						

[1]Franchise originated in Washington in 1961; transferred to Texas in 1972.

Managers of National League Franchises No Longer In Existence

Year	Manager	Finish
Baltimore		
1892	George Van Haltren	
	John Waltz	
	Ned Hanlon	12
1893	" "	8
1894	" "	1
1895	" "	1
1896	" "	1
1897	" "	2
1898	" "	2
1899	John McGraw	4
Buffalo		
1879	John Clapp	3
1880	Bill McGunnigle	
	Sam Crane	7
1881	Jim O'Rourke	3
1882	" "	3
1883	" "	5
1884	" "	3
1885	Jack Chapman	
	George Hughson	
	Pud Galvin	7
Cleveland		
1879	Jim McCormick	6
1880	" "	3
1881	Mike McGeary	7
1882	J. Evans	5
1883	Frank Bancroft	4
1884	Charlie Hackett	7
1885-		
1888	Not In League	
1889	Tom Loftus	6
1890	Gus Schmelz	
	Bob Leadley	7
1891	" "	

Year	Manager	Finish
Cleveland (cont.)		
	Patsy Tebeau	5
1892	" "	2
1893	" "	3
1894	" "	6
1895	" "	2
1896	" "	2
1897	" "	5
1898	" "	5
1899	Lave Cross	
	Joe Quinn	12
Detroit		
1881	Frank Bancroft	4
1882	" "	6
1883	Jack Chapman	7
1884	" "	8
1885	Charlie Morton	
	Bill Watkins	6
1886	" "	2
1887	" "	1
1888	" "	
	Bob Leadley	5
Hartford		
1876	Bob Ferguson	3
	BROOKLYN[1]	
1877	Bob Ferguson	3
Indianapolis		
1878	John Clapp	5
1879-		
1886	Not in League	
1887	Watch Burnham	
	Fred Thomas	
	Horace Fogel	8

Year	Manager	Finish
Indianapolis (cont.)		
1888	Harry Spence	7
1889	Frank Bancroft	
	Jack Glasscock	7
Kansas City		
1886	Dave Rowe	7
Louisville		
1876	Chick Fulmer	5
1877	Jack Chapman	2
1878-		
1891	Not in League	
1892	Jack Chapman	
	Fred Pfeffer	9
1893	Billy Barnie	11
1894	" "	12
1895	John McCloskey	12
1896	" "	
	Bill McGunnigle	12
1897	Jim Rogers	
	Fred Clarke	11
1898	" "	9
1899	" "	9
Milwaukee		
1878	Jack Chapman	6
Providence		
1878	George Ware	3
1879	George Wright	1
1880	Jim Bullock	2
1881	" "	
	Bob Morrow	2
1882	Harry Wright	2
1883	" "	3
1884	Frank Bancroft	1
1885	" "	4

Year	Manager	Finish	Year	Manager	Finish	Year	Manager	Finish
Syracuse			1888	Walter Hewitt		1894	Gus Schmelz	11
				Ted Sullivan	8	1895	" "	10
1879	Mike Dorgan	7	1889	John Morrill		1896	" "	9
				Arthur Irwin	8	1897	" "	
Washington			1890-				Tom Brown	6
			1891	Not in League		1898	" "	
1886	Mike Scanlon		1892	Billy Barnie			Jack Doyle	
	John Gaffney	8		Arthur Irwin			Deacon McGuire	
				Danny Richardson	10		Arthur Irwin	11
1887	" "	7	1893	Jim O'Rourke	12	1899	" "	11

[1]Franchise originated in Hartford in 1876; transferred to Brooklyn in 1877 and then ended.

Sources

The Baseball Encyclopedia, The Macmillan Company, Information Concepts Incorporated, 1968.

American League Redbook 1972.

Baseball Register, 1972 Edition, St. Louis: The Sporting News, 1972.

1972 National League Green Book.

Official Baseball Guide for 1972, St. Louis: The Sporting News, 1972.

Official Baseball Guide for 1971, St. Louis: The Sporting News, 1971.

Official Baseball Guide for 1970, St. Louis: The Sporting News, 1970.

The Sporting News, Oct. 21, 1972, Vol. 174, No. 15, St. Louis: The Sporting News, 1972.

SHOOT

by DOUGLAS FAIRBAIRN

A DELL BOOK $1.50
Soon to be a major Columbia movie

If you cannot obtain copies of this title from your local bookseller, just send the price (plus 25¢ per copy for handling and postage) to Dell Books, Post Office Box 1000, Pinebrook, N. J. 07058.

THE TAKING OF PELHAM ONE TWO THREE

a novel by
John Godey

"Reads faster than the speed of light!"
—*Saturday Review*

"Absolutely tops!"—*The New York Times*

"Can the hijackers get away with it? The answer will have you speed-reading . . . a taut and crackling novel."
—*Newsweek*

"A spellbinder that hurtles along like a runaway express train . . . harrowing, terrifying."
—*Business Week*

"A cliffhanger, fast moving and believable!"
—*New Yorker*

Soon to be a major UNITED ARTISTS movie
A DELL BOOK $1.75

THE BEST POLITICAL NOVEL OF THE YEAR

"Extremely moving . . . deeply felt . . . terrific!"
—Cosmopolitan

Wilfrid Sheed
People Will Always Be Kind

"A novel about an American politician that deserves to be ranked with two classic American political novels, Robert Penn Warren's **All the King's Men** and Edwin O'Connor's **The Last Hurrah**."
—Kansas City Star

"The inside dope on the dealing of politicians and on the sordid heights of campaigning. Amazing for its savvy, verve and toughness."
—The New York Times

A DELL BOOK $1.50

HOW MANY OF THESE DELL BESTSELLERS HAVE YOU READ?

Fiction

1. **THE TAKING OF PELHAM ONE TWO THREE**
   by John Godey $1.75
2. **ELLIE** by Herbert Kastle $1.50
3. **PEOPLE WILL ALWAYS BE KIND** by Wilfrid Sheed $1.50
4. **SHOOT** by Douglas Fairbairn $1.50
5. **A DAY NO PIGS WOULD DIE**
   by Robert Newton Peck $1.25
6. **ELEPHANTS CAN REMEMBER** by Agatha Christie $1.25
7. **TREVAYNE** by Jonathan Ryder $1.50
8. **DUST ON THE SEA** by Edward L. Beach $1.75
9. **THE CAR THIEF** by Theodore Weesner $1.50
10. **THE MORNING AFTER** by Jack B. Weiner $1.50

Non-fiction

1. **AN UNTOLD STORY**
   by Elliott Roosevelt and James Brough $1.75
2. **QUEEN VICTORIA** by Cecil Woodham-Smith $1.75
3. **GOING DOWN WITH JANIS**
   by Peggy Caserta & Dan Knapp $1.50
4. **SOLDIER** by Anthony B. Herbert $1.75
5. **THE WATER IS WIDE** by Pat Conroy $1.50
6. **THE GREAT EXECUTIVE DREAM** by Robert Heller $1.75
7. **TARGET BLUE** by Robert Daley $1.75
8. **MEAT ON THE HOOF** by Gary Shaw $1.50
9. **MARJOE** by Stephen S. Gaines $1.50
10. **LUCY** by Joe Morella & Edward Z. Epstein $1.50